GILBERT FRANKAU'S
SELF-PORTRAIT

Books by
GILBERT FRANKAU

Novels
THE WOMAN OF THE HORIZON
PETER JACKSON, CIGAR MERCHANT
THE SEEDS OF ENCHANTMENT
THE LOVE STORY OF ALIETTE BRUNTON
GERALD CRANSTON'S LADY
LIFE—AND ERICA
MASTERSON
SO MUCH GOOD
DANCE! LITTLE GENTLEMAN
MARTIN MAKE-BELIEVE
CHRISTOPHER STRONG
THE LONELY MAN
EVERYWOMAN
THREE ENGLISHMEN
FAREWELL ROMANCE
THE DANGEROUS YEARS
ROYAL REGIMENT

Collection of Tales
MEN, MAIDS, AND MUSTARD-POT
TWELVE TALES
CONCERNING PETER JACKSON AND OTHERS
WINE, WOMEN, AND WAITERS
SECRET SERVICES
EXPERIMENTS IN CRIME

Book of Travel
MY UNSENTIMENTAL JOURNEY

Verse
ONE OF US
MORE OF US
TID'APA
THE GUNS
THE JUDGEMENT OF VALHALLA
THE CITY OF FEAR
ONE OF THEM

GILBERT FRANKAU'S
SELF-PORTRAIT

A NOVEL
OF HIS OWN LIFE

THE BOOK CLUB
121 CHARING CROSS ROAD
LONDON W.C. 2

This Edition 1941

MADE AND PRINTED IN GREAT BRITAIN BY
EBENEZER BAYLIS AND SON, LTD., THE
TRINITY PRESS, WORCESTER, AND LONDON

SOME OF THE
PEOPLE IN THE STORY

Jack AKERMAN
Hylton ALLEN
Mrs. Eliza ARIA
Michael ARLEN

F. E. BAILY
Earl BALDWIN
Ralph BARRY
Beverley BAXTER
Kyrle BELLEW
Arnold BENNETT
Jeffery BERNERD
The Earl of BIRKENHEAD
Alan BOTT
Horatio BOTTOMLEY
F. S. BRADLEY
Mary Elizabeth BRADLEY ⎫
Mrs. Ellis W. JONES   ⎭
Lt.-Col. R. V. G. BRETTELL
Harold BROOKE-ALDER
Warwick BROOKES
W. E. BROWDER
Edmond BURKE
Clara BUTT

Sir Hall CAINE
Brig.-Gen. W. N. CAMPBELL
Joseph CHAMBERLAIN
Charlie CHAPLIN
Pauline CHASE
Betty CHESTER
Mrs. Cecil CHESTERTON
Dr. William CHRISTIE
Lt.-Col. C. A. CLARK

Rev. "Tubby" CLAYTON
Lt.-Col. D. R. COATES, R.F.A.
Arthur COLLINS
Ronald COLMAN
Bryan Ricco COOPER
Colin COOPER
Edmund CORK
Francis COVELL
Noel COWARD
A. L. CRANFIELD
Alice CRAWFORD
Capt. CUNNINGHAM-REID

Zena DARE
Clarence DARROW
Mrs. DAVENPORT
Marion DAVIES
S. C. H. DAVIS
Aimée de BURGH
Cecil B. de MILLE
Hugh DEMPSTER
James DOUGLAS
James Wedgwood DRAWBELL
Marie DRESSLER
Lady DROGHEDA
Dorothea DRUMMOND-BLACK
J. B. DUKE
Commander Geoffrey DUVEEN

Langley EDWARDS
George EDWARDES
Isobel ELSOM
Maurice ELVEY
St. John ERVINE

v

Dr Robert FENNER
Rex FLATAU
George S. FLINT
Dr. Alan FLYNN
Rosita FORBES
Arthur FRANKAU
Col. Claude FRANKAU
Edwin FRANKAU
Fritz FRANKAU
Jack FRANKAU
Joan FRANKAU
"Frank DANBY" ⎫
Julia FRANKAU ⎭
Pamela FRANKAU
Ronald FRANKAU
Susan FRANKAU
Ursula FRANKAU ⎫
Mrs. d'Arch SMITH ⎭

J. L. GARVIN
W. L. GEORGE
Sir Philip GIBBS
Sir Alfred GILBERT
Elinor GLYN
George GORDON
Sir Ernest GOWERS
Claude GRAHAME-WHITE
Alexander GRANT, K.C.
Charles GRAVES
Philip GUEDALLA
Ernest GUNDRY

"Owen HALL"
Cosmo HAMILTON
F. A. D. HANCOCK
F. J. HARDY
C. W. HARRIS
Charlotte HARRIS
Edith HARRIS
Frank HARRIS
Jack HARRIS
Mark HARRIS

Austin HARRISON
William HARRISON
H. M. HARWOOD
Clarence HATRY
Rev. E. M. HAWTREY
William Randolph HEARST
Alfred HEDGES, M.P.
Jesse HEITNER
A. P. HERBERT, M.P.
Sir Charles HIGHAM
Geoffrey HOLDSWORTH
Lord HORDER
Henry Percy HORNE
Lady HOUSTON
Sir Edward HULTON
Violet HUNT
Edward HUSKINSON
Sir George HUTCHINSON
Walter HUTCHINSON

Lord ILIFFE
Theodore INSTONE
Ethel IRVING
Sir Henry IRVING

Tennyson JESSE
"Solly" JOEL
Dr. Ellis W. JONES
Sir William JOWITT

Otto KAHN
Sir Frederick KEEBLE
Renée KELLY
Harry KENDAL
A. R. F. KINGSCOTE
John KIPLING
Rudyard KIPLING

Margaret LANE
Gertrude LAWRENCE
Col. R. E. K. LEATHAM
William LEES

Doris Leslie
Ada Leverson
Ethel Levey
Sinclair Lewis
Dr. Otto Leyton
W. J. Locke
Mrs. Belloc Lowndes
"Joe" Lumb

H. V. Macnaghten
Lillah McCarthy
W. A. McWhirter
The Marchese Malacrida
Hughes Massie
The Rt. Hon. Charles
          Masterman
Somerset Maugham
Lord Melchett
Lord Merrivale
Gertie Millar
R. J. Minney
Colleen Moore
George Moore
Henry Morris
Sir Oswald Mosley

Eveleigh Nash
C. R. W. Nevinson
Sir Henry Newbolt
Arthur Newton
Robert Nichols
Lord Nuffield

Auguste Oddenino
Phillips Oppenheim

Sydney Pawling
Ray Pinckney
Evelyn Platt
Sir Reginald Poole
Viscount Powerscourt
Sir Harry Preston
Crawfurd Price

E. T. Raymond
Lord Rennell
Frank Richardson
Cecil Roberts
Lt.-Col. F. J. Roberts
"Reggie" Rootes
W. E. Rootes
Lord Rothermere

Ellery Sedgwick
Sir Dehane Segrave
Edward Shanks
R. C. Sherriff
Henry Simpson
Upton Sinclair
Douglas Sladen
Greenhough Smith
Captain H. d'Arch Smith
Robert Alfonso Smith
Lord Southwood
Percy Spalding
Sir John Squire
G. B. Stern
William J. Studd
Sir George Sutton
Hannen Swaffer
Frank Swinnerton

Lance Thackeray
Sir Francis Towle
Lord Tweedsmuir

Heinrich Upmann

Russell Vick, K.C.

Edgar Wallace
Sir Hugh Walpole
Edgar Thomas Ware
Alfred Wareing
The Rev. Edmond Warre
Alexander Watt

Major Edric WELDON
H. G. WELLS
David WHITELAW
Clifford WHITLEY
James WHITTAKER
Herbert WILCOX
Oscar WILDE
Valentine WILLIAMS

Alice Muriel WILLIAMSON
Driver WILSON, R.F.A.
Col. the Hon. Maurice
WINGFIELD
Earl WINTERTON
Sir John WITHERS
Col. the Hon. Edward S.
WYNDHAM

FOREWORD

THIS is the story—in so far as it can be told without giving pain, causing undue offence, or landing my worthy publishers in the Law Courts—of my own life up to the age of fifty-five. I should esteem myself a poor hand at my present craft were I not confident that I could make it moderately entertaining.

One issue, however, causes me a distinct misgiving. All good tales are based on character. And to me my own character is still unclear.

The few who love me say that they understand me. Endowing me with various virtues, they diagnose one supreme fault—a passion for exhibiting and exaggerating all that is hardest in my nature. This, they attribute to the fear of being dubbed a sentimentalist.

But are the mild judgments of those who love us any more accurate than the severe criticisms of those who dislike us?

I doubt it—"little devil doubt" having been one of my earliest mental companions. "Der Geist der alles verneint" (the spirit of utter negation), my tutor, H. V. Macnaghten, called me before I was sixteen.

You may or may not draw some accurate conclusion from that remark.

Here is another remembered scrap of school-boy talk.

"Where did you get this word 'ruck' from, Frankau?" asks that same tutor correcting a Latin translation.

"From my mother, sir. She always tells me I must never be in it."

Sheer priggishness or mere lack of selfconsciousness? If will be for you, after you have read the whole tale, to decide.

You may also care to determine whether a four-year-old child who, according to family legend, on being informed that his two-months-old sister had died, remarked, "Then I shall have my nursery to myself now, Mumsey", was entirely artless or completely heartless.

Nor would it be playing fair with you to suppress a 1914–1918 criticism.

"It's all very well for you to say that", snapped my battery commander, after I had tried to assure him (this being the stark truth) that he was in no way to blame for some recent casualties. "But *you* only care for two things on earth—women, and what you writers call 'copy'."

As against which, set a much later judgment, also by a professional soldier, and one of my very few lifelong friends.

"There always used to be something of the predatory animal about his looks", recently remarked that very candid friend to another endover of virtue. "But now it's gone."

Meanwhile, living as I now do under a benign gynæcocracy which has so blunted my satirical pen that it dare not even name the alleged literary critic of whom my aunt, Eliza Aria, once said, "I can't help loving him because he's such an utter cad", I can only ask you study what follows with kindliness—and as much imagination as you happen to possess.

Omissions—as I have already hinted—are many. That virtue, at least, the self portraitist can claim.

G. F.

CONTENTS

Part One

ENTER AN EXHIBITIONIST

CHAPTER ONE

§ 1

AT the very back of my mind lurks an elusive silent picture of figures in scarlet and gold passing far below. This I have always presumed to be the first snapshot conveyed by the lens of baby eyes to the film of the immature brain.

Some faculty, maybe only imagination, connects the picture with Queen Victoria's Golden Jubilee in 1887. I had been born on the twenty-first of April three years before.

The next two pictures are more personal. Both were taken in the same room—my night nursery at 32a Weymouth Street, Portland Place, London. The outer wall of that room sloped. It had one long window protected by a high stone parapet—later climbable, peashooter at mouth or catapult in hand.

Opposite the one door was a coal fireplace, on to the hot bars of which I can still feel myself falling backwards as my feet catch the rim of the flat tin bath.

A nurse whose face escapes me saved my parents' first-born from auto-da-fé. But memory can still feel those burning bars on my childish posterior; and it is to this incident that I attribute my inordinate resentment of physical pain.

Snapshot number three is happier, more complete in detail—and enduringly miraculous.

In the tiny bed under the sloping wall a little boy sits prematurely wakeful. The same faceless nurse, or maybe another, gives him "his book". Under one of the crude line illustrations in that book—a sailor shooting at a shark which is just about to gobble up a swimmer—there is letterpress.

All of a sudden this letterpress, hitherto mysterious, assumes meaning. The little boy can read, can understand, every single word of it.

1

"And him not four yet", says nurse.

How proud was "Mumsey", how delighted "Pupsy", that day.

§ 2

"Pupsy", my father, had married at the age of thirty-four—purely for love—a girl fifteen years his junior, if we believe her own statement in *Who's Who*. (The birth certificate gives her three years more!) He was one of three partners—the others being his junior brother, Edwin, and his brother-in-law, always known as "Uncle G"—in the private firm of J. Frankau & Co., wholesale cigar merchants, originally founded by his father in 1837 to import leeches from France.

One early recollection of my father shows him taking off his coat and waistcoat, rolling up his stiff cuffs, and walking round the nursery on his hands. Bad at games, he was a great gymnast, and a tolerable shot.

He never owned a horse in his life. (All his money was spent on, or saved for, his family.) But he could and did ride anything hirable—though his seat was better than his hands.

He had a happy knack of caricature with a pencil, too, and a great love of learning. "If I could have had my way", he once told me, "I should have been either an artist or a professor."

As for his character, I can only write that—in all my experience —I have never met so perfect an epitome of the Christian gentleman, utterly honest, universally kind, and (for himself) completely fearless.

To which his ghost, for he had his sense of humour, bids me add, "Though he was an agnostic by conviction, very far from Norman by blood, and born at 22 Great Alie Street, Whitechapel".

My mother's character—I have grown to realise since her death —was infinitely more complex. Superior health (she might be alive now if Banting had discovered insulin a year or so earlier) gave her colossal energy.

She rode and drove horses as boldly (if not as skilfully) as my father. She bicycled furiously. She would play lawn tennis all day, and poker, baccara or bridge all night. She brought up four children. She had control of two businesses. She wrote a novel most years, articles galore—and four works on eighteenth-century colour-printing and engraving which are still standard.

She was as constant a needlewoman as a first-nighter. She read seven books a week. She founded, financed and ran a West End bridge club—the Cleveland. She changed houses whenever she had a mind to—and redecorated Verrey's restaurant in her spare time.

She was a co-founder, with the late J. T. Grein, of the Independent Theatre. She knew most people worth knowing—and quite a lot who weren't. She entertained like Maecenas. She travelled like Croesus. She collected prints, Toby mugs, jade . . . and a packet of trouble before she died at the age of fifty-five.

§ 3

No consecutive recollections fill the gap between 1888 and 1891 when I was sent to that "Morning Class for the Sons of Gentlemen" at 13 Somerset Street, Portman Square, which was always known as "Mrs. Davenport's"; though the leather-bound book entitled *Among the Stars* by Agnes Giberne awarded as a prize, my very first, for "General Improvement", is signed in correct copper-plate "Miss Woodman", her maiden name.

Figures supernumerary to the central character, however, begin to register. Ray Pinckney's dark face, long hands, and thin figure, for instance, can be as accurately visualised as the liver and white spaniel, reputedly eighteen, she kept at her flat.

From time to time various canaries, and an alleged pair of doves, both of which laid eggs, inhabited my day nursery. But no dogs—and, as far as I can remember, no cats—were ever allowed, in any of my mother's houses. My daily governess' spaniel, accordingly, excited interest.

So did an affectionate spanking she once gave me. It was not, however, until many years later that Rousseau's *Confessions* taught me why.

A kindly, competent, virtuous soul. Only the other day, I stumbled on her name in the obituary column of *The Times*—and blamed myself for never having attempted to find out what had happened to her.

Sentiment insists that I ought to have done so, and that she would have liked to see me again. But how can a man "twice condemned to alimony" continue to meet his liabilities if he let sentiment waste his working hours?

Subsequent to Miss Pinckney, appeared one, Oldfield, a Latin tutor of no mean repute.

Other figures in earliest memory are "Uncle G's", full bearded in a velvet house jacket and carpet slippers; and "Aunt Delia's". They, my father's eldest sister (one of three) and her husband—

who practised on his violin for one mournful hour daily, and nightly wrote up the diary which was burned unread at his death —lived in Ladbroke Grove, Bayswater.

Both their sons distinguished themselves in medicine. Albert, the eldest, who passed on before the 1914–1918 war, made one of the most important discoveries in pathology—but missed fame by his diffidence in not publishing the result of his researches. Otto, whom wartime prejudices forced to change the family name from Grünbaum to Leyton in 1914, became the leading diabetic specialist of his time.

He died in harness—knowing himself doomed unless he gave up working—a few months ago.

It was Aunt Delia, who—asking my five year old self if he preferred any particular portion of chicken—received the legendary answer, "I don't mind a bit as long as it's one of the white parts". And it was in her house, not very much later, that one would recite all seventy stanzas of "Horatius" word-perfect and costumed cap-à-pie, or throw oneself, in the same toy armour, from Otto's old rocking horse, which one pulled after one, declaiming, "Horse and hero fell".

You will observe that "Gu Gu", as I am still called by one of my cousins, was already being encouraged to become the exhibitionist. But at least my mother saved me from that distressing modern complaint, an inferiority complex.

For which—and the ambitions she instilled into me from the first moment I could understand reasonable speech—I am more than grateful to-day.

§ 4

I attribute most of the popularity I have won as a writer to the fact that I am so easily bored as a reader. And, since no form of reading bores me more than prolonged reminiscences of early childhood, I conclude this chapter with a few more quick sketches of the central and supernumerary characters in my tale.

Let me draw you Mrs. Davenport first.

Victoria's self was less the Victorian. I remember her primarily as "a presence", awesomely draped in what now appears to have been a teagown of coronation velvet, fastened at the breast with a colossal cameo brooch. There must have been other teachers at Somerset Street, but her figure has eclipsed them. "Dominant" is the only adjective which applies.

From her my childhood acquired the rudiments of Greek,

many more prizes, and a horror of macaroni, with which—cooked stringily à l'Anglais—we were compulsorily fed when we stayed for "afternoon class".

Of my companions at her establishment, memory recalls one Kuhn, whose long blond hair and sailor suits were deemed unmanly, at least two Ashmead-Bartletts, a Bonham-Carter, and my boon companion, "Garfy", son of an American dentist who lived in Harley Street, named Packe.

Independence was being instilled simultaneously with ambition. No domestic accompanied my daily walks to and from Somerset Street. Garfy and I, accordingly, enjoyed considerable freedom—only abused on one secret occasion, when we proved that human water will put out a coal fire.

This experiment—result of a controversy—took place at his house. At my own, other marvels of science were demonstrated, notably the electric light and the telephone then rare in the home.

Kuhn's astonishment when mere human breath failed to extinguish one of those first bulbs is still a clear memory. Yet more clear—maybe clearest of all early memories—is a tale.

My childhood stumbled on that tale, printed without illustrations in what must have been a bound volume containing various numbers of the same magazine, during a wet afternoon at Mrs. Davenport's. Reading it, I was transported, for the very first time, out of my own life into another's.

The magic, and the sheer misery, of this transportation—for the life of the child in the tale was as wretched as my own had hitherto been happy—lasted for nearly a week. But this thing I kept secret, even from Garfy. Because if it was shameful to "blub" for a physical hurt, how much more so to "blub like anything" over mere words in a book.

Never again, therefore, did I look in that book. Nor was it until a decade later that, reading Kipling's *Baa-baa Black Sheep*, I recognised it for the story—author's name disregarded, the very names of the characters forgotten—over which my child's self had cried.

Other tears, during the first conscious years of my life, must have been very few. Because the mind holds no recollection of them.

But that I must have already begun to live much in my imagination seems proved by the clarity with which I can still recall two dreams.

In one of these I slew, single-handed with bow and arrow, a

gigantic gorilla which had climbed the nursery staircase. In the
other I mysteriously acquired a coveted steam engine.

So vivid was this last dream that I could hardly believe my
eyes when, running to my toy cupboard before breakfast, I did
not find my dream engine on its proper shelf.

CHAPTER TWO

§ 1

FAR overshadowing my mother's distaste for dogs and cats was
her abhorrence of music. In my twenties, I took her to a little
music hall, long since swept away, at Mont Carlo, where a man
demonstrated his skill as a marksman by picking out a tune on a
piano with a repeating rifle.

"That", observed she, "is the only time I've ever seen a musical
instrument treated as I'd like to treat all musicians."

Accordingly—and although one, Henry Morris, secretary of the
Royal Amateur Orchestral Society, who also practised the violin,
even when our guest in the country, was among her greatest
friends—she never forced me to thump scales from the orna-
mental Ascherberg upright which silently decorated the double
drawing-room at Weymouth Street.

Near this piano, high on a pedestal, backed by the heavy lace
curtains which screened the front windows, stood a marble bust.

To that bust, and those curtains, an airgun presented by Henry
Morris, and one wax vesta of the period, my childhood owed its
release from a fear kept as secret as its tears over a story and its
vivid dreams.

Before my brother Jack (actually registered under the inappro-
priate names "Paul Ewart") was born in 1890, the domestic who
shared my room would leave me alone as soon as I had said the
Lord's Prayer, asked for a blessing on my parents, implored God
to insure my personal good behaviour and been put to bed.

All winter, there would be a fire in that room; and a terror, in
my childish imagination, lest dropping coals should set the house
on fire. But the air-propelled vesta with the flattened base did that.

Buffalo Bill himself never shot more accurately. At maximum
range—from the back windows overlooking the mews—the head
of the match exploded on the very nose of the bust. Thence, it

ricocheted on to the lace curtains, which burst into immediate flame.

I ran from the room shouting. The parlourmaid rushed up from the basement. Five minutes—I imagine she must have rung the alarm on our District Messenger call-instrument—brought the horses and the men in the helmets.

"Fire", I must have said to myself when I subsequently surveyed the wreckage, "is nothing to be afraid of. It can always be put out."

Anyway, that particular fear went from me—and hardly ever returns.

§ 2

Most parents of the period would have beaten me for my escapade. But both my father and mother were opposed to corporal punishment. By then, moreover, Mumsey had already convinced herself that her first-born was destined to be another Disraeli. Debate, therefore, took the place of the cane.

Wickedness did not enter into our discussion. But foolishness—and risk caused to others—were referred to at considerable length.

Later in life I heard my father's views (a) that I ought never to have been trusted with the airgun, and (b) that, as safety matches already existed, no others should have been found in the house.

About the same time as the arson episode, certainly before I went to prep school, occurred another. Faithful to her cult of independence, my mother insisted that the budding Disraeli, then taking his first lessons in horsemanship on the Downs at Eastbourne, should no longer suffer the indignity of a leading rein—and my pony bolted me back to its stable in the High Street from halfway up Beachy Head.

I stuck on. Subconsciously if not consciously, however, the terror of that two-mile ride must have haunted me. I never became the horseman my father was; and gave up riding altogether, as the result of a similar incident, some three years ago.

Another early adventure with the noblest of quadrupeds happened about the same time. My mother had hired a high dogcart. We were bowling merrily downhill when a wheel struck a stone. Hurled from my perch beside her, I grabbed for the slack of the reins as I fell. She jerked me safely inboard.

"We had an accident", I said on our return.

"Incident!" corrected my mother severely.

Thus early did she train me to a sense of proportion, and the correct use of words.

For already, in 1887, under the pen name of Frank Danby, she had won notoriety with her first novel, *Dr. Phillips, A Maida Vale Idyll*, published by Vizetelly in his one volume series.

Of this "advanced" book *Punch* wrote, "It should never have been written. Having been written, it should never have been published. Having been published, it should not be read".

Nowadays *Dr. Phillips* reads like a tract . . . or the precursor of my esteemed colleague, Dr. Cronin's, fortune-maker, *The Citadel*.

Forgive a quotation from its last chapter:

"The rage for surgical interference which is overriding the Pharmacopoeia" (sic!) "and demoralising the physicians of today has no keener champion than Benjamin Phillips. A terrible curiosity to unveil the mysteries of nature, and an absolute disregard for human life, characterise the surgeon whose magisterial aphorism to his pupils runs: 'When in doubt, operate; you may save a life, you are certain to acquire knowledge' . . .

"Benjamin Phillips lives to carry on his work, to unsex women and maim men; to be a living testimony of manual dexterity and moral recklessness. He is the idol of his clinic, the prophet of the new school; his name is in all men's mouths, and he can ably defend himself with pen and tongue against the attacks of his more timorous or more conscientious brethren".

My mother's fortune-maker, by the way, although it ran into many editions, earned her never a penny—because the firm of Vizetelly went broke.

§ 3

My father (why, I can't imagine, because he was born a British subject) received part of his education in Germany at the "Real-Schule der israelitischen Gemeinde", in Frankfort on the Maine. I still possess a rococo certificate signed by "Dr. S. Stern, Oberlehrer", testifying to his industry, tidiness, and civilised behaviour.

Civilised behaviour! A queer comment on the Germany of today. But Pupsy must have been an agnostic (though by no means an atheist) from the time he could think for himself. If he had any fault, it was a slight bias against certain members of the faith which his conscience had rejected.

The origin of his quarrel with that faith, I do not know. But he refused, absolutely, to permit any of the usual ceremonies at my own birth.

I remained in ignorance, until I was more than sixteen, of my ancestry; being "brought up Church of England", though the Reverend Brocas-Waters, curate of Holy Trinity, Albany Street, was not allowed to baptise me until "the child's old enough to understand things for himself".

Brocas-Waters, later translated to Jesmond Vicarage, Newcastle-on-Tyne, comes back as a tall figure with a beautiful voice and a dark beard trimmed to the traditional shape of his Master's.

He baptised me in August 1897. For years he sent me, towards Christmas, an illuminated calendar which set out my daily scripture reading. His was one of the best influences in my boyhood— and I never really doubted the wisdom of Protestantism until a winter's morning in Flanders, during the year nineteen hundred and sixteen. Nowadays, if I incline towards any form of credal religion, it is towards Rome's.

§ 4

Childhood's picture would not be complete without a few more impressions—photographed on the immature and retained by the maturing mind.

One of these impressions shows a colossal brass doorbell, set high out of reach on stone pillars. Past these pillars, up endless steps, I climb in to the rich presence (they drove behind their own horses) of my mother's eldest sister, a woman of great beauty, and her husband, a man of might with a golden beard.

Three of their children were already too grown-up for me to play with; but their youngest, Ashley, another of my boon companions, remains so to this day.

Reggie, Marjorie and Charlie were not relatives—but the best Red Indians who ever played at scalping in a Porchester Terrace garden. Reggie died for his country. Marjorie, disease took untimely.

She is pertinent to the story as my "first sweetheart". (Another vivid dream showed love so far consummated that we . . . shared the same nurse!) So are my mother's brother Jimmy who won a modicum of fame under the pseudonym "Owen Hall" by writing the "book" of *The Geisha, Floradora, The Greek Slave* and other musical plays; and her youngest and favourite sister, Eliza Aria, who survived her by many years to die in the company of the late Frank Vosper a few seconds before the curtain rose on the first London performance of *Grand Hotel*.

Eliza's daughter Nita was a constant companion of my Davenport and pre-Davenport days.

A blackly elfin creature whom one held in some contempt, and teased beyond the limit of her endurance from the first moment one discovered how easily one could make her lose her temper, Nita, too, disease took untimely.

Whereby hangs a macabre story, better left untold.

CHAPTER THREE

§ 1

THE maturing mind holds no recollection whatsoever of my arrival at my prep school, St. Michael's, Westgate-on-Sea. The one circumstance of which I am positive is that it caused me no unhappiness to leave home.

But the discovery of a new word lingers.

"What are 'dittos'?" I remember asking my mother as we surveyed the printed list of my sartorial requirements. And I remember further that the dittos in question ("a suit of clothes of the same material throughout. 1755" says my dictionary) were purchased at Swears and Wells, then in Oxford Street.

Other purchases included nightgowns; a wooden playbox and a cane trunk, painted with red and white hoops (all our family luggage bore that distinguishing mark) only just relegated to the scrapheap.

Nascent character can be indicated, I feel, by the self-expression of the period. Here is a fragment from a letter to my mother.

"I fell" (sic) "very well and jolly, was 4th in reading over. I am learning to play chess a little. The time here seems to be going so fast the end of the term will soon come. We had a Latin Exercise paper in which I was second only beaten by 2 marks by the top boy. I hope you are all right."

Note that "all right" is correctly spelt and that the superior intelligence is not named.

Another letter, to my father, contains the following:

"It is a round Association ball I want we are not allowed to play Rugby here, try and get a light one but it is preferable to get a full sized one. In reading over I was 5th but had top marks in classiccs. I am going to try and distinguish myself in football. I don't think

I shall be top this time but I shall do my best of course. P.S. It is that foreign paper" (writing paper) "of yours I want".

"Want", "top" and "distinguish" seem to be the operative words.

§ 2

Headmaster and owner of "Hawtrey's", as St. Michael's is still called, was the Reverend E. M. Hawtrey, aptly known as "the Beetle".

He passed on many years ago; but his wife still plays a great part in the enduring fortunes of the school, whose records go back to the 'fifties. Only recently she conducted me all over the two low houses which my childhood found so enormous—and carved at the Old Boys' lunch.

It was as we made our way out of the dining-room after the lunch in question that one cynical old boy, regarding the framed photo of another, asked, "Is it true, Mrs. Hawtrey, that you advised his being sent to Harrow because you were afraid he would never pass the Eton entrance exam?"

Will Lord Baldwin—for it was his photograph—forgive the jest?

Edward Hawtrey's father had been Vice-provost of Eton, later founding St. Michael's at Slough. (According to legend he fed his scholars so lavishly on such delicacies as strawberries and cream that the school came near to bankruptcy.) Beetle's handsomer brother, Charles, became the famous actor.

Beetle could act almost as well. His bulging bespectacled eyes, his reddening face, his threat (rarely carried out) of a "thorough good whipping" terrified even the boldest of us. His "stick to it like wax" (or, "like Trojans"), echoing stentorian across the football field, energised even the slackest. Broadbeamed in white trousers and a blazer on his creaking bicycle, he was a sight for the more benignant gods.

Aiding him scholastically one remembers, among others, "Daddy" Peach, who seemed to my "amorphous childhood" older than Jehovah, but lived long after the 1914–18 war. Memory suggests that he had a queer hole in one cheek, and white whiskers. His subject, mathematics, was not my forte. Neither did the attempts of the famous Miss Russell—who conducted that adjacent school whence "gorgeous girlhood joined in our dancing classes"—to interest me in history have any more success.

For had it not been dinned into me by my mother that I must "win a classical scholarship at Eton"? This scholarship to be followed by one at Balliol, and—prior to the Premiership—a career at the Bar.

Meanwhile hero worship concentrated on "Mr. Wheeler", a mighty athlete; and my

> "Illnesses, of whatsoe'r categories,
> 'Pussy' the matron cured with care and Gregory's".

The last rhyme is appalling, but less so than the remembered taste of that red laxative it commemorates. No wonder so many men of my own age suffer with their digestions. Consider the nauseous draughts to which any confession of costiveness condemned our youth!

§ 3

Except for a weekly visit to Bertrand's gymnasium and fencing academy, then in Warwick Street, and an occasional desultory afternoon in a field near Wormwood Scrubs, Mrs. Davenport's curriculum had been purely mental.

Football, hockey and cricket, accordingly, were new delights. Fleetness of foot soon earned me the soubriquet "Bunny"—and a friendly wrestle a broken right arm.

Diagnosed as a "green-stick fracture", this was set and healed at Westgate, then broken again and reset by our dissatisfied London doctor, Stivens—a great shot who, according to family report, had accepted a nouveau riche patient's invitation to a battue with the bluff words, "I don't mind, if you'll let me come disguised as a pheasant".

Months in a sling and a "water-glass" bandage, which dried as hard as stone, must have accentuated an early tendency. I fence (still at Bertrand's, under the grandson of my first master!) with my left hand, and shoot from my left shoulder. But I remained a right-handed batsman and hockey player. Why, I don't know.

Games seem to predominate over work in my early recollections of Hawtrey's—possibly because I found work so much easier, possibly because success at games earned the greater public approbation.

Bullying, I never suffered. As there were no dormitories—and hardly a moment when we were not under supervision—that phase of school life did not exist.

Snobbery, too—"Mr. Gossip" had not been invented, and anyway we read no newspapers—was unknown. To the ears of a later day that standing order, "Keep your five paces", vociferated by the master in charge to our Sunday "crocodiles" when encountering the humbler boy denizens of Westgate-on-Sea, may sound class conscious. But actually it was only a Victorian precaution against the risk of infectious disease.

We were simple schoolboys, yet not entirely devoid of malice. Memory recalls a story of "Mr. X", whom we deemed disdainful of cleanliness. Said the red-headed "Pussy", anxious to dispel the rumour, "He sends more washing to the laundry than any of the masters"—only to be answered, "He has to, I suppose".

The Beetle, according to another story, having surveyed one Sunday's rain through his study window, remarked, "I wouldn't send a dog out in this weather. Mr. X, you'd better take the boys for their walk".

§ 4

Of companions at Hawtrey's, I had many; of scholastic competitors only a couple—Charles Maude (auburn-haired like his lovely daughter Joan) who married Nancy Price, the actress, and Frank Mendl. Both excelled me in application; but neither could compete with the born examinee whom Beetle, suddenly opening his eyes, had to reprove,

"Frankau, you're making that up as you go along. Homer never wrote a word of it".

"I know that, sir", says Frankau. "But I thought you were asleep."

Of intimates, however, of boon companions, I had only one.

I have not seen Maurice Wingfield—or his elder brother Mervyn, now Lord Powerscourt, whom we reputed eccentric because he disliked company and abhorred games—for the best part of thirty years. My last recollection of them is in the uniform of the Charterhouse Volunteers at some long-ago Bisley.

Yet Maurice's only daughter is so like the boy I once knew that, meeting her fairly recently, a hundred older pictures came flashing into mind.

Maurice and I shared one of the few cubicles—over whose wood and glass partition we conducted mimic warfare with paper pellets. In the field, we played a curious two-handed cricket, without wickets, bowling alternately either as Lohmann or Spofforth, heroes of those far-off days. We walked side by side in the crocodile and discussed most things under the schoolboy sun.

The Powerscourts owned a huge barrack of a house in Portland

Place at the corner of Weymouth Street. There, too, Maurice and I consorted.

Eventually his parents let him invite me to stay with them in Ireland—a country I have never visited since then.

§ 5

Powerscourt is only a few miles from Dublin. Aetat 12, I travelled proudly alone. But pride suffered a severe shock before I had been staying with Maurice twenty-four hours.

"You said you could ride", remarked that scornful young centaur from his saddle, as the pony which had thrown me galloped back to his ancestral halls.

Since the incendiary episode with the airgun, my progress as a marksman had not been encouraged. Maurice possessed his own rook rifle; and exhibited his skill at venerie by stalking and slaying a rabbit. Envy gnawed at my boyish breast.

Maurice and Mervyn's parents were reputed "the tallest couple in all Ireland". To me they seemed like giants. The male giant had a huge beard, one glass eye, and—according to Maurice—so ferocious a temper that he once threw an undercooked joint, dish and all, at a footman.

I publish this story under reserve; but can vouch for the popularity demonstrated towards the entire family at a gathering of their tenants to which I was taken. If, as I have been told, Powerscourt remained unscathed throughout "the Troubles", the reason, to me at least, is clear.

There, surprised but too proud to admit the unusual, I ate off silver plates for the first time. There, too—it being August—I learned orally that the last grouse of the afternoon should be kept warm in death for the same night's dinner; and, from the framed cartoons which decorated the corridor outside our playroom, that the world's greatest villain was the statesman after whom the elder of my two brothers had been called "Ewart".

For another baby had been born to my parents, and registered under the names "Ronald Hugh Wyndham", two years previously in 1894.

§ 6

Visual memories of my few days at Powerscourt could still serve as the accurate background of a short story. The glimpse of a home life so utterly different from my own must have made a terrific impression. Envy, however, limited itself to my friend's prowess as a sportsman.

I coveted none of his possessions—except maybe his Irish terrier. The fact that his father was a peer and mine a cigar merchant did not even register. But the new word "bob-a-nobbers", used by him and his three sisters to describe those who paid their shillings to visit the mansion by the Dargle, did.

Meanwhile my father had given me my first camera, a Bullet Kodak; a Humber bicycle (mine, his and my mother's cost him, believe it or not, very nearly £100!); a stamp album; another album for crests and monograms—and, just before I went to Hawtrey's, I fancy, an experience of continental travel.

It was not his fault that our visit to Switzerland caused me the first real unhappiness of my life.

With us, to that village at the foot of the Beatenberg, went my barrister uncle, Fritz Frankau, who coxed one of the first English eights that ever rowed on the Continent, his wife Emily, and their two sons.

Tommy and Claude—I imagine—merely teased. But the effect was to make me detest the very sight of them. Keeping their behaviour secret from my father, my immature mind attributed most of the unhappiness to him.

My memory of this incident—except for a mental snapshot of Pupsy and myself on a mountain walk, the taste of icy water, and the ineffable joy of Mumsey's first kiss on our return—is a little dim. Colonel Claude Frankau, C.B.E., D.S.O., the distinguished surgeon of St. George's Hospital, might be able to refresh it. But we have not met for twenty-five years.

CHAPTER FOUR

§ I

I HAVE no idea why my mother called her second son by one of Gladstone's names. She remained a true blue Tory to the day of her death. Possibly this was a concession to my father's membership of the liberal Devonshire Club. Even more obscure is why she tacked the stage-famous "Wyndham" on to the "Ronald Hugh" of my other brother, now the radio star and comedian.

Fond as she was of the theatre, her liking did not extend to the players in it—one of her favourite axioms being that she would rather see one of her sons dead than married to an actress. Against which set another of her axioms, "When considering the words of people who write, always allow for a little literary insincerity", if you would arrive at the truth.

"S'Enry" at any rate—as Nita and I called the late Sir Henry Irving, first British actor to be knighted—plays no small part in these foreshortened memories of my early years. For he and my Aunt Eliza were already inseparables—and he grew to love my father better than he seemed to love most men, possibly because no man's character ever eluded those hawk eyes.

Children living in close proximity to a great personage rarely reverence him. S'Enry, to my eyes, was something of a comic figure—(Why didn't he get his hair cut? Why did he wear those preposterously floppy "wideawake" hats?)—until I had seen him in *The Bells* and heard him recite *The Charge of the Heavy Brigade*, "As Tennyson taught me to recite it, Eliza", while a fierce storm raged at the windows of his big suite at the King Arthur's Seat hotel in Tintagel, Cornwall.

I can still hear the hoofs beating as his voice boomed, to the very time and swing of Scarlett's climbing cavalry: "Up the hill . . . up the hill . . . up the hill . . . galloped the Heavy Brigade".

It was he, I believe, who told us the story of how Tennyson, asked by a lady fan to tell her what particular birds he had in mind when he wrote, "Maud, Maud, Maud, Maud, Maud, they were crying and calling" answered, "Rooks, ma'am. Rooks".

But for the following story I can vouch.

The scene is Aunt Eliza's sitting-room at the Alexandra Hotel, Hyde Park Corner. On the table by the window stands my mother's latest gift—a photograph of herself in a silver frame.

Enter S'Enry. He salutes my aunt, and walks to the photograph, which he lifts and examines with care.

S'Enry: "Your sister, eh. Exactly like her. Pity!"

For no man ever had a more diabolic tongue.

Memory conjures up another sitting-room, his own at the Bedford Hotel, Brighton, one of his favourite haunts. The table is laid for some half-dozen guests. In the place of honour next to the host sits that famous comedian of an older day, J. L. Toole, by then in his dotage. On S'Enry's left sits my father.

S'Enry, raising his glass with one hand and patting his guest of honour on the shoulder with the other: "Good old Johnny. The best fellow and one of the greatest actors in England". Aside to my father, while Toole drools and goggles: "He doesn't understand a bloody word I'm saying, Arthur".

A grimmish figure. But a great one—with many kindlier moments. You should have seen him as Coriolanus, storming:

> "You common cry of curs! whose breath I hate
> As reek o' the rotten fens, whose loves I prize
> As the dead carcases of unburied men
> That do corrupt my air,—I banish you".

You should have heard him call himself, in his set speech at the fall of the curtain, his audience's "Faithful, humbel and obediant servant". Would we had one like him on today's stage.

§ 2

During my last year at Hawtrey's (1897) the Egyptian Army under Major General Kitchener was still fighting its way up the Nile. But of this we children seem to have been told little and read less. For no faintest recollection of that warfare can now be conjured to my mind.

The only public event of the year which seems to have registered is Queen Victoria's Diamond Jubilee, for which we were given a whole holiday, first singing in the tin-walled chapel that still opens out of the boys' dining-room:

> "Where England's flag flies wide unfurled
> All tyrant wrongs repelling,
> God make this world a better world
> For man's brief earthly dwelling".

Afterwards we and the entire staff were taken on a picnic in two-horse brakes.

About this time, too—though it might have been two years previously, for the Road Act which compelled all mechanically propelled vehicles to be preceded by a man carrying a red flag had been abolished in 1895—my cousin Otto, already in his twenties, gave me my first ride in a "horseless carriage". The single-cylinder De Dion Bouton was started by lifting what is now the dickey and swinging the thus-exposed flywheel by hand.

Meanwhile I had to prove my mother's confidence and justify her first hope by winning an Eton scholarship.

That I should do so—in so far as I can remember—I never cherished the faintest doubt.

Not that I wanted the scholarship for myself. It was to be my gift to Mumsey. Credit that much. Debit the over-confidence which must have said, "It's never been any great effort to beat Maude or Mendl, so why make any supreme effort now"?

The Beetle, possibly not quite such an optimist, suggested a training gallop: "Let him try for a Harrow scholarship first—he won't get one, there are only three this year anyway, but it will be good experience".

Harrow, unlike Eton, added a "viva voce" test of "general intelligence" to the papers of which I remember no word.

"Now what", asked the bearded central figure of those three before whom the exhibitionist, only too anxious to demonstrate his superior intelligence, entered solitary, "can you tell us about the *Alabama*?"

"The *Alabama*", spouted the exhibitionist without a second's hesitation, "was a cruiser in the Civil War between North and South America——"

I can still remember the panic thought, "If he asks me which side she was on, I shall just have to guess it". But the sheer speed of the answer must have conveyed an encyclopædic learning; for that central figure, none other than Bowen's, to whom Harrow owes its song book, immediately asked another question, "Where was Lord Byron at school?"

Any fool could have guessed that correctly—and, thinking at top speed, "He wouldn't have asked me, if Byron had been at any other school than this one", I did.

Results: the third of the three scholarships; another whole holiday for the school; a letter from Bowen to Hawtrey, very unwisely shown to the successful exhibitionist, which contained the private information, "It was your candidate's viva which decided us in his favour"—and a youthful head swollen to bursting point.

If the walls of Harrow had fallen to the blast of my trumpet, Eton's would collapse.

§ 3

It is only in these after-years that I have realised the full nobility and the supreme unselfishness of my father's character. Not a rich man, he could so easily have said, "Why not let him go to Harrow now that he's taken a scholarship there, Julia? We shall save quite a lot of money".

But no such thought—the sequel was to prove—can ever have crossed his mind. Besides, Julia wanted me to go to Eton. She was light blue by conviction, though her father had been the artist-photographer of Bruton Street in the days when no languid young Etonian would have sullied his hands with "hypo", or posed New York beauties in front of his camera for the fattest fee.

My mother's father, by the way, must have been a fair wit as well as a fair hand with a paint brush. The latter is proved by at least one existing canvas; the former by a legend which relates how a more opulent relative, invited to dinner, appeared with grapes and a pineapple.

"Since he was feeling so charitable, Bella", remarked my maternal grandfather in the giver's presence, "why didn't he bring us some boots for the children as well?"

Isabella Davis, my maternal grandmother, was still alive in '97. Truth impels me to admit that, subsequently observing one of my male cousins lachrymose after her funeral, I expressed astonishment at the tears.

"She was such a disagreeable old woman," said my hard youth.

The Beetle himself took that hard youth to stay at Eton for the scholarship exam.

He must have entered another candidate, because memory's photograph distinctly shows three figures on the bicycles we must have taken with us dismounting from a pious pilgrimage by the railings of the original St. Michael's, which still stand where the Great West Road debouches into Slough.

But that other boy's name has been forgotten; and all I remember of the examination itself is my fallacious certainty that the Greek word "traumata" must mean "something drawn". Hence my misrendering of Xenophon's "having all their wounds in front", which guesswork, possibly mindful of South African tales by Rider Haggard, Englished "having dragged their wagons into a circle".

The Beetle, told of this, must have experienced black despair, and betrayed it—because even my confidence did not withstand the shock of learning myself so wrong.

For weeks after that visit to Eton I experienced a shattering conviction of failure.

Summer term (my disgraceful last!) was over. I made semblance of holiday with my parents at a house called Aston Rise near Henley, rented—memory says—from a legless sportsman who still hunted, though his groom had to lift him into a special saddle provided with two buckets, one for each stump. I played

lawn tennis. I played croquet. I bicycled. I bathed before breakfast every morning. But every morning when I awoke, every
evening when I went to bed, I reproached myself, "What will
Mumsey say, how will she bear it, when she knows I haven't got
that scholarship?"

Then, astoundingly, came the Beetle's cryptic wire, "Gilbert
placed twentieth on Eton indenture".

Twentieth out of twenty, even as third out of three! I have
often wondered whether the two results are significant of my
whole career. Nevertheless, I had won my scholarship, "although
he can't be admitted until January".

It was with Mumsey still jubilant over the Beetle's explanatory
letter that I first saw my father in his true colours.

"Let the boy go to Eton by all means", he said slowly. "But
not as a scholar. That wouldn't be fair. I can afford to pay the
full fees. And perhaps the parents of the boy who was just a
place under him can't."

§ 4

I wish I knew whether that twentieth scholarship was ultim-
ately awarded. I wish that my unselfish father had enjoyed life
half as much as his eldest son.

CHAPTER FIVE

§ 1

My mother, having interviewed "a young master called Macnaghten, he's not getting his house till the Lent half—they call it
half and not term, I'm sure I don't know why—but he's agreed to
take Gilbert," decided, "It's no good his going back to Hawtrey's.
He'd far better learn French".

Her own knowledge of that language—though she was partly
educated by Madame Paul Lafargue, the eldest daughter of Karl
Marx—is best demonstrated by her remonstrance to a Gallic hairdresser who had practised his art on the then-luxuriant curls of
my brother Ronald.

"Commong", cried she in those far-off happy days of an inter-
national gold standard, "doo franxs pour couper ung chevaux."

It was my more cosmopolitan father, accordingly, who discussed with Monsieur and Madame Robineau of Versailles the all important question of his first-born's bath.

Memory transmits, at risk of error, the professorial statement that the Versailles of 1897 possessed no single private house with a bathroom. Certain is that the tin utensil had been bought before I was left to wonder whether "Voulez vous un oeuf?" meant "Have you had enough?"

Robineau always asked that question when I refused a second helping—and the meaning of it puzzled me for at least ten days.

§ 2

Twice, recently, I have been reminded of Monsieur Robineau—irresistibly by Paul Muni's presentment of Zola in the film of that name and faintly by the schoolmaster in the play *French Without Tears*.

But of his wife—and a possible daughter—the mental camera holds no single picture, though I can still recall the setter I knew as "Fi-eno" (spelling and translation equally obscure).

Add, to complete the establishment, a *bonne à tout faire*, astounded at the daily lavations, Churchill and Sands.

Sands, I believe an American, was an old Etonian and a member of the Viking Rowing Club; Churchill indubitably a Harrovian, and Winston's brother Jack. Churchill was rising eighteen, Sands —from the photograph I still have—must have been a year or two older. To both of them these mellower years pay tribute for many kindnesses, and—above all—for the protection of innocence.

No word from either of them ever suggested—to a thirteen-year-old of more than average curiosity—what are now known as "the facts of life".

Occasionally Jack—who must, I feel, have been the fonder of children—used to hire a tandem bicycle. On this we would proceed, thirteen-year-old legs pedalling valiantly in rear, to Paris.

At least two years previously Nita and I had seen films demonstrated in the darkened lounge of a Scarborough hotel by an American who explained, much as a conjurer, "On a long film of gelatine we print from three to four hundred separate pictures".

But here, in Paris, were actual theatres on whose screens the pictures, instead of showing one a mere railway train, told tales—one, I remember, of a gentleman who took a strong dose of laxative by accident. Simple, silent fun!

Meanwhile, on occasional walks with Robineau and one of his

friends, I heard whispers of a different tale. "Le ministre m'a dit, Nous sommes dans les ténèbres", still sounds in the ears of recollection—and know I now, as not then, that it was of "l'affaire Dreyfus" those two spoke.

During this period of my life I was much alone, wandering happily round the gardens of the Palace and the Trianon. Pictorial memory must have been at its keenest. More than a quarter of a century afterwards—never having revisited Versailles—I set a scene in one of my novels there; and, checking the original dictation by map and photograph, according to my habit, discovered no mistake.

Exhibitionism, nevertheless, still took the place of industry. I "picked up" any amount of colloquial French, to the point of demanding the "gaufres" I adored "tout saignantes" from the fat lady who poured the honeyed mixture between her two hot irons.

But whether the word "gaufre" were masculine or feminine I neither knew nor cared.

§ 3

Arthur Collins, a relative of my mother, had been stage manager of Drury Lane Theatre, producing all the shows there, since 1886. In 1897—Sir Augustus Harris for whom he worked having died—he formed a company to take over the lease of the theatre and became its managing director, a post he held until 1924.

It was he who superintended the first command performance there (in 1911), and signalled his surprise marriage to the beautiful Jette Thom of Los Angeles with the laconic cable from California. "Bringing home winsome bride". His brother Frank, by the way —the brothers numbered eleven—is still one of C. B. Cochran's right-hand men.

I returned from Versailles—without escort—for Christmas. On the night of Boxing Day, my father and mother took me to the customary opening of the pantomime, "the first Arthur's done on his own".

This, I believe, was *The Babes in the Wood* with Herbert Campbell, the fatter of the babes lost in the aforesaid wood, wailing "Boo-hoo, I've got nothing to sit down on", and Dan Leno, the thinner, countering, "You've got plenty to sit down on, but nowhere to put it".

Indubitably Jimmy Glover played the God Save before the rise of the curtain—and not even a critic would have been admitted to the stalls in what fashion then called a "smoking jacket". "Tails" were as obligatory as "dittos" were taboo. As for smoking itself, one had to go to the music halls—whose balconies and promenades were only patronised by a certain kind of "lady"—if one wanted to indulge the palate at the same time as the ears and eyes.

It was Charles Morton, by the way, who first succeeded in luring "fashionable audiences" into a music hall, the Palace, whither my childish self was taken, as an almost too adventurous treat by Otto, to hear Lottie Collins, mother of José, sing "Ta-ra-ra-boom-de-ay" and a comedian who informed us:

> "Talk about the people in your mansions great,
>   We're as proud as any,
>   We've got the gas laid on,
>   Five hours a penny".

By January 1898 I discovered that the prouder inhabitants of H. V. Macnaghten's "scug house", as Eton called a house which had not yet won its football colours, to be less fortunate. Only candles illumined our separate rooms.

CHAPTER SIX

§ 1

ETONIANS have written their alma mater nigh to death—at which near-matricide I have done more than my bit. Recently, for sheer relief, I had to send three of my fictitious heroes to Harrow, whence one was sacked.

Rumour to the contrary, I did not suffer that grim experience. I was not even "requested to leave".

"M'tutor's" original house stood low on the present site of the Boer War Memorial between "Hoppy" Daman's and Williams'. You could, and did, thrust a red-hot poker clean through its lath and plaster walls.

From its camouflaging upper parapet, you could further—and did if you were sufficiently adventurous—"accidentally" drop a book close to the lame Hoppy as he took his last walk of the night.

But the six new boys—Barry, Cooper, Frankau, Platt, Schiff and Weldon—forgathered for the first time under that leaky rooftree, were in no mood for pranks. Even Frankau, one seems to recall, felt vaguely selfconscious—though he had left home, as usual, without a single qualm.

§ 2

Of Bryan Ricco Cooper, Royal Artillery, fighter at Gallipoli and an original member of the Irish Dail, there is a memoir by Lennox Robinson, who managed the Abbey Theatre, Dublin, from 1910 to 1914, and has won fame by at least two fine plays, *The Lost Leader* and *The Whiteheaded Boy*. From this, published in 1931, a year after poor Cooper's untimely death, I lift a précis of my own contribution:

"The House was a new one . . . As is usual in such cases, one boy became the butt of the rest. I always think that the main reason why Bryan Cooper became the butt was because of his marvellous good temper. In fairness to the rest of us I am bound to say that Bryan's personality was a little to blame for our japes. He resembled no character so much as the Beetle in Kipling's tale. Washing was a perfunctory affair. Hairbrushing ditto. Clothes meant nothing to him. He was very fat, with an enormous appetite and a disinclination for exercise, more especially football, which was compulsory and therefore disliked by us both".

Robinson comments, "It is difficult for us who remember him as one of the best dressed men in Dublin, always svelte and freshly tubbed, to realise that Bryan Cooper was a scrubby boy".

Evelyn Platt—whose elder brother Ernest now lives at Alassio and works hard for Anglo-Italian understanding—was Cooper's precise opposite, slim, dark of hair, with a girlish complexion and almost overneat in his dress.

Him, death took very gloriously in Flanders. He fought with his cavalry regiment from Mons to the first battle of Ypres. Out of the line, he chafed for action—and succeeded in getting himself transferred to the infantry. He should have been on the leave he had consistently refused to take the very day he was killed.

Ralph Barry, weirdly nicknamed "Hurtly", also joined the cavalry; and died from a pre-war polo accident.

Schiff is now Charles Burch, chairman of the Halesowen Steel Company; and Edric Weldon, though badly wounded, also survives.

We six, and some sixty other new boys, presumably as ignorant, were a little amazed at our first experience of communal Eton—a "pi-jaw" delivered in Upper School by "the Head".

On that occasion, the awesome figure of Edmond Warre sported its gown—and boomed for its peroration a deep-toned warning. We were to avoid, on pain of instant dismissal, "the filthy thing".

Not having been "put up", as the saying went, by either of my parents (both feared, I discovered subsequently, for my adolescent sensibilities), this phrase titillated my curiosity to fever point.

Always ashamed of confessing any ignorance to my equals, I demanded enlightenment from a superior, in the august person of the head of the House, one Stafford, to whom also my mellowing years pay tribute, not only as a protector of innocence, but for consummate tact. The details of that interview escape me. All I know is that I left Stafford's study unenlightened and unshocked.

Here again, compare the experience with Rousseau's in the monastery—which I have always felt to be largely fictional and conceived in a spirit of antagonism to the Roman Catholic Church.

And here, just for a moment, compare decent society's abhorrence of "amatory unorthodoxy" in Victoria's time with its toleration of the same vice today.

It would be useless to pretend that the "filthy thing" against which Edmond Warre fulminated was non-existent at Eton. As long as human nature remains human nature a system which educates lusty young fellows of eighteen and nineteen under the same roof as children of twelve, thirteen and fourteen, forbidding those lusty young fellows, at the identical pain of instant dismissal, the physical consolation of the opposite sex—so long shall we risk our children being contaminated.

But in the so-called "naughty 'nineties" unnatural practices were at least deemed filthy, kept secret, and tolerably rare. If Herbert Campbell or Dan Leno had put on high voices and waggled their hips—as so many of our modern London comedians when they wish to raise a cheap laugh—the audience would not even have known what they intended to convey. Knowing it, they would have hissed them off the stage.

This whole subject is unpleasant—and apparently dangerous. The *Sunday Referee*, now amalgamated with the *Sunday Chronicle*, whose courageous editor, R. J. Minney, author of *Clive of India*, recently attempted at my instigation to ventilate it in a series of articles entitled "She-Men", met with no support from any other newspaper. A book which described the trials of a handsome young man who tried to break his way into the "Fairy Ring" of modern theatrical management on a mere talent for acting was as good as ignored in the review columns.

Even my own letter applauding the *Referee's* attitude had to be heavily blue-pencilled—leaving it a mere attack on certain unnamed members of my own profession—before its mangled carcase tottered into the columns of Fleet Street's leading trade paper, *The World's Press News*.

Meanwhile the modern "pansy" flourishes like *The Green Bay Tree*—an unpleasant play which found immediate production; Oscar Wilde revivals are frequent, and it would take a battalion of Lord Queensberrys, running the risk of a thousand prosecutions for criminal libel, to clean up the sink.

§ 4

There were, as I have admitted, practisers of amatory unorthodoxy in the Eton of my youth. But personally I never came into contact with one; though hearsay—it was never more than hearsay—touched a name or so; and on one occasion Barry and I, taking hearsay for granted, indulged in running kicks at the possibly maligned pants.

Of "sackings", whether on this account or any other, memory recalls few; and none at "m'tutor's" between the Lent half of '98, my first there, and the Summer half of 1901, when I left.

As at Hawtrey's, bullying did not exist; and snobbery—at least between Etonian and Etonian—was unknown.

CHAPTER SEVEN

§ 1

FEW "lower boys" of my time came into personal contact with the Head—even their necessary castigations being executed by Austen-Leigh, the "Lower Master", naturally nicknamed "The Flea".

Warre carried this Victorian aloofness so far that one of us, on being rebuked by him for ragging that celebrated assistant at

Ingalton Drake's bookshop (now Spottiswoode's), "The Little Man", did not recognise the burly rebuker in the muffler, the flannel trousers and the rough blue blazer for the fulminator in the gown.

"Don't you know who *I* am?" thundered Warre with his words disregarded.

"No, I don't," piped one of us. "But you look like a bargee." What penalty followed, I also ignore.

My own acquaintance with the great man—he was indubitably that—began more happily. For no boy could have carried away from "Chambers" more of the three volume rewards with the signed bookplate, "Hunc librum honoris causa dono dedit Edmundus Warre Magister Informator Etonae"—or deserved them less.

Exhibitionism reached its zenith during this period. To a phenomenal memory which could repeat, almost without study, five hundred lines of Latin verse verbatim, was allied the cunning of the born examinee.

Smuggled cribs I despised. But had not Miss Woodman presented me with Pope's English versifications of the Iliad and the Odyssey, and the Head himself with the Aeneid translated by Conington, whose name sheer carelessness miswrote "Coningsby" (and passed it twice over for the printer) this very year?

While if one were a little uncertain of one's facts and dates in a Greek history paper, what easier than to conceal factual ignorance by writing one's answers in the language of Thucydides? This thing also, I did.

"He only works for prizes", wailed m'tutor in an early report.

"But what on earth else is there to work for, Mumsey?" cried the astonished acquirer of the many books.

§ 2

Hugh Macnaghten looked rather like a Greek god. A superb scholar, who—unlike his pupil—loved learning for its own sake, he was to send me in the after years, when he had become Vice-provost, his own verse translation of Horace's Odes.

He inscribed this book in a Latin which reads, roughly, "To Gilbert Frankau, once a fighter and now a writer for his country, his old tutor has given as a gift these songs of Flaccus, so poorly expressed".

Yet my boyhood's self—or so I imagine—he must have disliked as much as it was in his beautiful nature to dislike any human being. Nor can I blame him. My scornful puppyhood must have been among his greatest trials.

To an ascetic with an exaggerated sense of personal responsibility, indeed, the mere taking over of a house was such a trial that it caused him what would today be called a nervous breakdown. During one "half", the tall red-headed Conybeare, now Lower Master, deputised for him; during another "Pi" Ford, whose memory for names and faces was so phenomenal that, strolling on to the cricket field at Harrow, of which he was then Head, nearly ten years later, and seeing me there with my first wife and our two children, he came straight up and addressed me by name.

Subsequently "Macnaghten's" carried off every scholastic and athletic triumph. If ever you are in Eton see the wonderful library which Eugen Millington Drake erected to his old tutor's honour—and that memorial in Cloisters on which are graven the names of fifty-three who gave their lives for England, two of them V.C.'s.

But for our three first halves we remained a scug house. And our standard of learning is best shown by the ending of Stafford's first hexameter on the Chitral campaign under General Sir Bindon Blood.

"Ducente Bindine Bloodo", wrote Stafford, and was "torn for his bad verses". Whereafter he approached me—for I was always prodigal of my learning and soon recognised for a savant.

Alas, the savant's emendation to "Sub duce Sanguine Bindo" suffered a similar fate.

§ 3

Autumn and compulsory football gave me my first experience of human injustice. One communal lunch ended with stewed plums. Having partaken of these in all innocence, several of us were very mildly beaten by a certain fagmaster with ashplants on the ground that, "We ought to have known better than to eat fruit while we were in training".

We held an indignation meeting afterwards. Schoolboy loyalty, however, lodged no protest with our tutor. Thus the shot gangster, dying with shut lips.

There was something gangsterish, I feel, in our whole outlook on higher authority. Of an occasional "beak" (the Etonian generic for master) we might condescendingly approve. But between our secret lives and beakdom generally lay a gulf.

We knew them by unrevealed nicknames. The tiny bearded

Vaughan was "Toddy"; the large energetic Tatham, "Sweaty T"; m'tutor, "The Man".

One saying of his typified, to gangster adolescence, "The Man", who was clean mouthed beyond our measure and occasionally incapable of pronouncing his r's.

"Montgomewy", we would repeat to one another, "Montgomewy, did I hear you say 'Damn'?"

Oaths were heartier in those days; and our youth naturally imitated its elders. One of us at least could recite Kipling's: "He learns to drop the bloodies from every word 'e slings". And another possessed a tongue no less sarcastic than Edward Impey's, whose schoolroom abutted on the garden of his house.

"Let that be a warning to you. Never get married", Edward Impey would tell us when the high voices of his children at play carried in through the open window.

But the adolescent tongue of Edward Scawen Wyndham, more commonly known as the Vulture (afterwards to command the 1st Life Guards) bit even deeper. For it was he who, disputing some abstract point with "The Man", refused credence to a quoted authority with the words:

"I'm afraid, sir, that too much learning must have made him mad."

Ame damnée of the beaked Vulture, was the pale Ghost, then Lord Turnour, now Earl Winterton, whose modern dignity must pardon the chronicling of a certain occasion in a house debate on the question of London traffic conditions.

"I rise to maintain", began the Ghost, in The Man's fiery presence, "that the jams to be met with nightly in Piccadilly Circus are a positive disgrace."

"Jams" is a bowdlerisation of the operative word, which the sophisticated reader will have no difficulty in divining. Suffices, for a sidelight on gangsterism, that not a lip in the attentive audience quivered when our guests of honour missed the double entendre.

CHAPTER EIGHT

§ 1

WE soon moved from our first lath and plaster abode to Edward Impey's old house in Jordley's Place. It was into the cobbled yard below, which m'tutor adorned with those still-existent Greek bas-reliefs and tubs of marguerites and geraniums, that we hurled our tin baths and more fragile sanitary utensils on Mafeking Night.

Seen through the glass of personal memory that long conflict dissolves into a few pictures. Here is one.

I am driving beside my mother in a hansom cab. We pass what is now the Tottenham Court Road underground station. A pink and black news-placard flashes at us, "Spion Kop Lost". My mother's face pales. "How awful", she says.

In another of my pictures a forgotten comedienne sings:

> "He wrote to me he was a soldier bold,
>   A-fighting in England's wars,
> He wrote to me he was out at the front
>   Killing a lot of Boers—
> But last night I found him out
>   Mucking around the houses;
> So I says to him, 'You ain't out at the front,
>   You're out of the back of your trousis".

The songs of that day were legion, from Kipling's, "Will you kindly drop a shilling in my little tambourine for a gentleman in Kharkee ordered South?", to the pseudo-hawker's:

> "Wear a patriotic button in your coat,
>   Show you're no pro-Boer,
> Then you can wear your whiskers like a goat
> And they won't call you Krooger any more".

Recollection flings up the chorus of that masterpiece:

> "There's Baden-Powell and Kitchener,
>   And General French so bold,
> While the Bobs that I sells yer for a penny apiece,
>   They're worth their weight in gold".

And here is a last wisecrack of the period:

First Gentleman in Railway Carriage: "And what do you think about the war in South Africa, sir?"

Second ditto: "I can only pray, sir, that God will defend the right".

First ditto: "You adjectival pro-Boer".

Meanwhile a comparatively unknown Liberal politician called Lloyd George had barely escaped assault at Birmingham for

expressing similar sentiments; and all of us who were tall enough
had joined "The Dog Potters", otherwise the Eton College Royal
Volunteers.

§ 2

The E.C.R.V. of those days wore a diabolical legging; and you
could always tell when they were about to parade by the semi-
uniformed queues at the tailors' shops whose obliging assistants
strung the contraptions round our youthful calves.

Field days provided us with magnificent opportunities for
smoking—and why no casualties ensued from our custom of
inserting acorns into the breech of the long magazine Lee-Enfield
rifle prior to loading with blank cartridge, I shall never know.

Neither would I dare suggest that one R. E. K. Leatham, not
yet known as "Chico", a gangling red-head at m'tutor's, could
have been guilty of either practice. Since to do so might be a
libel on that distinguished ex-colonel of Welsh Guards.

My own interest in the Dog Potters was lukewarm. That I
should ever become a soldier seemed utterly impossible. It was
bad enough to be disciplined at sixteen. Later, it would be un-
thinkable. For by 1900, even the winning of prizes had lost its
thrill.

I could still win them, of course. But whither did Latin and
Greek lead? "To the Balliol scholarship", persisted my mother.

"To Oxford", I used to think. "And what's Oxford? Just a
larger Eton. I don't want to be at school any more. I want to be
grown up."

And from that some of my thoughts must have turned to my
father, from whom I had always refused to take more than five
shillings a week pocket money. But blindly—because so many of
my thoughts, at that time, were obsessed by a new aptitude.

As suddenly as it had been revealed to me in the nursery at
Weymouth Street that I could read words, so suddenly was it
revealed to me that I could write them . . . in verse.

That scene is the clearest, the most thrilling of my early—and
possibly of all my recollections. At one moment I sit reading one
of Nat Gould's yellow-backed racing novels; at the next I have
sprung from my wicker armchair to my open "burry", as Eton
still calls its writing desk, and my first poem is pouring from my
quill pen.

The thing came to me as easily, as naturally, as unaccountably
as that. I can no more explain it than I can explain why—having

been given what I still believe to be the light—I followed it so casually. My mother, possibly, was just a little at fault.

The legend runs how, while I was still at dayschool, and fidgeting her with questions, she looked up from one of her own manuscripts to tell me "Run away and write a book yourself".

Whereupon my child's self disappeared, and returned after several hours with its own bulky manuscript, which began:

> "Achilles' wrath, to Greece the direful spring
> Of woes unnumbered, heavenly Goddess, sing!"

Reproved, "But those are the first lines of Pope's Iliad", my child's self retorted: "Well, you told me to write a book, and that's the one I'm writing".

From which time onwards, I had never attempted originality in either verse or prose.

§ 3

The discovery that I could write verse synchronised with the discovery of the library, then housed in a long room over "New Schools", and a complete English edition of Dumas, which I devoured. The older poets I already knew. Then, on a summer holiday, Edward Berman entered me to Kipling—and I conceived the one literary hero-worship of my life.

That I should ever become a professional writer, however, seemed no less impossible than that I should ever become a soldier.

What was I to be then? Possibly a barrister. Possibly (blame Kipling!) an Indian Civil Servant.

My future was unclear. Clear only seemed the fact that my newly-found aptitude must be turned to account. More confident than ever, I decided to win the only prize Eton offered for English Verse, and sent in a poem on South Africa—one line of which ran (Apollo help me!):

> "On up the shell-swept slope to the murderous music of the Maxims".

The final stanza alluded to the calm heroism of "Our women—alone by their firesides all deserted". To my horror, to my amazement, to my utter contempt for "a lot of blasted pedagogues who don't even know the meaning of poetry", I did not win.

That finished it. No power on earth—not even Mumsey—should send my headstrong youth to Oxford.

But, first, Eton should have "a really live newspaper".

"Turnour's going to be my sub-editor", I told my father. "I feel I can make it pay from the first number. But you can give us the block for the cover if you like."

The original capital for our venture was instantly provided —£1 3s. 4d.

CHAPTER NINE

§ 1

SPORT, love, and the winning of my "Boats", my only colour, mingle with my memories of founding the *X Magazine*.

At that hotel in Cornwall where Irving would recite not only *The Charge of the Heavy Brigade* but whole scenes from Byron's *Manfred*—and whence he would drive out in a hired barouche to strow golden sovereigns all along his triumphal way—I had met a pale dark girl of about my own age called Gladys. Her father was dead. She travelled with her mother, and "Captain P".

Schoolboy love of the most romantic—without even a kiss to sanctify it—followed. Gladys was produced in Weymouth Street —and a parti carré approved for the Christmas holidays.

Armed with my first twelve-bore and several dozen of Mr. Hellis' cartridges, I took train for the inn at Boscastle, kept by one Ince. There I shot my first partridge. There, I first rode with a pack . . . of harriers. Thence I paid my first (but by no means my last) visit to the big white house above Honiton in Devonshire where my friend Edric Weldon—whom the 8th Hussars will remember best as "Tubby"—still lives.

It is just possible that I was vaguely love-lorn for Gladys. We certainly exchanged photographs. We indubitably wrote each other constant letters.

But the affair which followed was of a different texture. On one holiday occasion I bicycled the hundred and eight miles from London to Bournemouth in nine hours exactly for a single embrace.

I name no name, although—surprising as it may seem to a more sex-conscious nowadays—there is no reason for such reticence beyond the fact that the lady is still alive.

She was in her middle twenties. Our kisses left us breathless. But all we ever contemplated was honourable matrimony. And after I had been confirmed we took Communion together.

In the meantime Turnour wrote in a mottle-covered copybook which I still possess, "The X's Book. Dec. 6th, 1900".

Three hundred copies of a circular announcing the new periodical were sent out with copies of that austerer organ the *Eton College Chronicle*, on December 18th, 1900.

Our venture, we decided, must be—in so far as it concerned our readers—anonymous. But since we had also decided to break down all the traditions of Etonian "ephemerals" by accepting paid advertisements, the principal canvasser introduced himself with the personal pasteboard, "Gilbert Frankau, Editor of the X. Care of R. Ingalton Drake".

A quarter page facing matter—the book tells—cost five shillings. Winter, from whom I hired my outrigger, bought half our back cover for two pounds five shillings, a rate subsequently reduced to "four pounds if you'll take it all".

One seems to remember that the line between canvassing and blackmail was rather thin.

My own handwriting records our birth pangs, with which I will not bore you; quoting only a few gems from "our feuilleton".

This tells: "How surprised would the Mrs. Grundys of Salter's Court have been, how shocked perchance, had they known that Amy Tristock was a Coryphée at the London Theatre".

But Amy died gloriously saving her baby brother, for whose sake she had adopted the shameful career of a chorus girl, from the fire raging behind the iron safety curtain, in front of which stood "a sturdy Colonial, an Englishman in every bone and sinew of him", who, "by God's providence had brought his revolver".

"Sit down, every man jack of you. If any man, or any woman either, leaves his or her seat, I shoot", cries my sturdy Colonial while "sheer surprise held the audience to their seats for ten eternal seconds, and then the band struck up, 'There'll be no Show tonight'."

It is in a heavily leaded "box" at the end of this, my first effort as a storyteller, that my maturing self reads, midway between tears and laughter:

"Though our pleasure is marred by the irreparable loss that has befallen the Empire within the last few days, we go to press with one thought in our hearts, one sentence on our lips—God Save the King!"

CHAPTER TEN

§ 1

VERY rightly Time has gilded, romanticised (and made profitable for public entertainers) the memory of Queen Victoria. Truth, nevertheless, compels me to state that the Eton College Royal Volunteers, forcibly turned out for her funeral, were dry-eyed to a man.

On a night in the previous May we had marched resentful to Windsor Castle, and serenaded her, with uplifted torches, living. On that morning in January—Guardsmen behind us—we lined the steps down which her body was to be borne.

"Stand at ease", repeated the sullen Coldstreamer behind me as that order reached us. "Stand and freeze, I calls it."

After which all I remember is bringing my rifle to the present, and the sheer hypnotic effect of one figure in the procession which followed the coffin.

A plumed helmet of glittering silver capped that figure in the gorgeous uniform. Its fierce black moustachios were up-brushed; its withered arm concealed.

The Pomper of Potsdam looked all of a war lord, even if he did bolt to Doorn like a rabbit.

The Neurasthenic of Nuremberg and his gangster stooges look ... the hooligans they are.

§ 2

Queens might die, but the *X Magazine*, with a circulation of "318 at Eton 100 to Subscribers" had to go on.

Number Two appeared punctually on February 12th and contained a brace of news scoops, awfully headed "X-clusive". The second still seems worth subbing to read:

"Messrs. Waring and Gillow of Oxford Street, London, were engaged on a recent mournful occasion to drape the catafalque at

Osborne. A gentleman entered the room and stood watching for some minutes.

"'You are doing that the wrong way,' he said, with a slightly foreign accent. 'Here, get down from the ladder and I will show you.'

"The gentleman then mounted the ladder, and, taking hammer and nails, with a few deft touches rearranged the draperies.

"The workman from whom we had the anecdote added admiringly, 'He did it for all the world as though he were a born upholsterer. He said mourning draperies should be in long lines and very straight, and draperies for festivities looped and curved. A few lectures like that—and there would never be another mistake in decoration.'

"But unfortunately Messrs. Waring were unable to arrange with the gentleman in question for a series of lectures, for in the intervals of his other occupations he governs the German Empire!"

"Our Feuilleton" was entitled, "The Parting of the Ways. A Tragedy in Three Scenes".

Modesty forbids more than a précis of the final scene in which "Olive"—an "honourable woman" who has given her word to marry Charles Vaston but cannot help loving Archie Thelston—"is alone".

"Outside the sea toils mournfully up the beach and the breeze sighs among the rose bushes"; until, "Boom! Far away out at sea, the blue haze is cut by the red flash of the first discharge"; and Olive knows that there "grimy men in barbette and battery are slaving at breech and shell to keep England's flag flying and England's shore inviolate".

Olive, my second heroine, died of failure of the heart's action at the psychological moment when "a British torpedo boat darted from our lines and headed for the enemy's flagship".

"Good-bye, Archie", she murmured at the last. For although she had seen the enemy's flagship blow up "with a deafening report", she knew, somehow or other, that "the brave torpedo boat, with Lieutenant Thelston and its crew", must have "sunk the next instant under a sleet of shot".

Pride, refusing complete anonymity, initialled that masterpiece "G. F."

§ 3

I was on sick leave when the third number of the *X*—which contains, *inter alia*, several bits of spicy gossip about various masters and an "Answers to Correspondents" column reminiscent of the then famous *Pink 'Un*—was sold out to the last copy.

Turnour's telegram about the next issue, which I still possess, reads: "Head refuses to allow publication *X* without interview with you Hatchett and I in despair please return at once".

My interview with Hatchett, manager of Spottiswoode's, who took over Ingalton Drake's business just before we began publication, escapes me. But memory has not lost the picture of Edmond Warre booming from his desk in Chambers:

"The very worst features of yellow journalism. Let it cease".

So cease the *X* did—though my pleading secured the august permission to supply our last number, already printed, to outside subscribers.

The exhibitionist signed the obituary notice with his full name, ending:

"We may have been personal but we have never been dull; and since those who are older and wiser than ourselves have deemed it fit for us to depart, it is in a perfectly gentlemanly way that we retire from the arena".

Having read this, my father took pencil and drew a caricature which showed my top-hatted self disappearing, *X Magazine* under arm, through a doorway marked, "Gents".

CHAPTER ELEVEN

§ 1

THAT summer my first volume of satiric verse, *Eton Echoes*, was published by George New, whose bookshop happened to be outside the jurisdiction of the authorities. The prose dedication reads:

"To the Lord High Executioner beneath whose unswerving axe fell the martyred *X Magazine* in the first flush of youth this little volume is dedicated as a peace-offering by its author, the quondam editor of that ill-fated periodical".

Yet already the pursuit of literature, like the pursuit of learning, had lost its thrill.

It may have been that I wrote verse, as I had won prizes, too easily. It may have been that the failure of my first journalistic adventure had soured me more than I realised. It may just have been mere greed. It may have been—as one of my mother's novels was to suggest later—that deeper, finer, more worthy processes were at work in an eldest son who had begun to realise his father's constant goodness.

Remains only the fact that I told her, "I'm sick of Eton. And I don't want to go to Oxford. What I want to do is to go into the pater's business".

"You mean—you want to help him?"

"Well, I could. He isn't very fit, you know. Couldn't I write up the books and that sort of thing?"

She had dreamed me another Disraeli. She told me, long afterwards, how nearly that boyish determination broke her heart. Yet all she said while I pulled our boat slowly upriver was:

"Pass into Oxford first, just in case you change your mind afterwards".

That much, carelessly, taking less than twenty minutes over each two hour paper, I did.

§ 2

Looking back, it seems just possible that another circumstance swayed my decision to leave Eton before I reached Sixth Form or was given my Upper Boats.

My first real love affair—though still innocent—was at its zenith. Absurdly pledged to marry, I may have yearned for escape. But my ambition (mine, this time—not Mumsey's!) to join my father in a business of which I knew nothing except that it "sold cigars, and held the sole agency for the Upmann brand", predominated. Flaming enthusiasm could not even wait till that summer half ended. My "leave book", the usual Lyte's *History of Eton College*, is dated June 1901.

It appeared that I must learn German, and subsequently Spanish. By the middle of July, accordingly, my father was presenting me to Heinrich Upmann, who had retired from Havana to Hamburg but still took a lively interest in the Cuban banking,

cigar manufacturing and general commission business which bore
his name.

To him—though I could understand no word he spoke—I took
an immediate spite. A tall old bachelor with the iron-gray hair
and moustache of the typical Prussian, who lived alone in a big
house facing the waters of the Alster and never sallied forth
except in black tails and a bowler hat, Heinrich Upmann radiated
all the arrogance of wealth and Germany.

The very politeness with which my father treated him was an
offence in my young eyes.

We lunched, with others of the same ilk, at his "Stammtisch"
(perpetually reserved table) in the Hamburg Rathskeller. He
drank his whole bottle of wine. We went back to his house. He
and my father talked business for two hours; and continued their
conversation next morning.

If ever one man's lies shortened another man's life, they were
Heinrich Upmann's lies to my father that morning. But of this I
knew nothing at the time.

Hamburg German—the pater thought—was not as pure as
Bremen's. To Bremen therefore, where he did business with a
marine insurance company, we went. And there he left me,
cocksure that I should be speaking and writing the language
perfectly within three months.

The widow Hagen's little house, unlike Robineau's, contained
no other Englishman; only a Herr K., son of a chewing-tobacco
manufacturer, who was serving the usual three-year apprentice-
ship with another firm, and left punctually at 7.15 every morning
to collect their letters from the public post office, and a Herr H.,
similarly employed.

Liking neither (K. chewed the paternal product!), I used both
for my one purpose—supplementing their unpaid German lessons
over our frugal meals with four solid hours a day at the local
Berlitz School. Of English acquaintances I made but one, a
musical Yorkshireman of my own age and education.

Basil Whitaker and I wrote a song together. The refrain ran:

> "Give me horses and dogs and a gun, sir,
> And the women can go to hell".

For I was no longer engaged to marry and still vierge du corps,
if not du cœur.

§ 3

I bought my first dog—an alleged fox terrier—in Bremen; and named him "X" in memory of my magazine. But, except for that ludicrous song, the pen no longer tempted me; and a request from the editor of a famous quarterly to write an article on "Contemporary Eton" met with the astonishing sententious reply that I had decided to devote myself to commerce.

Turnour functioned in my stead.

The Etonian side of my life—or so it seemed to my furious concentration—must be wiped out, and even home forgotten until my purpose was accomplished. For sole relaxation I rode, alone in the Bürgerpark or in company at the school, where I took an informal cavalry course.

Our instructor was a veteran of 1870. From him, also, I took my first lesson in national hate.

"You should have heard," he said to me once, "the stories my grandmother used to tell of the way Napoleon's troops behaved when they invaded Germany. Then you would understand the joy I felt at Mars-la-Tour."

This instructor, according to legend, was a great lover of the sex, and kept a collection of peculiarly personal wax models in a locked cupboard at his home. The rest of my acquaintances were good dull burghers, grave monogamistic merchants or insurance brokers—far too polite to ventilate, in the company of a young Englishman who affected a green check waistcoat with brass buttons and trailed a dog they called a "fuchs" in his wake, the current slanders about our behaviour to the Boers.

CHAPTER TWELVE

§ 1

WITHIN three months of arriving at Frau Hagen's I wrote triumphantly to my father that my knowledge of German was "good enough for anything".

"I'm only wasting my time here", I went on. "What I ought to do now is to learn business."

And I made a suggestion to which he at once agreed.

His cheque paid for two tickets—"ein mann, ein hund"—to Frankfort on the Maine. There my widowed Aunt Ida, who could still remember hanging the Union Jack out of her window when the Prussian troops marched through in 1866 to defeat the Austrians at Sadowa—and had a horror of dogs which exceeded even my mother's—welcomed me but not X, banished to the stables where her youngest daughter was the most celebrated equestrienne of her day.

What happened to that animal, I forget.

Of Ida, I like best to remember that no more unselfish woman ever lived. She was to perish, stone blind, some time after the 1914-1918 war—just prior to which her foreign trustees had insisted on selling out the British securities my Uncle Edwin left her to buy German, thus reducing her income to nil.

From one who took care of her and watched over her in her last years, I have the following tale.

Some weeks before Ida's actual end she relapsed into a coma which should have meant death. Artificially revived after many hours of unconsciousness, the first thing she said to this watcher was:

"Why did they bring me back? Never be afraid of dying. *There's nothing there*".

§ 2

Aunt Ida possessed a host of friends. Among these, Frau R., who owned a small vineyard, had a daughter married to a cigar manufacturer, by birth a Dutchman. To him, furnished with a letter of introduction, I went—taking an hour's train journey, first to Hanau, thence to a village called Gross Auheim.

Philips, a ruddy eye-glassed man in his early thirties, was a Roman Catholic. He welcomed me courteously, but held out little hope of my becoming a "voluntär".

"I don't like unpaid workers' , he said. "And there is an even greater difficulty. All our books are kept in shorthand."

"But supposing I learn shorthand?"

He smiled at me, "If you could do that, I might take you".

"You don't believe I can then?"

"Frankly, no."

The challenge alone sufficed. I went back to Frankfort. I demanded, "A professor of shorthand—the Gabelsberger system is the one they use". Next day, I began.

Gabelsberger shorthand, unlike Pitman's, is alphabetic. I could soon write the symbols. But the challenge, elaborated before I left Philips' office, had insisted I must be able to take down a letter.

So a "business school", in the top floor of a big building on the Zeil, supplemented exclusive tuition. Meanwhile I had written home asking for, "an allowance of £3 a week if you can manage it".

For was I not seventeen and a half, and quite capable of "living on my own"?

By the end of October I found a single room whose high windows looked down on the Kaiserstrasse and the huge glass-roofed railway station. Breakfast was provided by the landlord. Lunch and dinner, I took at restaurants. For a shilling or two, in those days, one could eat and drink copiously. Quite decent cigars cost a penny apiece—a workman bought five for the same price.

Horse-riding, too, was cheap—and motor cars still so rare that when one skidded clean round in the wide street below my bachelor windows the trivial circumstance registered itself as an event.

I made various German acquaintances during those early days in Frankfort; but no friends.

My friends were mainly Englishmen of about my own age, supposed—by trustful parents—to be learning the language. We used to forgather in the Palmengarten, a local concert hall, beer garden and recreation ground combined.

There Albert Stern, fifteen years later Director-General of the Mechanical Warfare Department, one of the pioneers of the tank, had a dispute with a German officer which ended in a challenge to a duel.

Stern invited his challenger to the adjacent shooting gallery; set up several visiting cards edge-on—and cut them clean in half with pistol bullets at twenty paces. The duel did not take place.

My own apology to a gentleman of similar type, on to whose immaculately overalled leg I had unwittingly dropped a cigar butt, was quick enough to arrest his sword when only halfway out of the scabbard.

Neither did I have any such trouble as a young English acquaintance of mine who was recently bawled out and threatened with arrest by a Berlin policeman for dropping a used match-carton. The "Schutzleute" of those far-off days were happy enough clubbing the unemployed, and arresting their fellow citizens for lèse-majesté.

"The Emperor is a fool", said one of these; and with the hand of the law on his shoulder, "But I meant the Emperor of Austria."

"There is only one Kaiser in Europe to whom that remark

could apply", pronounced the Schutzmann; and took the offender to jug.

I believe you will find this same tale in the excellent autobiography of my friend, Valentine Williams, who married that beautiful woman and fine actress, Alice Crawford. He could have related a better one: how, returning from Burgos to Paris, he informed a very literary young lady, "I've just been interviewing Franco".

"And how is our dear Gilbert?" asked she.

Lèse-majesté is not unknown even in modern Germany. Witness the jest about a certain general, eight months married, but of whose capacity as a father the populace begged leave to doubt.

"If it's a boy", ran that jest, "he'll send a thousand aeroplanes flying over Berlin. If it's a girl, he'll send five hundred. And if there should be no happy event, he'll send his chief-of-staff flying."

But men have been sent to concentration camps for less.

§ 3

Christmas would have found any normal youth anxious for a holiday at home with the father and the mother who adored him, with his two young brothers and a sister already five years old. But my own youth—possibly altruistic, possibly merely selfish, certainly abnormal—disdained the proffered fare.

"I've got an appointment with Philips for the second of January", I wrote—and on that day I presented myself at Gross Auheim with a certificate from the business school saying that my shorthand speed was eighty.

"Unmäglich (impossible)", laughed Philips; but I took down and read back the letter he dictated; and next day I caught the 6.35 to work.

The factory, built round a cobbled yard, employed some two hundred hands, mostly girls. In a private office next to the proprietor's worked the "prokurist", or manager, who never signed more than his surname, "Stoll". In the outer office abode a very fat book-keeper slightly reminiscent of Bryan Cooper, a very thin book-keeper, myself, and a young office boy.

Stoll and the fat book-keeper cuffed this boy's ears daily. It was the normal routine whenever he made a mistake, and soon adopted by me.

I was set to keeping customers' accounts and to deducting

health and unemployment contributions—then unknown in England—from the wage sheets. Some of the men piece-workers earned seventeen marks (the mark then being worth one of our shillings) weekly; no girl more than twelve. Summer working hours were 7 a.m. to 7 p.m. In winter one hour less.

In the courtyard lived chickens; and a colossal blue "deutsche Dogge", such as you see in the old pictures of Bismarck. This beast, loosed nightly, was reputed unapproachable except by Salm the watchman.

Doubting this, and hating to see any dog chained, I put repute to the test at one midday break. An adjacent fowl perished; the workers scattered screaming. But the terror of Gross Auheim, his immediate hunger satisfied, followed me obedient to lunch; a meal I used to take, privileged, with Stoll and Philips at the one inn.

We were served—among other things with potato pancakes, the recipe for which I have never been able to discover—by a dark wench named Käthi.

Towards the middle of February Käthi's figure showed a definite change. Philips remarked on this.

"Jawohl", smiled Käthi. "Es hat gut gefangen. Bald bin ich verheiratet." ("Rather. It's taken well. I shall soon be married.")

For such was the custom in philoprogenitive Gross Auheim. I remember being rather shocked.

CHAPTER THIRTEEN

§ 1

It is curious how a chance phrase will stick in the mind for the best part of forty years. Shortly before I went to Philips' I met a young man named Koch, son of the famous Frankfort jeweller, who had just joined his father.

Naïvely—perhaps fearfully—I asked him how he could tolerate the monotony of going to the shop at the same hour every morning and leaving it at the same hour every evening.

"It gets into one's flesh and blood", he answered.

This truth was as patent to me as Käthi's condition by the time I had been catching the same 6.35 a.m. train to Gross Auheim for six weeks and is even more patent today.

Later, acting on Philips' suggestion, I gave a "fest" to his workpeople. A huge barrel of beer and a vast supply of the hot sausages we used to munch for our "elevenses" cost about £2, and did something to enhance my popularity.

The unpaid voluntär's position, nevertheless, was rather grim.

Bad feeling between the two nations had been roused, nearly three years back, with the Kaiser's telegram of encouragement to President Kruger. I had heard Hayden Coffin's song:

> "Hands off, Germany; hands off, all!
> Kaiser boasts and Kruger brags".

Our government silenced Hayden Coffin. Then as now, however, the German propaganda machine disdained manners as easily as truth.

You have only to read Kipling's poem "The Rowers", published shortly after the conclusion of peace in South Africa, "When Germany proposed that England should help her in a naval demonstration to collect debts from Venezuela", to realise the kind of newspaper articles on which Philips' workpeople were fed.

Kipling wrote:

> "There was never a shame in Christendie
> They laid not to our door".

And after those two savage lines, "Our dead they mocked are scarcely cold, Our wounds are bleeding yet", he went on:

> " 'Neath all the flags of all mankind
> That use upon the seas,
> Was there no other fleet to find
> That you strike hands with these?
> Of evil times that men can choose
> On evil fate to fall,
> What brooding judgment let you loose
> To pick the worst of all?
> In sight of peace—from the Narrow Seas
> O'er half the world to run—
> With a cheated crew, to league anew
> With the Goth and the shameless Hun".

This, I believe, was the first time the word "Hun" found its way into our common speech.

Those English pacificists, afterwards to jeer at Lord Roberts for preaching conscription, who deprecated "The Rowers", could never have visited Frankfort's biggest music hall, "The Orpheum", where a comedian named Otto Reuter always evoked the biggest laugh of the night with a song that told how an English nurse in South Africa was shot in the breast.

Our women being proverbially less generous of bosom than Hunland's, the last lines of the song ran:

> "The doctors found the bullet,
> But they couldn't find the breast".

Meanwhile in Philips' workrooms hung German Navy League posters screaming, "Our future lies on the sea" (which slogan I saw plastered all over Italy in the summer of 1938); one of the wooden moulds used for making the fillers of cheap cigars, flung by an undiscovered hand, might have broken my spine as I walked between the rolling tables; and even Philips believed his *Frankfurter Zeitung* to the point of assuring me, "You'll never beat the Boers".

I shall never forget the astonishment on his face and Stoll's when—in the middle of our hottest dispute over the lunch table—Käthi swelled in with the news that peace had been signed at Vereeniging.

"Unmöglich", cried both.

§ 2

Such disputes, and the perpetual lies I read about our cruelties to our prisoners, affected me—curiously enough—very little. I saw nothing prophetic in them. They did not even prevent a lukewarm liking for Stoll, and a few others who "weren't too bad for Germans".

The companions of my free time, nevertheless, remained English or American—and before my eighteenth birthday I once more fell in love.

Edith and her tall sister Marion were Bostonians. They lived with their mother, and their father—Frankfort representative of the American Shoe Machinery Company. Once again, only marriage was contemplated by either of us—and no solitary jaunts allowed.

Even our kisses, as I remember them, would have passed muster with a modern film-censor—"parlour courtship" being the operative phrase.

Marion used to sing "Melisande at the Well" to the family while we sat in a corner holding hands.

Memory suggests that we considered ourselves engaged. But of this I am not certain. What I am certain of is that Edie's influence—though the realisation of this would have shocked her sweet soul to its Puritan depths—kept me away from certain narrow streets behind the Zeil.

I had no craving for that kind of adventure, only for what I considered romance. And even romance—as I now see it—must have occupied a very subordinate position in my thoughts. Otherwise I should hardly have decided to spend four evenings weekly —the Saturday half-holiday was unknown and I never returned to the Kaiserstrasse before 7 p.m.—learning Spanish from a lady whose eruditions far exceeded her beauty. Neither should I have written, purely for my own satisfaction, a "General Report on the factory of August Philips and Söhne, Gross Auheim", which runs to seventy pages of foolscap, and still amazes me with its sketches, its calculations and its technical knowledge.

Witness only pp. 34 /35 on "Cutting the Wrapper"; and the "Genealogical Tree showing the 189 colours in sorting", to which is appended the note, "9 shades × 7 colours × 3 surfaces. $9 \times 7 \times 3 = 189$".

I spent three weeks alone at the one wooden-walled inn of Heyerode in the Taunus, where we had a branch factory, to learn "clean-sorting", as the book calls it, and three months at the tables moulding fillers and rolling them in the wrapper.

And before I left Philips' I could tell—by merely smoking it— which of the fifty different tobaccos in our storerooms had gone to the manufacture of a particular cigar.

But this was no feat of the palate compared with the one performed by Philips' wine-merchant brother-in-law on a certain occasion when we visited his mother at her vineyard on the Rhine, and she sent us home with a picnic basket.

"This wine", said Herr R., having opened and tasted the bottle in that basket, "must be wrongly labelled. It doesn't come from my mother's vineyard. It was grown on the other side of our wall."

Subsequently I was to see, in Cuba, two fields without even a hedge between them producing entirely different tobaccos down to their very boundaries. In this case, inquiry proved Herr R.'s judgment to be exactly right.

I had been a smoker since I was fifteen. (The Round Tower of Windsor Castle, with its unparalleled facilities for observing the approach of hostile forces, is still recommended for that purpose to precocious Etonians.) Even my father's offer of "a nice cigar instead of those cigarettes"—though deadly in its subsequent effect among the shrubberies of Glen Cottage, Maidenhead, where we made holiday in the summer of 1900—had not weaned me from my fat Gourdoulis and Melachrinos.

To the juices of hop, grape and apple, however, I came untrained.

Drunkenness, in Germany, was still esteemed a virtue. "The man who's never been tight", ran the proverb, "can't be a good fellow."

I made my début as a good fellow with one of the factory's commercial travellers on hard cider in the suburb of Sachsenhausen, feeling very manly if a trifle sick.

April 21st, 1902, nevertheless, called for a birthday celebration —details of which are still remarkably clear.

Some four of us, all English, dined at a restaurant called Malepartus, whose sign was still hanging over its doorway when I last visited Frankfort in 1932.

There we drank Rhine wine, and topped it up with brandy. Whereafter we promenaded the town.

Memory recalls watching a "Liebesmahl"—which has nothing to do with love, being a regimental dinner—through the windows of the Frankfurter Hof, in whose bar we also celebrated; and further alcoholic peregrinations till long after midnight, when the one sober member of the party said:

"The trams have stopped. I'll walk you home".

So we walked—Rex Joseph, the sweet singer, and I—arm in arm till we reached the outer door of 73 Kaiserstrasse; and there he suggested, "Hadn't I better take you upstairs and put you to bed?"

"I was so certain you were sobering up", he told me afterwards, "both from the way you answered me and from the way you took out your latchkey, that I left you."

Thus left—all this being still as clear to me as though it had happened yesterday—I relocked the outer door, climbed five flights of stairs, found myself facing the door of my own "pension", kicked out the top half, which was of thick glass, climbed over the splinters, entered my own room, turned on the incandescent gas lamp, and climbed into bed.

Hours of blissful unconsciousness followed. The usual maid woke me. Then I heard her scream—and the landlord rushed in.

"Um Gottes Willen!" he screamed; and turned off the gas which I had forgotten to light.

Fortunately, I always slept with one window open. I remember remarking on this, assuring my landlord that I would pay for the broken glass, washing certain wounds which might have handicapped me as a father, changing my shirt, and donning the awful readymade coat and trousers, the black felt hat, I had bought out of my £3 a week.

My coffee, I could not drink; but 6.33 to the second found me showing my second-class season at the barrier; and that morning, as was occasionally made necessary by alterations in the time table, I walked the two miles of pavé from Hanau to the factory; where I related my achievement—not, maybe, without a touch of vainglory—to Stoll.

"Better still", said he, "if you had remembered to put a collar and tie on."

But even that day, I worked through; and all that year, still refusing to go home, I would take no holiday.

"No more exhibitionism", I must have been saying to myself. Yet unconsciously. For that I had not learned to reason, is quite plain.

The urge to speak and write two foreign languages perfectly, to master every detail of a business which had little or no relation to my father's—however good or bad the underlying motive—was purely emotional, mere self-fulfilment.

A casual line in one of my mother's letters, received just before my return, tried to point this out.

She quoted Tennyson's, "You have but fed on the roses and lain in the lilies of life".

This to me, who had never asked for a shilling beyond my allowance while I laboured fourteen hours a day for six days weekly.

How hotly, how unfairly, seethed my resentful immaturity, as I penned my reply.

CHAPTER FOURTEEN

§ 1

My last week in Frankfort I did take as a holiday. Memory's pictures are limited to two. In one, lonely at the Café Bristol, I devour column after column of the *Daily Telegraph*, which is reporting the Hartopp, most famous of all "society" divorce cases, verbatim. In another Edie and I—duly chaperoned—are watching a performance of *Alt Heidelberg*, better known in its modern musical guise as *The Student Prince*.

"Karl Heinz", wailed the deserted heroine in the last act of that play, "du kommst nie wieder." ("You're never coming back.")

But I promised that I would; and I believe that we kissed each other goodbye at the station. Though this I cannot be sure.

Sure only is the utter strangeness of homecoming to a new house, 11 Clarges Street, Mayfair, which—according to my mother—had once been Emma Lady Hamilton's. A footman unpacked for me; he and a butler served the Christmas dinner. But on Boxing Day morning my father decided that he would "just run down to the office and see if there's anything in the post".

The peculiarity of this proceeding did not then strike me. I demanded to go with him. A hansom cab clip-clopped us over woodblock paving to 30 Gracechurch Street. The Havana mail had not been delivered. The "post" consisted of two circulars and one receipt.

We returned to Clarges Street in time for lunch. As usual, the family had seats at the Lane, where the dark Madge Lessing, whom I thought very lovely, sang:

> "I'm the rose of all the Riviera,
> Pluck me if you can,
> Buttonholes are coming into fashion,
> I should make a nice one for a man
> Who likes a flower with all its petals open . . ."

It's queer how the words of old songs stick in the mind.

§ 2

My father's younger brother Edwin had died while I was in Germany, leaving him the bulk of a fairish fortune. Hence

Mayfair (not yet a byword for extravagance and stupidity); Julia's (my near-manhood no longer called her Mumsey) brougham and victoria; and Clover Cottage, Eastbourne, whose exiguous drawing-room she—mocking at superstition—hung with a peacock wallpaper.

But my father had no zest for the Mayfair game.

"Now you can feel a gentleman again", he used to mock me when he opened our mahogany front door with his latchkey—he hated ringing for his staff at any time—of an evening. The only unfair remark I ever knew him to make!

Yet even my hot youth could not resent that unfairness. Because by the time I had been accompanying him to and from the city for a few weeks I began to realise—far better than my mother—just what those lies spoken in Hamburg were costing him in health and faith.

He and his two partners had built up, with their own money and their own hard work, the Upmann cigar business in Great Britain. Their word as good as their bond, they had never demanded that the verbal agreement for a sole agency, already of thirty years' duration, should be put into writing.

Sheer loyalty to this association had caused them to refuse a magnificent offer by J. B. Duke's Tobacco Trust, which had recently acquired the bulk of the Havana factories, to amalgamate with another firm and thereby control most of the trade.

All three partners had agreed, "We can't let Upmanns down".

The reward for this loyalty was gloriously Teutonic—Upmanns insisting that Frankaus must share their sole agency with our two principal competitors.

Outwardly my father took that blow with his chin up. But even my youth could feel that the treachery had broken his heart.

The shock of learning that his trusted associates had no conception of business honour turned his iron-gray hair nearly white. He was a sick man—with his only surviving partner, Uncle G., now a widower, verging on seventy.

In imagination, he saw the business ruined.

"What a bloomer", he used to say. "My God, what a bloomer. I backed the wrong horse."

§ 3

I had to endure the full purgatory of "shellshock and neurasthenia" as a grown man myself before I really understood all that my father must have suffered during the last three years of his life.

But enough of those sufferings were already plain to me; and I am always glad that I managed to help a little—even if only by stealing out to buy him those round tins of his favourite "Three Castles" cigarettes.

It was not the Edwardian thing to smoke Virginia cigarettes at half a crown a hundred. Even as late as 1914 a young friend of mine, newly commissioned to a regiment of yeomanry, suffered stern rebuke for offering a case full of "cheap gaspers" to his superior officer.

And especially was it not the thing at 30 Gracechurch Street, where Uncle G. and "our Mr. Musgrave"—a relative by marriage who acted as manager—puffed fat Havanas all day long.

Yet with the green tin at his elbow empty, my father—standing to write his letters at the high mahogany desk which had served his father before him—would fidget and fidget for another.

I used to open that other tin, and put it down beside him, and watch his hand go out, feeling more sorry for him than I had ever felt for any human being in my whole young life.

Curiously, his hands were always steady—and the only time I ever saw him near to losing his temper was when he accidentally opened a bill addressed to me.

That bill, from a bootmaker named Selzer in Frankfort, who made as good a shoe as Peal's of Oxford Street for a very moderate price, had been rendered once before.

"Why haven't you paid it?" stormed my father.

"Well, I've only had the bally things three months."

"Three months! You've no right to keep him waiting a day. Write him out a cheque immediately. Immediately, I tell you. And you'd better send him a letter of apology."

And over lunch, by which time he had simmered down, he told me a story of my Uncle Edwin who—asked if Frankaus would give a banker's reference—retorted, "We bank at the Bank of England, sir. But our reference is cash".

Edwin had been the financier of the firm, and also its buyer. My father was its principal salesman: at which job—since all men loved and none distrusted him—he excelled.

"When Edwin first went to Havana", he told me on another occasion, "there was so much money about that they had their horses shod with silver."

Thus gradually I learned the whole history of the business, whose present managing director, George S. Flint, was our office boy when I joined.

My grandfather's first warehouseman, Shepherd, who came to

him in 1837 and was pensioned after fifty years' service, still used to visit us in 1903—and Pedder, who came in 1887, did his fifty years, too.

Shepherd's original job must have been a messy one. He received and despatched the leeches my grandfather used to import from France. Then leeches began to go out of fashion; and my grandfather turned to sponges. Not yet his son-in-law, Uncle G. was sent to Smyrna to buy the first consignment. "Lovely girls there", he told me in a rare mood of expansion.

But my grandfather died at forty-four; and by 1857 my father was being told by the head of the ring who controlled most of the sponge trade, "We've got it here, Frankau", tapping his forehead, "and we've got it here, Frankau", tapping his pocket, "and you're not coming in".

My father used to enjoy telling that story, and how he beat the ring within two years, and how—by sheer accident—he and his young brother and Uncle G., the faithful clerk who had married their eldest sister, drifted from sponges into cigars.

"All our customers were chemists", the story went on. "And when the doctors of those days began to advise their patients to give up smoking pipes and take to cigars instead, the patients took the advice as though it were a prescription. They asked their chemists for cigars; and the chemists began to ask us for them. So one day I bought a few boxes."

The chemist who bought those few boxes of cigars from my father—Westmacott of Manchester if I can trust my memory—was still our customer in 1903.

§ 4

It is difficult to depict my father without overstressing his many virtues. I shall never forget his Quixotry when Harry Savory, the Piccadilly cigarette manufacturer—one of the best accounts in the West End, who had never bought a cigar from us in his life—shouldered his way into the private office one morning.

"Those b——s So-and-So", shouted Savory, "have been cheating me, Arthur. I'll never buy a ruddy box from 'em again. You can have the whole of my business."

"I can't believe they've been cheating you", said my father. "You always were a hot-tempered chap."

Harry Savory's hansom was at the door. A few minutes later my father had coaxed him into it. They went round to So-and-

3

So's together. When my father returned, I remonstrated with him. So did Uncle G.

"The chap had only lost his wool", he explained. "He and So-and-So have been friends ever since I can remember."

Yet that this Don Quixote of Gracechurch Street was always a cheery Mentor to my youthful Telemachus, I cannot pretend.

In the presence of our small staff, which included one of the few female stenographers then working in the city, or when customers came to see us, he could play the part of the successful merchant. But alone with me in the upstairs office—it was horse's work to drag him away from his desk of an evening—his selfcontrol would go.

"You don't understand", he used to rave. "That one mistake of mine has ruined the business. I should never have let you come into it."

And on one occasion I had actually to unlock the private ledger and show him his capital account, just over six figures, before I could persuade him that we were solvent.

Poor Pupsy, who never harmed a human creature, what a trial you could be in those moods!

CHAPTER FIFTEEN

§ 1

MODERN medicine might have diagnosed my father's condition as the reaction of an enfeebled physique to a prolonged mental strain. But of the enfeebled physique, my mother and I knew nothing; and, although we were terribly sorry for him, both of us resented his "nerves".

Naturally optimists, full of a joie de vivre which demanded (and seized on) every opportunity for personal enjoyment, we could not understand why he should be so gloomy. But this our common loyalty would not discuss.

I had my work in the city, largely clerical during my first year she, having "relapsed into novel writing and published *Pigs in Clover* 1902" (again to quote her own statement in *Who's Who*) was once more busy collecting material for another work on colour printing and engraving, *The Lives of James and William Ward*.

Jack, as we always called my brother Paul Ewart, was rising

twelve by then, Ronnie just over nine, and my sister Joan (actually christened Aline) two years younger.

They also kept my mother busy—especially Jack, a strange, restless, troublesome character, who had been sent away from his first school for refusing to say his lessons except with a waste-paper basket on his head; and who—loosed from the leading rein for the first time—was subsequently observed at full gallop facing his pony's tail.

"It's so easy to ride the right way round", remarked Jack at seven. "So I thought I'd try the other."

But between me and my brothers and sister lay the gulf of adolescence—to be bridged only after the passing of many years.

I cannot honestly say, looking back on this period of my life, that I had any affection for, or any interest in, either Jack, Ronnie, or Joan. All my loyalties were concentrated on my father, and the bulk of my affection on my mother . . .

Till yet another love affair—still of the calf variety—intervened.

§ 2

About the time I returned to England from Germany, Marjorie, my childhood's sweetheart, in training to be a singer, was learning Italian from a lady of such astounding loveliness that—having shared some lessons—I decided to continue the studies à deux.

My passions—alas!—were only reciprocated by a book which I still possess inscribed "al mio incomparabile allievo" ("to my incomparable pupil"); but how strong they must have been is shown by the fact that they led to the first and only breach between myself and my mother.

Julia lent me her brougham one evening. I was to fetch her from the house where she had been dining. I fetched her punctu-ally, but not alone. She had promised an aunt of mine a lift. My ladylove and I were forced to take a hansom. Imagining Elvira to have been insulted, I sulked with Julia for a week.

"Pupsy rather enjoyed that week", my mother told me long afterwards. "Because he had you all to himself."

The judgment was sound, if not altogether kind. My father's love for me did contain that slight tinge of jealousy. He never felt quite happy if I went out with a girl.

Accordingly I told him nothing of my first holiday plans—a platonic journey with my new ladylove as far as Florence, to be followed by a meeting with Edie and her family in Rome.

The journey really was platonic, though an Italian sailor in

our crowded second-class carriage accused us of being on ou
"viaggio di rose" (voyage of roses), a nice phrase—and subse
quently enlightened my ignorance, alone towards dawn in th
swaying corridor, "You Englishmen are poor lovers", wit
numerical boasts of his own prowess.

Nor did Rome provide me with the experience I still lacked.

Returning solitary I found myself—for the first and only tim
in my life—penniless; and hereby pay belated acknowledgment t
a nameless American gentleman who treated me to breakfast o
the train.

In themselves, the above incidents are hardly worth chroniclin
But they had a peculiar sequel. Home again, thwarted affection
sought the consolation of the pen.

The story was entitled "Seamew and Pantheress", and heade
with the appropriate Swinburne couplet, "You could not tam
your light white seamew nor I my sleek black pantheress". I
relates the Italian journey of one "Juan" who loved two ladie
a blonde and a brunette.

Juan's brunette woke alone to remember "the night when sh
had glimpsed, for the first time, the innate bestiality of the othe
sex". How much his blond glimpsed, I have forgotten. Certainl
too much for the *Saturday Evening Post* or the *Strand*.

§ 3

Acting (for once!) on my mother's advice, I did not off
"Seamew and Pantheress" to an editor. Besides, my ambition
were still purely commercial; and my selfconfidence still so ove
whelming that—by the end of my first year in Gracechurch Stree
—I felt certain I knew everything there was to know about buyin
and selling cigars.

My father and uncle—it seemed to my youthful impatience-
were altogether too old-fashioned, and too cautious. Laughingly
used to tell Julia Uncle G.'s pet aphorism, "If I had my way abou
sending out the Havana orders this week, I shouldn't send out an
at all".

And once, I remember, when my father, at his very gloomies
said, "If anything were to happen to me, Julia, I don't kno
what would happen to the business", I broke in, "Don't yo
worry about that. I'd run it for her".

That made him laugh.

He was beginning to laugh again by October of that year 190
The anticipated ruin of the business had not occurred. His o

customers remained loyal. One or two new "Independent" factories—notably "Romeo y Julieta", whose new proprietor, the tiny "Pepin" Rodriguez, had visited us, and left with a sample order that summer—were starting up in Havana. He began to talk of going there, "only it's so difficult for me to get away".

November brought good trade—and sent me down to Eton, at m'tutor's invitation, for the first time since I had left.

Chance has preserved a list of those who sang "Green grow the rushes, Oh!" and "One more river to cross". The thirty-four names include Turnour, Wyndham, Barry, Cooper, Platt, Schiff, Weldon *ma* and Weldon *mi*, Pender, now Governor of Cable and Wireless Holdings Ltd,, Leatham, and Thorne *ma*—who was to play his part when the Worcesters retook Gheluvelt, thus saving the Ypres Salient, in 1914, and is now that general affectionately known to the army as "Bulgy".

In that list also is James (G. C. B. if memory is adequate) whose story I interpolate, because it is one of the finest I know.

James was the first captain of the house. Thanks to him, we won our football colours—and a place on the river.

At the outbreak of war James visited m'tutor.

"I can't volunteer for at least two years", he said. "I'm in business now, with all my people dependent on me. But if it lasts that long, I shall be all right, because by then I shall have been able to train other people to do my job."

At the end of his two years he volunteered for the infantry— and was killed before he had been in the front line twenty-four hours.

CHAPTER SIXTEEN

§ 1

In the opening chapter of George Meredith's almost forgotten masterpiece *Lord Ormont and his Aminta* you can read how the bigger boys at a certain school "revelled in the devilish halo of skirts on the wheel encircling Lord Ormont's laurelled head".

No Lord Ormont, I made Christmas holiday chez Maxim in Paris at the age of nineteen and a half.

Champagne supplied courage for that first experience. But the experience itself—dictated partly by curiosity if mainly by the code of a day which condemned male ignorance as sternly as it insisted on female innocence—supplied no delight.

Sentiment revolted at the cash transaction—and pitied the purveyors of such disappointing romance. I discussed this matter with my father, whom not even Helen of Troy could have weaned from an innate asceticism.

You can judge the code of the day by his answer, "That class of woman is a safety valve".

Abolish it—he suggested—and thousands of decent girls would be seduced.

"Avoid artificial complications" was another maxim he produced during that discussion—and for a while I did, confining myself strictly to business, which provided me, in the January, with my first really responsible job.

A fire at the Haydon Square warehouse had destroyed almost our entire bonded stock. "Prepare the claim", said my father.

When I showed him the calculations, he grinned:

"There'll be a row about this. You've put everything down at selling price".

"Well, isn't market value the same as selling price? That's what it says we're insured for in the policy."

Whereupon he told me the reason for that ambiguous phrase "market value"; how, after a great boom in cotton which had ended in the usual slump, a colossal fire broke out in the Liverpool cotton warehouses.

"The companies had to pay purchase prices in that case", he went on. "And they didn't like it a bit, because they could have replaced the cotton for half."

"There was some talk of incendiarism, too", said Uncle G.

My father's prognostication proved correct.

"I'm afraid you've made a mistake", said the assessor. "Selling price! You mean buying price in Havana, don't you?"

"Buying price in Havana?" I queried in my best Etonian debating manner. "But how can that be market value? After all, *we* are the market."

We disputed the point in the dock-sample room—till he insisted on seeing "one of the partners". I took him upstairs. My father said, with a touch of pride, "I agree with my son. It seems to me your company wants to have it both ways. When we asked them to insure us at purchase price they refused".

The assessor talked of "replacement value" and said he must "take instructions". He returned the next day. The company stuck to its decision. So did we. You can't replace vintage wares at the original cost.

"But if I settle with you at selling price", wailed the assessor, "and other claimants get to hear of it . . ."

My father fired up at once.

"We're not asking for any special treatment", he began. "Either the claim's just, and you pay it. Or it's unjust, and you refuse."

"You mean, you'd go to law?"

Pupsy shrugged his shoulders. The assessor departed again—and returned with a suggestion for compromise. Supposing we added compound interest at five per cent. per annum to the Havana prices?

"I'll get my son to work it out", smiled my father.

He checked those final calculations himself. Uncle G. cross-checked them, grumbling, "This is absurd. Here is a case" (10,000 cigars) "we have had in stock for fifteen years without being able to sell it—and they pay us ten times its value. On the cases which came in last week and were actually sold we lose our profit".

"But the insurance company", said my father, "saves its face."

You should have seen the assessor's face when he found that the compromise worked out at some £12 more than our original demand, which had been approximately £12,000.

"I don't quite see", he told us, "how I can pass the extra amount."

"Then we'll let you off the £12", said my father—and we settled on those terms.

§ 2

I have told the above story at some length because it has had a lifelong effect. Only last year, reading of a case in which a life insurance company, issuer of a policy without a suicide clause, avoided payment to the unfortunate creditors of a man who had shot himself by standing on its obscure legal rights, I was so infuriated that only the wisdom of my friend A. L. Cranfield, then editor of the *Daily Mail*, prevented me from dashing into print.

I consider the insurance company in question—having established its legal point, that, suicide being still considered a crime, the executors of the criminal cannot benefit from it—should have paid up in full as a moral gesture.

A happier effect of that long-ago dust-up over a policy was that my father and Uncle G. decided to award me a bonus.

This I invested—for a brief two years—through the giver of that old airgun, Henry Morris, my mother's stockbroker and the only real dandy I ever knew.

Henry—tall, bald, with a beautiful figure and a dark "imperial" on his chin—once donned a blue flannel suit and a straw hat instead of the regulation topper, morning coat and striped trousers for a Saturday morning in his office.

"But I carried a tennis racket under my arm", he told Julia. "Just to show I really was going away for the weekend."

And on another occasion he arrived at our house in a great state of distress with the news that his pet trouser-artist at Poole's in Savile Row—where he bought all his clothes—was "not looking at all well".

"I can't take the risk of anything happening to him", said the dandy. "So I ordered *eighty* pairs."

Henry's manners were as perfect as his clothes. He adored music as much as he adored children—and was always discovering "prodigies", for whom he used to give parties at his house in Hamilton Terrace.

Taken to one such party while I was still at Hawtrey's, I had met three young ladies, all unsophisticated.

The eldest and largest of these sang to us.

"Most of Henry's swans turn out to be geese", scoffed Julia as we drove homewards. "That girl nearly deafened me."

It serves further to explain my mother's lack of musical sensibilities when you realise that the girl who nearly deafened her was . . . Clara Butt.

§ 3

That year, 1904, the Japanese were fighting the Russians. But until December—when a panicked Russian admiral opened fire on our Doggerbank fishing fleet, which he mistook for hostile torpedo boats—no one in England worried very much about that.

Apart from business, my own recollections of the spring and summer seem to centre on an American musical comedy called *The Prince of Pilsen* at the Shaftesbury Theatre, where I laughed myself sick over an unknown comedienne, the "Prince's" daughter, who wore a sausage made of diamonds on her prominent bosom and was listed in the programme as "Marie Dressler"; and my Uncle Jimmy's entertainment of the same nature, *Sergeant Brue*.

This last succeeded *A Chinese Honeymoon*, which had beaten all

existing records by running for a thousand nights at the Strand.
Zena Dare was in the cast; and a sweet woman who subsequently
became one of our greatest tragediennes, Ethel Irving.

Another of Jimmy's singers became even more famous. Dame
Marie Tempest made one of her first successes in *The Geisha* at the
Old Gaiety, just being pulled down in 1904, with Wych Street
and other slums, for the building of Kingsway.

But the Strand itself was still that narrow thoroughfare of
which one sang:

> "You needn't go trotting to Norway,
>   You'll find 'em in every doorway;
>   You'll see them in their glory
>   If you'll only take a run
>   Down the Strand,
>   That's the land
>   Of the Midnight Sun."

There stood the old Tivoli music hall. Nearer west, you had the
Empire, whose promenade was the main lady-market and its
final turn "The Bioscope", as its management still called the
cinema; and the Moorish-looking Alhambra, where also one found
ladies. The Alhambra is now the Odeon picture house; and
"the Pav", famous for its chucker-out, has also degenerated to
films.

These—or the Oxford, next door to Frascatis—I had learned to
frequent. The land of the midnight sun, however, was still terra
ignota. One experience had sufficed.

That year I eschewed those later markets, the Continental
Hotel at the foot of Waterloo Place; or the Globe in Leicester
Square, where, according to legend, if you joined a lady at her
table, you were apt to be presented with the bill for her week's
suppers; or that even more exclusive haunt, red-blinded on the
site of the present Piccadilly Hotel, of which the song ran: "You'll
find her at Jimmy's transacting her biz"; and the chorus:

> "For at things which are snide,
>   She is almost as wide
>   As the wide wide world".

I had never even supped in a restaurant—except on one occasion when Barry and I celebrated long leave from Eton by
daredevilling it at the Trocadero—till a night when I fell in with

3*

"mad Carlow", as his schoolfellows called the present Earl of Portarlington, who insisted on my accompanying him to the Carlton, and introduced me to a particularly luscious . . . pink foie-gras.

But that may have been in 1903. For among the 1904 memories is the lovely face of my Italian teacher seen against the dark-red mahogany panels of the narrow old Savoy restaurant, long before it was enlarged by the addition of the present balcony and ballroom.

We entered from the Embankment by the little lift you can still use. The absurd curfew was already in force—and the modern night club unknown. A waiter removed our 8s. bottle of champagne at midnight.

Only hansoms and "growlers", as we called the four-wheel cabs of the period, waited outside—and at home my father, who never slept till he heard my latchkey in the door.

Not that I should have funked a wigging if . . .

But that—alas!—was never to be.

CHAPTER SEVENTEEN

§ 1

UNLIKE most children of the period, I had never been afraid of my father. Increasingly, however, during my first year in business, I had been afraid *for* him. Why, I don't quite know.

He may have seemed—to my adamantine adolescence—so much too decent for a world in which ancient associates broke faith, and even insurance companies only lived up to their policies if threatened with the law. Fear may have sprung from those terrible headaches which sometimes sent him to bed for two whole days, or merely from increasing affection.

Anyway, there the thing was; and with it a further sense of responsibility. The pater mustn't be worried. The pater must be cheered up. If the worst came to the worst and his nerves couldn't stand the strain any longer, I must be able to run the business for him.

And of course—repeated absurd selfconfidence—I could.

In my own imagination, our positions were already reversed—I the father, he the child. Recognising his experience, I could not

dmit that he had drawn wisdom from it. Cognisant of his utter
goodness, I could not bring myself to believe in his strength or his
ability.

Then—all of a sudden—his whole outlook on life seemed to
change; and my fear vanished.

Vanity attributed the change to my own influence.

"He'd never have made up his mind to this Havana trip", I
told Julia, "if I hadn't persuaded him that I could look after the
business while he was away. It's bucked him up no end having
me with him."

That was in June.

§ 2

The change in my father lasted till he went away. He had been
doing business with Cuba for the best part of thirty years without
once crossing the Atlantic. In New York dwelt the one boon
friend of his youth—Martin Beckhard, then (and still) high in the
confidence of Kuhn, Loeb, the bankers.

He would spend a whole week with Martin before catching the
Ward Line's *Morro Castle* to Havana. And for Havana, he must
have some new clothes.

Memory recalls, fantastically, the grin of sheer boyish enjoyment on his face as he came through the drawing-room door at
11 Clarges Street to display one of the white day-waistcoats he
had bought for himself.

Waistcoats in a Cuban summer! Edwin had always made his
buying trips just after Christmas. But then Edwin hadn't travelled the provinces—Liverpool and Birmingham, Manchester,
Glasgow and Sheffield—selling the stuff. The pater was still doing
that.

He went in July. He wrote to my mother, as he always had
written to her, every night—posting his first budget when he
reached New York.

A wonderful trip. He felt like a two-year-old. It was so good
of Gilbert to give up his own summer holiday. The boy must
have a really good one in the autumn.

Next mail brought us descriptions of a trip up the Hudson. And
from Havana he wrote rapturously, sending us photographs of
himself in the factories or on muleback in the plantations.

"I ought to have come years ago. My Spanish isn't as good as
Edwin's, but I manage to get on all right. Tell Gilbert it looks

like being a really fine crop, and that I've given quite a lot o orders. Between us we ought to be able to sell them."

We wrote back. "Don't forget that Kipling quotation". Foi we had made a family joke of:

> "He eats and has indigestion.
> He toils and he may not stop.
> His life is a long-drawn question
> Between a crop and a crop".

Then he cabled us that he was returning on the *Etruria*, ending his cable with the family code-word "Pullman", which meant "feeling even better than first class".

So we decided to meet him at Liverpool. Why we did this, I don't quite know—any more than I know how Julia and I bore it when, out and down from that high, black-hulled, clipper-built liner of an older day, tottered a ghost.

Only the ghost of the happy man to whom we had said goodbye eight weeks back let me help him to the train.

"I was taken ill on the ship. I had to stay in my cabin most of the time", he explained. "But I'm all right again now." And he tried to smile at us, to reassure us.

"Don't you think you ought to see Otto?" suggested my mother.

"Not until I've been to the office. I've a lot of notes I simply must give to old G—and Gilbert of course."

We were back in Clarges Street—the boat had arrived in a rainy dawn—by lunch time. He would have gone to Gracechurch Street in the afternoon; but we persuaded him to lie down, and stay in bed for dinner.

"He hasn't even smoked a cigarette since we met him", I said to my mother. "Don't you think you ought to send for Otto?"

"No. He wouldn't like it."

"But we can't let him go to the office."

"I don't see how we can stop him."

"Julia—he isn't going to die, is he?"

"Of course he isn't. Don't let that ridiculous imagination of yours run away with you."

"Could we have the brougham tomorrow?"

She looked at me curiously, before she said, "All right. Go and ring up the stables".

"Is this the snobbish sort of habit you've got into while I've been away", protested the pater, when the coachman drove up after next morning's breakfast.

He had eaten nothing.

"Yes", I lied; and helped him in.

§ 3

We lunched in the office that day—"old George", who had been with us in Shepherd's time, fetched us two chops from the Lombard Restaurant next door.

I made my father eat half of his and drink a cup of coffee; but the cigarette I gave him afterwards choked him at the first puff.

"He looks ghastly", said Musgrave, when I went downstairs. "I've just been talking to your uncle. He says he ought to see a doctor at once."

"We're doing our best to persuade him", I told Musgrave. "I'm just going to ring up Otto."

I told my cousin Otto what I could of the symptoms. His voice sounded grave.

"Get him here tonight if you possibly can", he said. "I'll wait till I hear from you."

The brougham came back for us—on my orders—at five o'clock. By six, I had coaxed the pater to my way. I remembered, as we went clip-clopping for Harley Street, that this was the first time he had ever consented to travel either from or to the city in one of the carriages. I think I knew the very worst on that drive, during which he never spoke a single word.

I certainly knew it within the hour because I forced it out of Otto in the few moments we had alone after the consultation.

"About how bad is he?" I asked. "Is there any hope? Don't lie to me about him."

Otto hesitated.

"He's about as ill as he can be", he said at last.

My father had caught some obscure form of galloping consumption in Havana. On board ship, there had been hæmorrhages. He coughed on the way home, and I saw the red stain on his handkerchief. Next day, one lung collapsed. Then he rallied.

This seemed miraculous. For the modern operation of artificially collapsing the infected lung was still unknown.

Hope kindled again when Otto said he might be taken to Clover Cottage; and rose higher when we heard that his friend, Henry Irving, who was not to die for a twelve-month, had lost a lung years ago.

My Aunt Eliza (Mrs. Aria) told us this. I cannot vouch for the story; but I know that it cheered me up tremendously. So that when the invalid began to fidget, "That boy really must have his holiday", I kept a rendezvous in Berlin.

Julia's telegram reached me at the Adlon the very night I arrived. I returned to London by the first train; took a hansom from station to station, and made Eastbourne about teatime. A "fly" rattled me along the parade and up the hill. A weeping servant let me in to Clover Cottage.

With Julia, in that tiny drawing room still papered with peacocks, sat only her brother Jimmy.

Jimmy took me upstairs. A nurse and, I think, Otto were standing by my father's bed. As I approached him, his eyes opened; and he tried to smile.

If you remember what the lady who was dying of cancer said to Rousseau, you will know what happened next.

Pupsy smiled again when that happened.

"You observe, Gilbert", he managed, "that your father is at least dying in the odour of sanctity."

Those were his last conscious words.

CHAPTER EIGHTEEN

§ 1

IT would be absurd to pretend that my mother was heartbroken at my father's death. To the best of my knowledge she shed no single tear for him. But then tears had never been her way.

Neither were they mine. Yet the journey from London to Woking, the cremation ceremony itself, brought me to a point of hysteria which has always made me sympathetic to young people who find it difficult to restrain their laughter at funerals.

And, looking back, I realise that Julia and I mourned all the more deeply because we made so little public exhibition of our grief.

I had lost more than a father—the only man I have ever met whose life was completely selfless. She had lost more than a husband—the only man, as she herself told me, who ever won her complete respect.

It seems all the more curious, therefore, that the lessons he spent his life in teaching us should have been so soon erased—partially at any rate—from both our minds.

§ 2

Christmas 1904—barely a month after my father's passing—saw me again in Paris, imagining myself very much the man. No longer a purchaser, I experienced a sufficiency of delight—and my first ride in a taxi-auto, motorcabs being still unknown in London.

Montmartre was still Montmartre in those days—or so at least it seemed to a boy not yet twenty-one, shepherded to L'Abbaye Thélème, to the Rat Mort, and the Café Hanneton, and the Filet de Sole, where Triquette and I breakfasted after our taxi-ride in the Bois.

Years later I was to make good literary use of that short holiday and others like it. But for the moment my ambitions were still commercial.

Not only in Clarges Street would I occupy my father's room! His will had been proved by then. Written on a single sheet of the firm's notepaper, it read, "I leave everything of which I may die possessed to my dear wife, Julia Frankau, absolutely".

By then, too, Julia and I had both realised the implication of that peculiar deed drawn up in the middle 'seventies by which the entire goodwill of the family business reverted to "Whichsoever of the said three partners, Arthur Frankau, Edwin Frankau or Joseph Grünbaum shall survive the others".

What neither of us realised was that the larger lunacies are rarely committed by the unintelligent; that the highly strung and the over-imaginative can make far worse mistakes in life's major issues than the placid and the unenterprising folk on whom they so often look down; that her extraordinary courage, her overwhelming love for, and her misplaced confidence in her "wonderful son, Gilbert" were the worst allies for a temperament more literary than businesslike—and the peculiar chivalry of Uncle G.

Egged on by my continued insistence, "Of course I can manage the business", Julia was already resolved for the larger lunacy when she consulted her new solicitor, John Withers, then in his earliest forties (he had married the daughter of an old friend, Doctor Giffard Ransford), about that deed.

"You'll have to buy Mr. Grünbaum out", said Withers. "And as the business is making £7,000 or £8,000 a year he'll be well within his rights if he asks £10,000 to £15,000 for the goodwill."

Told of this interview, Uncle G. cuddled his gray beard, and retorted, "That may be the legal position, Julia. But I was supposed to be a very sick man when Arthur and Edwin inherited the business and took me into partnership. They had no idea I could possibly survive them. So morally I cannot see that I am entitled to a penny".

Nor—despite all my mother's attempts at persuasion—would he accept more than the return of his capital, plus a token payment of, I think, £1,000, and a nominal salary to act as chairman of the private limited company which Withers advised us to form.

"I'd really like to retire," he told my mother. "But I feel I ought to stay on for a year or two just to advise Gilbert."

My father's barrister cousin Fritz Frankau—also a director of A. Frankau & Co., Ltd., manufacturers of the B.B.B. pipe, originally founded by a member of the family but not otherwise connected—agreed to join our board for the same tutorial purpose.

Another innovation was the appointment of a firm of chartered accountants, Messrs. Gundry, Straus and Soper (now Gundry, Cole & Co.), to audit the books.

The Strauses, father and son, still plead my cause with the Income Tax Commissioners. But Ernest Gundry has gone. One of the last names he mentioned on his deathbed was my own. You may perceive a reason for this as the tale proceeds.

Suffices, for the moment, that I became managing director of the newly-formed company on my twenty-first birthday (April 21st, 1905); and that, metaphorically speaking, our next-door neighbours, Christy & Co., the hatters, were already finding it a little difficult to fit my city self with a large enough size.

§ 3

In the meantime, home life had also undergone changes—as may have been foreseen by my father when he used to chaff, "When I die, Julia, put my ashes in the leg of a poker table. Then you'll never be away from me very long".

At poker Julia lost so rarely, being both lucky and plucky, that Edward Hulton, who was just meditating sallying down to attack London's Fleet Street from his journalistic fastness in Manchester, once said to her, "I'm sure I don't know, Mrs. Frankau, why you ever bother to write".

But then Hulton, at whose country house, Downside, I happened to be staying when he eventually sold out his newspaper interests for a cool six million pounds sterling—cash on the nail and no shares, thank you—always considered writing rather a mean trade.

At auction bridge—still in its infancy—Julia was not quite so expert. Memory recalls a dialogue at Almack's, one of the first "cock and hen" bridge clubs in London, which we both joined.

Her partner, on losing a big rubber: "You must be a very wealthy woman, Mrs. Frankau".

Julia, modestly: "Far from wealthy, Colonel So-and-so. Comfortably off, shall we say".

Her partner: "But you can't have less than ten thousand a year—otherwise you couldn't afford to play ten shillings a hundred".

Poker, bridge, and continual flutters on the Stock Exchange, however, represented only the smallest part of my mother's activities. My father's health had made entertaining difficult. Now she revelled in giving lunch parties, and especially dinner parties, at which the wine flowed freely—and talk was not always discreet.

Unusually for the period, coffee and liqueurs were always served with the ladies still at table; and so potent, on one occasion, proved the brandy—to say nothing of Julia's capacity for putting her guests at their ease—that another gallant colonel interrupted a discussion about an ex-royal favourite with the words:

"Three hundred pounds for a couple of hours. But, by Gad, Mrs. Frankau, she's worth every penny of it".

Unconscious laughter-maker on a later occasion was George Moore, one of my mother's oldest friends, who drew the principal character of his novel *Esther Waters* from my wet nurse, and who said to me, the first time I ever met him, "If your mother had only become my mistress when I asked her to, she would write better English".

My Aunt Eliza, he further suggested, had enjoyed that unique honour. For, like most men of limited loving-powers, nothing gave the greatest of our prose stylists greater pleasure than such imaginary successes as the one he immortalised in his apocryphal story of the mysterious lady with honey-coloured hair who, on the day she departed enceinte for America, explained the real reason for a whole month of amorous dalliance with him in Dublin by saying:

"I came to you because Texas has no literature".

On this occasion, however, the "White Slug", as my mother always called him, was on his best behaviour. Present, among others, were the lovely Alice Muriel Williamson, her husband, and Sydney Pawling, one of the partners in Heinemanns, the publishers. Guest of honour was the author of that latest bestseller, *The Old Wives' Tale*. Only after the honoured guest had taken his departure did George Moore ask, joining thumb and first finger of his right hand in a characteristic gesture:

"Now tell me, Juliah. Who is this fellow Bennett? Does he write?"

Poor Arnold Bennett, how often I wanted to tell you that story—only restraining myself because you would be so dignified —while you were alive.

CHAPTER NINETEEN

§ 1

THE more I look back on those twelve bachelor months I spent so happily with Julia in Clarges Street, the more I am amazed that the multitude of my own activities should have surpassed even hers.

That most of the activities were futile is beside the point.

I was rarely home before two o'clock in the morning. But at Gracechurch Street I worked—not unsuccessfully—for at least eight hours a day. Uncle G.'s pessimism still chafed my optimism. But otherwise we got on well enough.

Loyal to his memory, Arthur Frankau's customers continued to buy from his son.

Memory brings back various figures—Hickson, a grand old John Bull of a man, always in high collar and Ascot tie, who bought for Thomas Porter & Son, the Sheffield wine merchants; John Bird, who controlled the wine and cigar department of John Mark & Co., the Manchester grocers, full-bearded, in his black morning coat, with the gold albert watchchain of the period looping his high waistcoat; Harry Preston, whom I was to know better in the post-war years; Oddenino, the famous restaurateur, always short of time and usually of temper; Frank Towle of the Midland Hotels, very Cambridge and aloof, who bought mostly from another firm; his brother Arthur, now married to Margery Lawrence, the authoress; that great gentleman Alfred Hedges of

Benson and Hedges, who became Liberal Member of Parliament for Tonbridge in 1906—and many more.

These, fortunately, did not share the opinion of my junior clerk, George Flint, who recently confessed to me, sitting in my own old managerial chair, "How I used to hate you every time I came upstairs to fetch your letters"; or of the two competitors whose conversation I chanced to overhear—in that very 1905—at Verrey's.

"And what do you think of young Gilbert?" asked one of those competitors.

"Well", answered the other, after a judicial pause, "his father was a gentleman."

A different character might have been hurt. I was only flattered. Had I not conceived a supreme contempt for "popular boys" in my schooldays? Was not my very unpopularity proof of my success?

§ 2

It was not the custom then, as it is now, for city men to lunch in the West End. Restaurants were scanty, London's only public motor-transport consisted of a few solid-tyred petrol-driven omnibuses, and Big Business still clung to its old haunts east of Temple Bar.

But it had always been my father's habit to lunch at Romano's on a Saturday. And to this custom—wild women would not have kept me from the office on a Saturday—I adhered, frequently in the company of "Brookie", several years my elder, and my bachelorhood's bosom friend.

Harold Brooke-Alder, to give him his full name, was a director —with his brother Gilbert, who has also passed on—of N. J. Fenner and H. B. Alder, the paint manufacturers. He had been brought to our house in my father's time, by Ada Leverson, prized for her wit.

"A little woman who runs up your blouses and skirts", Ada was the first to say. "Now that's what I call a really little dressmaker." And it was she, I believe, who nicknamed Harold "my first footman" on account of his prematurely white hair.

Ada wrote a novel or so, in the same light vein. Her greatest friend was Frank Richardson, also a writer, who described his recreation in *Who's Who* as, "The Whisker Question", and achieved maximum publicity by attacking what he called "the odious custom of wearing face fungus" at every possible opportunity.

Thinks a retired judge in one of Frank's novels, as he turns to look at the club out of which he is just sauntering, "Forty years ago, when they elected me, I was the only bounder in the place. Now it's simply full of them".

Another friend of Ada Leverson's—"the veiled woman in black" who sat all through both his trials, and sent him violets and met him when he came out of prison—was Oscar Wilde.

How Harold, almost your typical hunting man, ever drifted into Ada's Bohemian milieu, he never told me—possibly because I talked about myself so much that I never gave him a chance.

His experience got me out of more than one scrape—the worst just before my majority. The lady in that case was both fair and kind; but my second rendezvous at her flat in St. James's Court found her entertaining three other gentlemen who were just sitting down to a quiet game of cards.

Would I play poker? Would I not? Would I care to increase the modest stakes when I was winning? Well—if the other gentlemen really wanted to. Would I wager £120 on four queens—having thrown a useless ace into the discard? You bet I would.

Whereupon I was shown four aces—making five altogether! And even my inexperience began to wonder if the game could be quite straight.

Violet, who had been sitting beside me throughout, kindly suggested that I had lost enough. The gallant captain who had displayed those quadruple aces, learning that I was not provided with a sufficiency of cash, produced—even more kindly—a cheque form.

I compromised with an I O U; and was on the phone to Harold before half-past eight next morning. He arrived while I sat breakfasting with Julia, to whom I had made full confession.

"There's a private detective named Conquest", said Harold; and to Conquest we went, receiving, in the course of a day or so, a dossier of cardsharping activities which made me think it impossible that I should ever be pressed for payment.

Yet pressed I was, with a solicitorial document addressed to the office, demanding "£120 plus 6s. 8d. being the cost of this letter" under threat of an immediate writ.

"I shouldn't answer", advised Harold.

The verbal opportunity, however, seemed too good to be missed; and, having annotated the document in red ink, "Did your clients inform you (a) that I am a minor and (b) that there were five aces in the pack with which they attempted to cheat me", I sent it back.

This incident did not quite disrupt the uneven tenor of my way with Violet, who supped with me the same night. Our relations, nevertheless, soon became a little strained.

A while later she figured in the newspapers. Considering her lovely eyes, her slender figure, and how many defrauders of dressmakers have escaped scot-free in the interval, the prison sentence a pre-war judge meted out to her still seems rather stiff.

§ 3

Another "very beautiful and very honourable lady of my acquaintance"—as Brantôme, whom I read avidly at this period, would have phrased it—was Mrs. J., who kept one of the last aristocratic "houses" in London and would supply any quantity of lovelies for a bachelor country-house party on receipt of a wire.

I had met her originally in Paris, whither she would take selected members of her troupe for holidays. We were never on visiting terms; but on one occasion she showed me her "nest egg", which she always carried on her person in a washleather bag. I never saw better diamonds, or a woman who looked more like a duchess, even with an uplifted skirt.

The police never interfered with Mrs. J.; and I would hazard that, if she still lives, it is in decorous retirement—a pillar of local good works. But that Sascha Tarnowska can be anywhere on this planet I very much doubt. Because she was just a little blond of the demimonde, only to be mentioned here because she inspired a bestseller of the period, *The Sands of Pleasure*, by the late Filson Young.

He called her "Toni"—hence the couplet in my own satire:

> "Where man drops down life's ladder, rung by rung,
>   And Sascha-Toni catches Filson young".

Sascha-Toni, unlike her consoeurs of 1938, did not appreciate worldwide publicity. "That man!" I can still hear her ejaculating. "He ask me to sleep with him; and when I say 'No', he go away and write his damn novel."

"If ever you write a novel", quoth Julia about this time, "you'd better call it *A Voyage Round the Half-World*."

Yet my interest in the ladies of the town—though frequently

academic, their lives seeming so much more colourful than those of the young ladies I met at dances—worried her. She preferred to know me in my old bedroom, now furnished as a study, exercising what she once called my "fatal facility" with the pen.

For I had begun to write again, purely as an amateur—though I did not scorn the first three guineas I ever earned for an article, bought by the editor of a weekly paper called *The World*.

On acceptance of the article, I visited the editor in person—discovering him tall, thin, pale of face, and extremely dignified in a black frock coat with silk lapels. Such was Cosmo Hamilton, four and thirty years ago.

§ 4

In my father's lifetime, Julia's travels had been severely restricted. Now she developed a passion for sleeping cars; and either that Easter or that Whitsuntide we went—accompanied by Jimmy Davis' wife, Esther—to Aix-les-Bains.

Joseph Chamberlain was there. I remember him as a spare, rather tremulous figure, still with his orchid and his eyeglass, both hands rested on a stout stick, sitting in a garden; and Julia's words: "Why won't they listen to him? We must have Protection".

But I had no interest in politics then, being far more obsessed with learning to drive a ponderous open Renault.

"Declutch, monsieur. For the love of the deity, declutch and change down or she will slide backwards over the precipice with us", my teacher used to shriek as we lost speed on the dusty mountain roads.

Of an evening, I would take Julia to the casino where—because we always walked arm in arm—one of the painted ladies was overheard to mutter, "But it is disgusting, I tell you. Simply disgusting. A liaison between a woman of her age and a young boy like that".

And at Aix—greatly daring—I scraped acquaintance with a member of the Gaiety chorus, very lovely with red hair.

Gaynor and I were never more than platonic friends. But she opened up a new world for me—the world of the stage door, of "Oddy's" and Romano's at curfew hour, of the Saturday supper train to Clacton, and the discreeter houses in St. John's Wood.

Over that world presided the magnificently moustached figure of George Edwardes, always known as "The Governor".

"The Governor's in front tonight"—Jimmy, keeper of the stage door, used to inform me—"so Miss Rowlands won't be out till after the finale." And the yellow-wheeled brougham one could hire for half a guinea from the Coupé Company would have to wait.

So many ladies of title graduated from the Gaiety that one writes of it with diffidence. But one of them, I hope, will pardon the reporting of a scrap of criticism from a lowlier colleague overheard while her horses pawed the just-laid paving of Aldwych:

"Gertie Millar. Gertie Mil*lar*! Feathers as long as your arm in her hat and a carriage and pair to take her home. But when I first knew her, dearie, she was just Gertrude Mill*er* in a pair of clogs and a shawl".

All the more honour to the Dowager Countess of Dudley if the story be true.

That year Gertie Millar starred in *The Spring Chicken*, with sweet Kate Cutler; and plump Connie Ediss, who used to smoke cigars down to the butt by transfixing them with a hatpin; and Teddy Payne the comedian; and Lionel Mackinder, a joyous dancer who volunteered the day the 1914–1918 war was declared and was killed before the first Christmas; and George Grossmith, whom the programme still called "junior", because his father, whose humorous piano entertainments had delighted my earliest boyhood, was still alive.

But the men of my own age patronised the show mainly for its chorus. You rarely went in till the first of the two acts was over— and if you were sufficiently épris and sufficiently wealthy you took a front-row stall for the run of the play.

§ 5

About this time, I again relapsed into verse with a short satire— a parody on that Horatius I had recited from the rocking horse— which I called "The X.Y.Z. of Bridge". Julia, on whom I inflicted the stanzas, thought them worth publishing. P. S. King & Son decided they might sell if illustrated. Pawling recommended a young artist named Lance Thackeray, who came to dinner, and did a marvellous job for a ridiculously small fee.

Lance, whose pencil had more than a touch of genius, died untimely in 1916. Our joint effort, published at a shilling, died the day it was born. I doubt if there is a copy extant beyond my own, which is minus its paper cover.

Curiously, the lack of recognition left me completely cold.

I was far more interested in selling "fourpenny" and "sixpenny" Havanas—then obtainable at every public house—by the case of 10,000 at cut prices than I was in making a mere hobby profitable.

Even after I fell seriously in love with a "nice girl"!

Part Two

FAMILY MAN

CHAPTER TWENTY

§ 1

THE pukka sahib is out of date, except as an object of derision. Nevertheless I should deem myself guilty of unkindness and unfairness—both of which my riper years hold to be major vices in social relationship—were I not to preface the tale of my first marriage with one expression of profound regret.

The major fault, throughout, may have been mine. Inevitably, such tragedies cause pain. The only excuse I can now offer—not that excuses ever seem worthwhile to my philosophy—is that, as a young man, I could never see anybody's point of view except my own.

§ 2

Obsessed with my work, with my hobby of writing, with my academic peregrinations about the half-world, with my platonic trips to the stage door, and one other adventure—too curious to chronicle—with a soi-disant countess who turned out to be a morphinomaniac and nearly landed me at Vine Street, I did not realise how seriously I had fallen in love until late in the summer of 1905.

Even then—Julia and I and my father's other three children were holidaying on the Thames at Wargrave—I only found myself missing, and that only occasionally, a pleasant companionship which had never progressed farther than flirtation with a young lady somewhat older than myself, whose figure was exceptional, whose red hair was completely natural, who possessed the readiest wit, and a knowledge of the poets equalling my own.

A chance reminder spoken by a female cousin, "What's happened to that nice girl I met you with at Aunt Eliza's? I thought you seemed rather gone on her", sharpened recollection. Returning to town I renewed acquaintanceship; and took Dolly first to a picture gallery, afterwards to tea at Charbonnel and Walker's in Bond Street.

As a journalist, she was allowed more freedom than most young women of the period—about as much as would be allowed to a modern girl of fourteen. Still, we drifted into the habit of spending Saturday afternoons together; and every now and again she permitted me to drive her home in a hansom. The stricter code eschewed even that mild form of unchaperoned conveyance as "fast".

Meanwhile I continued to take supper with Gaynor; and had been asked, by my Uncle James, to try my hand at writing lyrics for one of his shows, which looked like being a flop.

"They seem to think I can fill a theatre with Gabs Ray and Maudi Darrel", he wailed, naming two minor if superbly attractive stars. "For God's sake give me a funny song. Two of 'em if you can manage it."

But my one and only effort came back with the characteristic note, "We must at least wrap up our indecencies in tissue paper".

For, although his mild quips in *The Geisha*, which made the audiences of its day rock, excited positive scorn when it was revived recently, Jimmy's wit off-stage could be as unbridled as his expenditure.

I only wish I could quote his remark about the receiver who examined him in bankruptcy, and to whose question, "Don't you think it was rather extravagant to keep a personal valet?" he retorted, "Do you expect me to clean my own boots?"

Jimmy's whole career was so extraordinary that it seems worth recording. In 1869 he took his LL.B. at University College, London—and practised as a solicitor till 1886, when he became a barrister member of Gray's Inn.

Chucking the law, after unsuccessfully contesting Dundalk as a Conservative against Sir Charles Russell, later Lord Chief Justice, he founded his first weekly paper, *The Bat*, which failed; became dramatic critic of the celebrated *Pink 'Un*, and assistant editor of Galignani's *Messenger*, the English newspaper in Paris; founded another weekly, *The Phoenix*, which also failed despite his historic answer to its dunning printers, "Sir, I *never* pay printers"; wrote the books of seven successful musical comedies; owned racehorses, country houses and town houses—at one of which he gave a colossal reception with the brokers' men drinking vintage champagne in the pantry; and spoke his own epitaph when he said, with that charming smile which endeared him to all Bohemian London:

"You can trust me with anything except a pretty girl or a sovereign".

A slight exaggeration which excluded his prime virtue, kindness. But he loved to exaggerate, as witness his statement:

"Every Saturday night of my life I ask the loveliest girl I know to Romano's and order the very best supper I can think of. And every damn Saturday night, just as we're being served, in comes George Edwardes with a girl I'd much rather have and orders himself a supper I'd much rather eat".

I may have been telling Harold that very story—we were certainly sitting in that very restaurant after one of our usual Saturday lunches—when I suddenly made up my mind to propose.

§ 3

Seen in cold print, that operative word "suddenly" seems preposterous. Preposterously, nevertheless, it is the exact truth.

During my lunch with Harold, I decided—without any previous consideration—that I would marry Dolly. It is possible that I told Harold of my intention, and that he attempted to dissuade me. But of this I am not quite sure.

Anyway I left him and drove straight to a house in Dorset Square, No. 13 if memory can be trusted, where I found Dolly alone. It took a whole hour of alternate coaxing and bullying before she would consent.

Julia was out of town till Sunday evening. I met her at the station with my extraordinary news.

"Well, you've always known your own mind", she said. And that was all.

Many years later, she told me her immediate reaction:

"I hated the way you were racketing about. I was always frightened you might get into some terrible mess. But more than anything else—after what your father and Uncle Edwin had told me about its morals—I was terrified of your going to Havana alone".

For that business trip had already been arranged. So why not combine it with a honeymoon? Dorothea Frances Markham Drummond-Black and Gilbert Frankau were accordingly married at Saint Margaret's, Westminster, within six weeks of their engagement being announced, on a foggy day of December 1905.

By a curious contretemps—my best man, to whom I had grandiosely and characteristically left all arrangements for the ceremony, did not look up the rules till the last moment—we had to procure a special licence, an enormous and expensive parchment, secured only just in time from a little dark office in Doctors' Commons.

But a worse contretemps occurred after the reception at my mother's house. In my excitement I forgot to kiss her goodbye. This unkindness haunted me for years. For no mother ever gave her eldest son so much that he wanted—including a sufficiency of money to marry his first wife.

§ 4

Looking back, I often wonder how much I was in love with Dolly, how much I was in love with love, as the saying goes, and how much with a new adventure—marriage. An element of chivalry seems plain. I could give the things her youth craved. Plainer still, however, is the fact that my main love, my overwhelming passion, must have been for myself.

That marriage might entail any personal sacrifice never crossed my mind. I anticipated—mainly if not entirely—an enhancement of my own pleasure.

Fatherhood had no appeal whatsoever. I trusted that we should have no children—at any rate for some years.

CHAPTER TWENTY-ONE

§ 1

DOLLY and I spent the first week of our married life at the old Hotel Bristol in Paris. Our suite—an aristocratic waiter informed us—had often been occupied by "Le Roi Edouard Sept".

My bride was curious to see the celebrated Maxim's. There another slight contretemps occurred—Sascha, who occupied a nearby table, calling across to me, "So you've brought a new one this time".

Fortunately Sascha spoke in German, a language Dolly did not understand.

Julia, passing through on her way to Monte Carlo, visited us, and took us to lunch. She brought some letters—including one that enclosed a cheque for fifty American dollars from a magazine called *The Smart Set* to which I had sent an over-clever short story.

This money was duly invested—in two hats for the bride.

Followed a journey to Liverpool, where we caught the old *Campania* for one of her worst winter trips. Bad sailors, we spent most of those nine days in our cabin. One huge wave, our steward told us, actually broke glass on the captain's bridge.

America had long been the land of my business dreams. I knew Ida M. Tarbell's recently published *History of the Standard Oil Company* almost by heart. To me, Rockefeller, Carnegie, Pierpont Morgan were far bigger heroes than Lord Roberts or Lord Kitchener.

Absurdly, I yearned to emulate them, not for the sake of their millions, but for their power.

It seemed to me when I tottered on deck carrying a heavy locked satchel of business papers, and looked on New York for the first time, that no game could be as much worth the playing as this American game of Big Business.

Forgive my horror, therefore, when the receptionist at the Waldorf—possibly deceived by a fur coat eventually sold to defray storage charges in late 1918—took me for an orchestra leader, whose name, though written differently, was pronounced in the same way as my own is, Franko.

§ 2

The old Waldorf Astoria comes back to the mind as a colossal mausoleum, hideous red brick without, frightful mahogany within.

Humour recalls the dumb denying face of one of its porters when ignorance asked for directions to the "Peacock Gallery", as the slang of that day called a certain lounge where travelling salesmen or their grass widows were alike presumed to find consolation against loneliness—and Dolly, waiting at a side door for a lady with black eyes whose two ramping black horses waited neither for man nor woman.

"The only time", said I, when my young wife returned from a shattering trot along Riverside Drive, "that you've been on time for an appointment since we arrived."

She could no more help being unpunctual than I could help being exactly on time. For this, my youth already found it difficult to make allowances. Otherwise, however, the New York of early 1906 with its many brown-stone houses saw us happy enough.

We duly admired its tallest building, the twenty-two storeyed Flatiron, which now looks like a cottage when seen from the hundred and fourth storey of the Empire State.

We supped in joyous company at the old Savoy Hotel, now the Savoy-Plaza—and alone at Sherry's and Delmonico's, the crack restaurants of their time. At Delmonico's, to our British amazement, I was told that either Dolly or the cigarette she had just lighted must be put out. American ladies did not smoke in public—then.

We lunched, marvelling at its luxury, at the old Saint Regis—still one of the very best hotels in the world. We strolled along Fifth Avenue where nearly every house was still a private mansion. That January every woman on the Avenue of a morning wore a bunch of violets over her heart; so Dolly must do the same.

But the heart of Fifth Avenue, for me, was that enormous downtown building, No. 111, which housed J. B. Duke and his Tobacco Trust. One day I would rule the roost in offices as large as that!

Martin Beckhard's brown-stone house—on 87th, I believe—also fired an embryo magnate's ambition; because it had a telephone in every room including the toilet.

To be so busy that one could not escape from the phone even at toilet time seemed the very apotheosis of Big Business. Pity, therefore, a young woman of no wild ambitions dragged half across the world to . . . buy cigars.

There were no Havana cigars to be bought in New York. Five days there, one courtesy-curiosity visit to No. 111—and we were off by rail for Havana, making short stop-overs at St. Augustine, Florida, almost empty, and a tiny town called Miami, these being much less expensive than Palm Beach.

In Miami, there were only two hotels; and the one which we happened to choose possessed no elevator.

"Why?" explained the receptionist when I asked him to throw light on this phenomenon. "Well, it's like this, see. The other hotel belongs to Henry M. Flagler."

"The Standard Oil man?" asked one of Ida M. Tarbell's few British readers.

"Sure. But he's a railroad man, too. And our elevator—we being independent—has been held up on his railroad for the last six months."

Big Business—on the grand piracy scale! That was how I wanted to play the game myself.

My own big business opportunity followed.

Walking out from that four-storeyed elevatorless hotel after our first night there, I was accosted by a persuasive young land-salesman.

"Real estate in this township of Miami", began he, "is going way up. If you've a few dollars to invest, you can't do better. Let's say a hundred dollars. I could sell you a nice two-acre lot for that. Right back of the depot."

"Nothing doing", said the embryo magnate.

I occasionally wonder what those two scorned acres back of the railway station sold for in the post-war boom days at Miami. Call it a hundred thousand pounds sterling—and you won't be far wrong.

A missed fortune, and the little wooden pier, the small cabin of the Miami Yacht Club behind us, we crossed Florida north-west for Tampa—and an hotel of which the less said the better. Thence a toy steamer with tin decks shipped us due south down the Gulf of Mexico to Havana.

This sea journey, as I recollect it, took a day and a night—and included one transhipment. For in 1906 Flagler's rails did not yet run along the coral to "Caya Hueso", the old Spanish bucca-neers' Quay of the Skeletons, more familiarly "Key West". Nor had the Wright Brothers yet succeeded in lifting themselves from the ground.

§ 3

Unless she stayed with friends, the Cuba of three and thirty years ago was no place for a young woman accustomed to ordinary English comforts, far less if she happened to be an expectant mother.

This happening was not definite by the time we made Havana. I still blame myself, nevertheless, for the youthful blindness—it was only that, not unkindness—which made me keep Dolly there for a whole month.

We put up at the best hotel, the Louvre—and I killed what looked like a woolly-bear caterpillar, only it was a good six inches long, with the heel of a shoe on the tile flooring before we went to bed under our mosquito curtain the first night.

Next morning's "housemaid" materialised in an open-neck shirt and a pair of cotton trousers with a large cigar odoriferous between his teeth. I couldn't understand why the smell of fairly good tobacco should make anyone sick!

Every morning I would be away for the factories by six o'clock, not returning till eleven. Then we would be entertained by one or other of my manufacturers. These lunches could be terrific—one, with Manuel Lopez, the proprietor of the "Punch" brand, lasted from twelve till four, neither he, his wife, nor any of the other guests speaking a word of English.

After that—for me—more work.

The sun blazed all day, but could not abate one mite of my own furious—and so often misdirected—energies. The evenings and the nights were delicious. I simply could not understand why Dolly should be so tired!

After about a fortnight a queer incident, for which I still find no explanation, occurred. Slightly indisposed, I took to my bed. Within twenty-four hours a cable arrived from Julia, "Feel positive you are ill wire truthful news immediately".

Up and about again I wired back, "Self Pullman but we shall need house and not flat on our return". For by then the unwanted happening was definite enough.

"Do you think she'll understand why?" asked Dolly.

I told her that Julia and I always understood each other; and went on with my job. Slightly acclimatised, we made a few friends—notably the recently married Aida, tall and lovely daughter of Calixto Lopez, one of the handsomest men I ever knew, whom Havana nicknamed "Don Quijote". He died years ago; but you can still see his face on the labels of the cigars that bear his name.

Calixto had built himself one of the largest factories in the whole town, with the entire top floor as his family dwelling place. It was always cool there—and you could have marked out a lawn-tennis court in the principal room.

The Upmann factory, too, was grandiose; and the attached bank, where you could see the big silver dollars stacked by the thousand, in high repute. Still their predominant English buyer, I did my damnedest to get our sole agency restored to us—not realising that the job would take me another eight years.

There were so many things I did not realise on that morning when we left Havana. But of one thing I was positive: Since there had to be a baby—and goodness knew how much happier I should have been without one—at least let it be a boy.

CHAPTER TWENTY-TWO

§1

f subsequent experience has taught me anything about woman-
ind, it is that no man's utmost efforts ever succeed in reconciling
omen of conflicting temperament. And if ever two women—each
ith her own excellent characteristics—possessed diametrically
pposite temperaments, they were my mother and my first wife.

Between those two, adored by one, married to the other, stood
1y boyhood's self—callow, self-centred, pleasurably obsessed by
1e responsibility of carrying on a business; and with no more
:nsitivity, no more sense of psychology, no more feeling for the
:ttle niceties that control personal relationship than the figure of
1e Japanese samurai in full armour I wanted to buy—only Julia
·ouldn't let me—for the narrow hall of our little corner house,
4a Great Cumberland Place.

Julia had acquired that house—long since pulled down to make
·ay for Lyons' Cumberland Hotel—on receipt of my cable; and
·as already panelling its walls with silk and canvas for us when
·e returned to London. Generous to a fault, she furnished it to
1e last tooth glass. Philoprogenitive, she looked forward to a
·andchild with rapture.

If only I could have shared that delight!

We moved in by the spring of 1906. Julia had just tired of the
·ouse in Clarges Street, reputed Emma Lady Hamilton's. The
:itz was newly opened. She established herself, her personal
1aid, the French governess and her other children there. One
·ight, when she was going to a party, I asked if I might have
1e use of her sitting room.

She gave me a curious look; and mentioned the name of a lady.
. admitted that the lady would be dining with me in the restaur-
·nt. Julia shrugged her fine shoulders.

"I only want to have a private talk afterwards," I said
·uthfully.

For already, after less than six months of matrimony, I had
:ached that point when youth must have its confidante. And
·ow could I confess, either to my mother or to Harold? Loyalty
·rbade the first outlet, pride the second. But Marie, I knew,
·ould understand.

She had been married, not too happily, herself. Once lovers,

4

we were still friends. After dinner we went upstairs. I took he
in my arms and poured out my heart to her.

"Do you want me back?" she asked.

"No," I said, again truthfully.

Marie (that is not her real name) made me release her, an
looked at me soft-eyed for a long time.

"You're still in love with your wife", she said at last.

"I suppose I am."

"Of course you are. It's just marriage itself you're hating
I always knew you would. You're much too young for it."

Just before we parted, after a final kiss, my boyhood begged
"You won't tell anybody about tonight, will you?"

They say women can't keep a secret. Imagine what the worl
would be like if they couldn't keep them better than men!

§ 2

The scanty reasoning power I possessed at two and twent
must have acknowledged Marie's judgment correct. But ther
reason stopped dead.

Soon, our few hours at the Ritz were as good as forgotter
Still emotionally satisfied with my marriage, I put nearly a
my doubts aside.

My days I continued to spend at Gracechurch Street, where—
by one of those unhappy accidents which ruin so many gambler
—my first year as managing director had produced a balance shee
that made the shrewd, bullet-headed, rusty-haired Gundry sa
"If it goes on like this, we shall have to be thinking how to inves
our surplus profits".

My salary had been raised to £1,000 a year by then. We pai
Julia £5,000 in dividends—and transferred the other £6,000 t
reserve. Unwisely I boasted of that result to a young woma
whose financial ignorance was abysmal—failing, as usual, t
make any allowances for a mind that could not see eye to ey
with my own.

Business, to me, was a game, my one objective to expand it, t
sell more cigars than my competitors. The Standard Oil Compan
if one could trust Tarbell, had run many of its competitors out
business by ruthless price-cutting. Why shouldn't I do th
same?

Eventually this infantile behaviour resulted in a round-Robi
protest by my competitors to Pepin Rodriguez, already one of th
leading Independent manufacturers. Pepin, a shrewd, kindl

eat-handed Cuban, as short as the French King his namesake,
emonstrated. In vain.

This absorption in the immediate job—from which I still suffer
–added to a false and deplorable sentimentality must have been
qually to blame for a major conjugal mistake committed at this
eriod of my existence.

I made no effort to enlighten my young wife's financial ignor-
nce. She must not be worried with money matters—decreed
entimentality—until after the baby had been born.

§ 3

All that time Dolly was courage, Julia kindliness itself. My
wn secret attitude I can only describe as resentful neutrality.
A son might just be tolerable. But it was no use pretending that
wanted, or that I had ever wanted, this complication of a child.

Horses still drew most of London's traffic; and you could always
ell when a happy event was expected in the better-class neigh-
ourhoods by the straw used to deaden the sound of the hoofs.

With September quarterday approaching, I ordered my van
oads. That Dolly might be in any danger, that her ordeal would
e a painful one, may have occurred to me. But memory registers
o apprehension.

It might, I think it would, have been salutary for my blunted
ensitivities if Dolly had followed the example of another newly
narried wife of our acquaintance—and insisted on my presence
ntil the very last moment of decency. Instead she insisted on my
eaving her long before the worst pains began; and I was fast
sleep on a sofa in the alcove of our silk-panelled drawing room
vhen Julia woke me with the news:

"It's a girl. Dolly was too marvellous. She never even whim-
ered. She's all right. So you'd better go to sleep again".

I did.

That happened at about three o'clock in the morning. At five
Julia went home. At a quarter to eight a slightly surprised par-
ourmaid woke me with tea. Dolly—the nurse told me—would be
etter left alone.

At the usual 9.30 I took the twopenny tube, as we still called
he Central London Railway—in contradiction to "The Under-
round", on which locomotives still belched steam—to the office,
nore depressed than I had ever felt in my whole young life.

The confession sounds utterly brutal. Yet at the time I was
ot aware of any brutality, only of a black cloud, overhanging all

my existence. Later I learned that my father—with his exag
gerated sense of personal responsibility—had always dreaded
large family. So possibly I was the victim of inheritance.

My father, however, from the moment they arrived, loved h
children, especially his eldest son and my baby sister. I neve
even liked either of mine until they were nearing womanhood.

This, they both know. For this—and much else—they have fo
given me. Sometimes—especially when they are in quandaries—
they acknowledge the superiority of my worldly wisdom. Constantl
they refuse to accept my own estimate of my own character.

"Hard-boiled", they laugh. "You!" And that is when I ar
most afraid of liking them too much.

§ 4

Dolly and I christened our first daughter Ursula Nannett
(Why, I don't know. Humour subsequently suggested that th
Latin word "ursula" might be dog-translated into "the child sh
bare".) By a stroke of good luck we secured one of those legendar
Nannies whose slogan is Mrs. Micawber's. Anyway *she* neve
deserted Dolly; and is nurse to Ursula's Timothy, our three-yea
old grandson, as I write this.

The nursery, I have already made plain, saw little or nothing
me. Soon, however, my mercurial spirits banished depressio
With Dolly up and about again, we had quite a lot of fun.

I taught her, though she never became an expert, to pla
poker. She tried to teach me, though she might as well have trie
to teach a hippopotamus, the piano—on that very Ascherber
(another gift of Julia's) in which I had once seen goldfish swir
ming after the arson episode with the airgun.

On Saturday nights we frequented the Supper Club, whic
used to meet—on that night only—at the Grafton Pictu
Galleries. This club—in those far-off days—was the only reputab
place in the whole of London where members and their gues
could sup and dance after the theatre.

Thither, on one occasion, came Julia, trailing in her wake
shy, awkward, semi-silent companion, still in his early thirtie
and not yet married to the daughter of Doctor Barnardo.

"Dull dog, isn't he?" said I to Dolly. "I never know why sl
wants to be bothered with these literary people. Still, *Liza*
Lambeth wasn't a bad slum novel. I always liked that charact
who was never out of the family way and kept on saying, 'Oo-e
I em a naughty girl, I em' ".

"He's got a new play on—*Lady Frederick*. They say it's quite good. We might go one night", said Dolly.

And so we dismissed . . . Somerset Maugham.

Better known at the Saturday Supper Club was a certain Mrs. W., whose constantly-changing youthful escorts were popularly supposed to be rewarded with black-pearl tiepins. Hence my line, "Where the bold boy might earn the pearly gage".

Memory further recalls "the beautiful Mrs. Patterson", a voluptuous blonde, and a certain Mrs. Saunders (maybe Sanders), dark and petite, and reputed the best performer of the "new dances", the double Boston and the two-step, in town.

"Marie" used to come there, too, usually with Harold; and an adorable little Dresden-china-shepherdess of a young woman with prematurely silver hair, who loved horse-racing even then; and later took to it professionally.

Who would have thought that Helen Vernet with her tiny hands and delicate appearance would ever stand—the only woman bookie—to take our bets across the iron railings? Yet she does so to this day.

Helen represents Ladbroke's. A grand chap from the same stable, "Tommy" Graves, now a peer, was the most energetic of all our masculine performers. But Hughie Bagot-Chester, brother of the famous "Bubbles", ran him close.

Hughie's business, at any rate during the post-war years, was a peculiar one. He specialised in the insurance of racehorses. We met him for the last time at the Cavalry Club this very year.

"How goes it?" I asked.

"Pretty badly, old chap. I've got to have another operation. There isn't much chance, I'm afraid."

He died under the anaesthetic within forty-eight hours.

CHAPTER TWENTY-THREE

§ I

THE inevitable conflict between my mother and my wife began with a slight skirmish in the spring of 1907. Julia wanted to see Italy. The aunt of the huge brass doorbells and Ashley would accompany. Dolly, with one baby to look after and another on the way, could hardly be of the party. But why—suggested Julia —shouldn't I make the fourth?

My selfishness adjudged Dolly's mild protest wholly unreasonable. The thought of yet another child renewed my depressions.

"A holiday will do me good," said I—and went.

The journey is not worth chronicling, except for my aunt's heartfelt ejaculation after being dragged round yet another picture gallery.

"I don't want to be blasphemous", she panted, sinking heavily into her armchair at the Grand Hotel, Rome. "But if I have to look at many more sacred pictures I shall begin to wish that the Madonna had never had that child."

Returning to London from Milan—after one horrified half-hour in that house known as the "Casa della Marchetta" (The House of the Brass Check) which actually adjoined the cathedral—I found Gundry preparing another balance sheet.

In this, despite a swelling turnover, low prices and increased expenses—I had tempted the manager of their cigar department, Jack Bishop, away from Joseph Travers & Sons, the wholesale grocers—already told their tale.

Still, we could pay the same dividend. So why worry? Especially with our original reserve fund, about £20,000 worth of what we imagined to be gilt-edged securities, intact.

§ 2

That summer, 1907, Ronnie went to Dyer's house at Eton. (Some of my contemporaries may remember Dyer's exhortation— he taught mathematics—beginning "A practical man".) The enigmatic Jack had already decided on becoming a farmer—to Julia's astonishment and disgust. But my Uncle Jimmy, dead in the April, had sold her for £50 the plot of a story; and this was absorbing most of her time.

Where she and Dolly made separate holiday, I do not remember. Most of my own August was spent in London. Late on a hot evening I dropped into the Savoy Grill, to encounter Platt supping two lovely young stage ladies, with one of whom—a slim blonde— he was obviously much enamoured, "pour le bon motif", I realised, knowing my Evelyn Platt.

He invited me to make the parti carré. Supper over, we taxied the ladies to Paddington Station—and Evelyn, at his heartiest, pulled me into the carriage just as the nonstop train pulled out for Maidenhead.

Platonic refreshment at a charming cottage followed. It was

wo o'clock in the morning when the horrified Evelyn looked at his vatch.

Lads of these enlightened days would have demanded to sleep on the premises. But, under Edward the Seventh, ladies were still compromisable—and no cars for hire.

My suggestion of seeking that hotel where Marie and I had once sojourned, moreover, was instantly vetoed.

"Mother", said Evelyn, "will have a fit if I'm not home before she's awake." And he suggested, the last train having long since departed, that we should walk, in tail coats and "pumps", if you please, to Slough.

Sober (I stress this) and sorrowful, we marched away till we reached Maidenhead Station. There, a wondrous sight—a train moving very slowly in the correct direction—met our young eyes.

We clambered railings, leaped, escalated an open truck piled with granite; and were still congratulating ourselves when—at Taplow, a mile or so up the line—the train stopped and a lamp lashed in our faces.

"This train's called the Stony", a gruff voice from behind the light informed us. "And this is as far as it goes."

The five or six miles from Taplow to Slough, with the white dust of that bygone road caking between our silk socks and the thin heels of our low shoes, seemed a hundred. There, we caught a workman's train, that landed us back at Paddington by six.

"Jolly good fun", said Evelyn. "I'll be home in plenty of time. She really is the loveliest girl. I wish to goodness I could persuade her to marry me."

But Pauline Chase—J. M. Barrie's original Peter Pan—married somebody else. I hear she is now a widow; and trust she will pardon my harmless tale.

§ 3

Pepin Rodriguez, tired of remonstrating, at last cut off our supplies of Romeo y Julieta. This made Bishop—and Musgrave, still with us—gloom. I decided another visit to Havana absolutely necessary—even if it meant being away for Dolly's confinement, which we had decided on entrusting to a new doctor, Bob Fenner, one of the grandest chaps I know, who is still practising at seventy.

One Saturday afternoon, about a month before I sailed, there occurred an incident which was to end in a cause célèbre.

Still, as I thought, a member of Almack's cock and hen bridge

club, then housed in a big ground-floor flat at the bottom of Ha:
Hill, I dropped in for a game of bridge, and, losing the firs
rubber, gave the card-room steward a small cheque.

He returned almost immediately with a message from the
secretary, Sir Hugh Stewart. As I was not a member, the chequ
could not be cashed. Asked why I was not a member, the stewar
said I hadn't paid my subscription.

Julia had a new house, 64 Grosvenor Street. I borrowed the
few shillings I needed from an acquaintance; and hared thither in
a taxi.

"I thought you'd paid the damn thing", I told Julia. "Yo'
did last year."

"Didn't they apply for it?"

"I'll swear they didn't."

"And you certainly weren't posted. Or I'd have seen it on the
board."

After a short consultation we rang up John Withers at his
private house in Gloucester Terrace.

"You'd better come along", said he.

I went alone. On Monday Withers asked the club for an apology
—and my reinstatement. Both were refused. I issued a writ
"This was succeeded" (I quote from my mother's pamphlet "An
Impression from the Law Courts", privately printed the following
year) "by an attempt to deprive me" (her) "of my rights as a
member of the club." On which she also issued a writ.

These events, though annoying, did not disturb my equanimity
Early December found me being driven from the New York docks
to the old Knickerbocker Hotel. On the way I observed a queue
of several hundred people waiting to enter one of the offices of the
Guaranty Trust Company.

"There's some panic on", said that famous character, James B
Regan, the proprietor of the hotel—and he offered to cash any
sterling cheques I cared to write on my London bank at ten per
cent. over the usual dollar rate.

In his cigar department I was told that they could not clear a
single case from bond unless their bank certified the cheque, and
that people with five thousand dollars to their private credit were
being allowed just enough to pay their household expenses.

The usual dealings on Wall Street were suspended. But one
could still buy for spot cash. And Steel Common stock stood at a
nominal seven dollars.

Here, I felt, was opportunity knocking at my very door. The
Bank of England would lend us £10,000 on our reserve fund. I

abled for that amount to be remitted by cable, stating the
purpose for which I wanted it.

Next morning brought an answer, "We cannot approve of your
gambling", signed by both my "tutors", Uncle G. and Fritz.

Before I returned from Havana the Harriman (I think) panic
was over; and the shares I had wanted to buy at 7 stood at
approximately 70.

Net loss—in the imagination—another hundred thousand
pounds.

§ 4

That time, I sailed direct from New York to Havana on the
Ward Line's *Morro Castle*; and stayed at the old Miramar, a tiny
hotel on the Malecon, where the celebrated Canfield used to set up
his double-zeroed roulette wheel.

My room was marble, and overlooked the sea. To it, while I
unpacked, came the usual presents of cigars from our manufacturers—and a note on perfumed paper that read:

"Dear Mr. Frankau,

"I do hope you will enjoy your stay and that I shall be seeing
you one of these evenings. I have several new importations—and
should like you to sample them before our climate gets in its
deadly work".

The high-powered sales-letter did not attract the family man.
Neither did the shop windows of San Ysidro, where five thousand
unfortunates exposed themselves nightly in their narrow ground-
floor cubicles. I preferred to watch different professionals playing
"Jai-Alai", as South America calls the Basque pelota—one of the
most exciting games in the world.

The three-sided court is about twice as long as a racquet court.
The ball, as hard as a racquet ball but about twice as large, is
slung from a basket scoop strapped to the player's wrist. One such
caught a brother cigar merchant on the forehead and nearly killed
him. Excited Cubans gambled with the bookies on every shot.
The players were allowed to bet, too. Naturally, they made
money. I was told that the physical strain was so great that most
of them died early of heart disease. So why not?

I made great friends, during those weeks, with three young
Americans—the two brothers Staples, who were in charge of the
Trust cigar factories, and a grand Texan called "Billy" Williams.
Most nights we played poker.

4*

Billy always won. The Staples boys usually broke even.
always lost.

"And you'll go on losing", said Billy, "until you learn not t
come in on a pair of deuces when the openers are jacks."

I owe that boy a lot. He taught me that poker is less of
gamble for the expert than bridge; and gave me Curtis's invaluab
book on the game, which I still possess.

Another member of our "school", the black-browed Garcia
gave me a copy of a picture that hung over his office desk, which
coveted because it seemed to express my own attitude toward
life. From a shack on a mountainside issues a miner. He holds
revolver in each hand. Underneath runs the slogan, "Live eac
day so that you can look every damn man straight in the eye—an
tell him to go to hell".

Another friend I made was Don Luis Marx, the greatest gourme
and bon viveur of his day. He took our poker school in his enor
mous Mercedes to spend a night on his plantation. On the way w
stopped for lunch—and his chauffeur produced a dish of ho
partridges and two magnums of iced champagne from the luggag
trunk.

This, remember, long before the days of the thermos bottle o
the frigidaire.

The plantation itself, seen from the window of the room I share
with Billy, looked exactly like Brooklands racetrack; because a
the tobacco grew under flat tentings of cheese cloth, almost th
same colour as concrete—and the plant grows taller than a mar

Don Luis had been to the docks that day—and bought up ar
entire consignment of pâté de foie gras. His chef served one c
these, *hot*, with our dinner.

Said Billy Williams, "I could do with some of this for break
fast".

We went to our room in the small hours. At 6 a.m. precisel
one of Don Luis' retinue tapped on the door.

"Your breakfast, señor", said he to Billy; and deposited
pâté as big as a baby's cranium, piping hot, on a little tabl
between our two beds.

The Lone Star State bore the ordeal like Sam Houston; bu
degenerate Britain took its hang-over to the toilet; and gave uj
everything except the ghost.

CHAPTER TWENTY-FOUR

§ 1

EUROPE and America might dance two-steps, double Bostons or even cake-walks, but Havana stuck to the "bailé", as being more suitable to its climate and temperament. This dance was a very slow "maxixe", which Gay had taught me, performed almost stationary, but with much movement of the hips.

In the huge dance hall were two bands. When one stopped, the other carried on immediately. Skilled couples revolved for a whole hour—their pride being to remain within a six-foot circle. Great adept at this was the exiguous Pepin.

We remained on the friendliest terms. He regaled me on "pollo con arroz" (more rice than chicken), on "poté Reguladora"—a thick soup, named after the restaurant which served it, deemed ill-cooked unless "the spoon will stand upright in the dish". But to sell me cigars, he utterly refused.

Seeking a substitute for his brand, I made the acquaintance of an ex-foreman just starting his own factory, whom Havana affectionately nicknamed "Chocolaté", from his favourite beverage. I gave Chocolaté his first English order, for "Fernandez Garcia", just before Christmas 1907.

After the war he became one of Havana's most prosperous independent manufacturers, controlling, among other brands, Punch.

Just prior to Christmas 1934 I received a parcel of Punch "Coronas", every band printed with my own name—this though we had never even exchanged a postcard for more than twenty years!

§ 2

The great sight of Havana was its carnival—all the loveliest brunettes you ever imagined (you had to court them through barred windows for the rest of the year) throwing confetti and streamers from four-horse coaches. The young men had not yet taken to throwing bombs.

Even then, however, the Cuban of the working class was handy with his revolver. I had a glimpse of some masons who had struck for higher wages taking pot shots at the blacklegs on a scaffolding—and ran like a stag.

More dangerous, however, proved an attack of ptomaine poisoning, contracted after eating fish at a celebrated restaurant way out on the Vedado. Dressing happily for dinner, my legs gave under me—and I had to crawl along the floor to the telephone.

Doctor Lainé found me supine on the bed; and hardly able to see his face.

"Keep awake if you value your life", he ordered. "Take one of these every half hour. And you'll be all right by tomorrow morning."

Calomel and putrescine (unless it was that other ptomaine, cadaverine) fought it out till the sun rose over the shark-infested Caribbean. Then calomel won.

Two days later, preceded by a cable to 111 Fifth Avenue which ran, "Frankau on *Morro Castle* with some of our dollars don't let him get away to England with them Staples", I arrived in New York, and was sitting in a private room at the old Holland House by five o'clock.

Who made up that poker game I forget—but J. B. Cobb, the tobacco magnate, certainly sat in it. We played in green eyeshades, and started gingerly, doubling from a dollar.

Towards eight o'clock we stopped for planked steaks and beer. Towards midnight I was the winner of about a hundred dollars. They started doubling from two dollars about then. By 2 a.m. it cost twenty to open a pot—and I began to be a little nervous.

"He's playing so tight you couldn't get a grain of sand between his lips", remarked, in effect, a gentleman in shirtsleeves who had discovered I was not coming in under three of a kind. "But we'll get those dollars back before we're through."

The more I won, the higher they made the stakes.

Someone dealt the last of the ace pots at 5.30 a.m.—having previously put up the requisite hundred and sixty dollars (£32). I, still a winner, came in on a pair of sevens for three hundred and twenty. The third man in made it six hundred and forty to play.

Curtis and Billy Williams forgotten, I put up my money; drew the miracle, those other two sevens—and boarded the old *Mauretania*, after regaling the entire party to a caviar breakfast at the Knickerbocker, with something like two thousand dollars in my pocketbook.

This, my first really big game of poker, was to have a most peculiar sequel in my last one, as you will learn before I finish the tale.

§ 3

My second daughter, Pamela, was born on the 3rd of January, 1908—only a few hours before I arrived at Great Cumberland Place. Officially she is still non-existent—as I forgot to register her birth.

Towards the end of the month I found Julia slightly annoyed. It transpired that the jobmaster from whom she hired her two carriages at £75 a quarter had asked her to help him by paying a whole year's hire in advance. Having cashed her cheque, he promptly filed his petition in bankruptcy.

"I shall buy a car", she decided, writing off her loss with a smile

Someone—it may have been that slim young artilleryman, Captain Beasley, now the *Daily Mail* bridge expert, and more familiarly known as "Pops"—recommended the "Dustless Spyker", a forty-horse-power machine manufactured in Holland.

On this imported chassis Mulliner fitted a colossal landaulet body. French chauffeurs were still deemed to possess a more magic touch than English. But Julia's six-foot black-moustachioed swanker from Paris touched her pocket a little too magically over his petrol and repair bills.

Item, he was so terrified of the whole contraption that we always proceeded down Bond Street in low gear. I, more daring, attempted the slight gradient from St. James's Palace to Piccadilly in top; and stalled my engine.

A horse bus of the period promptly rammed its steel-shod pole through our back panel, to the consternation of my passengers, Julia and Sydney Pawling, and the intense delight of all onlookers. Motorists were not too popular in 1908.

The damage repaired, Julia found a new chauffeur, a young Englishman named Carter, whom I encountered recently, very posh of livery, at the wheel of a glittering Rolls. He reminded me, wistfully, of the day he was trapped with stop watches doing "between fifty and sixty" along the front at Eastbourne, and fined a fat pre-war tenner.

Once again, Julia paid up.

§ 4

On the 12th of February, 1908, the defence in what came to be known as the "Almack Case" was at last delivered.

Followed, again quoting from Julia's pamphlet in which she describes herself as "half Celt and wholly impulsive" (she may have been born in Dublin), "applications for postponements, particulars and yet more particulars, pleadings, legal quibbles called interlocutory motions, interminably argued, delaying the day of justice till the 24th of June".

Withers, taking no chances, had briefed Lord (then Sir Edward) Carson, who brought down Oscar Wilde and was to become the hero of covenanting Ulster, to "lead" Sidney (later Mr. Justice) Rowlatt, already Junior Counsel to the Treasury, and another junior of whom he held a high opinion, Horace Avory.

Carson's brief was marked three hundred guineas—the others according to custom a hundred and fifty and seventy-five. At a final consultation in Carson's chambers that eagle with an Irish brogue decided—the legal position was extremely complex—that I had suffered an "ouster". At a final conference in Withers' office at Howard House, Arundel Street (the firm he founded there with one clerk today occupies the entire building), I rehearsed my "proof of evidence" as carefully as though it had been a stage part; and was further instructed:

"Don't wear a straw hat. The Lord Chief Justice" (Alverstone, who was to try the case) "simply loathes them."

This is how Julia describes her own feelings, her own impressions of the opening scene.

"The great building, the wide hall with its statues and stillness . . . We were piloted to our destination up the stone staircases and through corridors all cool and gray.

"The Court was crowded . . . I met smiling faces, heard sympathetic voices. My lawyer" (Withers), "rather cold in manner, temperamentally opposed to myself, but unerring, untiring . . . begged me to sit quietly beside him, not to greet and converse with friends, strangers and pressmen.

"The judge entered. I had met him once in private life. He looked little different in his robes . . .

"Then there uprose my leading counsel, tall, saturnine and dark . . . He was taking the case on its most vital and serious issue. Honour was at stake. The deep voice, the music of the familiar brogue held me. How beautifully the rounded periods held the music of my early reminiscences. The lovely days of my childhood came back to me. It was right it should be from Ireland my advocate came."

§ 5

Carson's best effort that morning was, "This assassin's blow struck at my innocent cloient". The innocent cloient then mounted the box.

The story I told in examination was the truth, the whole truth and nothing but the truth—and nobody enjoyed the telling of it better than I. Even the judge's reproof (he looked a little like Warre only more benign), "You mustn't call me Sir, Mr. Frankau. My correct title is My lord", did not shake me.

"The old boy rather liked that juvenile touch", I remember thinking; and when the late Lord Merrivale (then Henry Edward Duke, K.C.) rose for his courteous cross-examination, all I wanted was an opportunity to score.

He gave me my only one with his final question:

"Now tell me quite frankly, why are you bringing this case?"

"Well, sir", said I, "if you really want me to be quite frank it's because I don't see how anyone could stand people saying that he'd been turned out of the kind of club you're representing."

But Avory's sarcasm bit deeper than that.

He spoke only one sentence during the entire proceedings, and that was an aside just after the unfortunate Sir Hugh Stewart had taken the oath.

"You are a captain?" Duke asked him.

"Yes. In the militia."

"Did he say militia or malicious?" rasped Avory to Rowlatt, in a voice that stiffened even the bored jury to attention. For they had decided the issue privately on the first day of the four it took to try.

I did not know this. Duke's smooth what's-all-this-fuss-about opening, his masterly handling of an almost impossible defence, plus the enormous publicity given to the affair by the press, had shaken even my selfconfidence over the weekend adjournment, which I spent at Burhill playing mediocre golf.

And when Alverstone summed up in the same Dukely strain, "You may think that this young man—though his conduct is not in question and the club seems to have disregarded all its own rules—you will remember that his name was not even posted—would have done better to lay his case before the committee than to consult his solicitor", only a kindly usher saved me from despair.

"Don't you worry about what he said", whispered that usher as I escorted a shaken Julia out of court to await the return of the jury. "Don't you worry about anything the old man said. They made up their minds after they heard you in the witness box. One of 'em told me so."

The jury answered all questions put to them in my favour. They awarded me £50 damages. My mother's action was settled "out of court"—no damages, but the club to reinstate her as a member and pay all her costs.

Immediately, we proceeded on foot through brilliant sunshine to the Savoy Grill and lunched some fourteen of our friends.

The fact that the jury's decision might be taken to the Court of Appeal cast no gloom over our merriment. We gloated over the posters, "Club Case. Verdict for Plaintiff". We quoted the current gags of two music hall comedians: "You can't come in here"; "Why can't I?" "Because you're not a member": "But I am a member": "Then why haven't you paid your subscription?": "Because I thought mother had".

Neither did the Court of Appeal reverse the verdict—they only deprived me of those £50 damages, leaving me my costs.

The total costs of this little affair—which had its true origin in a difference of opinion between my mother and the lady who subsequently married the innocent Sir Hugh—were in the neighbourhood of £9,000.

Our expenses, *after deducting what the Court allowed us as winners*, amounted to £1,500. The club, having paid the balance, liquidated, reconstructed, and can still be found, minus its hyphen, in Savile Row.

Julia at once found an opposition club, the Cleveland, in St. James's Square. This also flourished for many years at different addresses—one of these, by a curious coincidence, her old house, 11 Clarges Street.

I still feel that Withers advised us properly; and that if we had followed Lord Alverstone's suggestion and put my case before the committee we should only have met with a rebuff.

It was fortunate for me, nevertheless, that an ex-member of Withers & Co. happened to be practising his profession in India some four and a half years after the Almack Case set all Britain talking; and could enlighten his fellow exiles.

"Frankau?" perpended a committeeman of the Bombay Yacht Club, scrutinising my proposal for temporary membership. "Gilbert Frankau? But isn't that the young chap who was turned out of some London club or other for cheating at cards?"

CHAPTER TWENTY-FIVE

§ 1

THAT summer, 1908, Uncle G., taking his usual cure at Kissingen, walked out of the hotel one morning; sat down on his customary seat in the woods; fell asleep, and never woke. Fritz only came to Gracechurch Street for board meetings. The main financial brake was off!

We had had another goodish year. One of Gundry's clients, I. R. Barkoff, who manufactured Sandorides cigarettes, needed a little capital for his new factory in Chryssel Road, Brixton. I—already feeling that there could be no fortune in the cigar business—needed scope for what I believed to be my stupendous financial abilities.

Surely I could make myself a second J. B. Duke!

To him—father of that Doris whom today's press describes as the richest woman in the world—I had already been sent by a slow-spoken Virginian from Danville, Edgar Thomas Ware, newly appointed to take over the Trust's cigar interests in England.

J. B. Duke comes back as a huge shambling figure with a florid clean-shaved face, dressed carelessly, and wearing a curious pair of black-laced gout boots. He received me alone; looked me over; decided—as I see now—that he could not use me; and vented an aphorism I have never forgotten:

"There are only three things you need to know in business. The first's men".

He paused.

"And the second?" I asked.

"Men", he answered smiling. "And the third's men, too."

Then he rang for his cashier; said histrionically, "I'm going out to lunch and I haven't got any money. Let me have a hundred pounds, please", and dismissed . . . the son of the man to whom he owed the bulk of his fortune, though the pater was not alone to blame.

The pater told me this tale himself. So I know it is a truthful one.

At the very moment when young Duke, desperately short of money in America and totally unable to dispose of an immense stock of his (I think) Bull Durham cigarettes, had cut the selling price in half, there walked into the office of J. Frankau & Company, London, a little Frenchman.

"My name", said he, "is Bonsack. I have invented and provisionally patented a machine to make cigarettes. Your firm has been recommended to me as honest and possessing sufficient capital for my modest requirements. For £5,000 I will give you a half share in my invention."

My father and his two partners promised to think the matter over, and asked Monsieur Bonsack to call next morning.

"We're very sorry", they told him. "But we have come to the conclusion that there is no real future for cigarettes."

Bonsack caught the next boat to New York. He saw young Duke, whose cigarettes were selling like wildfire at half price.

"If you make them on my machine instead of by hand", he said, "you can go on selling them for the same price at a good profit."

Duke believed where my father and uncles doubted. The Bonsack machine was the foundation of the American Tobacco Company, whose competition with Ogdens and similar brands led to the formation of our own Imperial Tobacco Company, and, after a prolonged struggle and a law case which first brought F. E. Smith (later Lord Birkenhead) into prominence, to the formation of the British American Tobacco Company, a joint venture in which the battlers pooled their export businesses—with Duke and his associates controlling, at that time, fifty-one per cent. of the shares.

But I. R. Barkoff, with his little shop at No. 5 Old Bond Street, still made all his cigarettes by hand.

§ 2

Needless to say, I took J. B. Duke's aphorism very seriously—and promptly increased my staff. I also invested in a cigarette machine—and decided to launch an advertising campaign.

Shortly after we had installed our machinery my office boy announced, "Mr. Charles Higgem".

"Bring him right up", said I.

At the time Mr. (afterwards Sir) Charles F. Higham had just succeeded in persuading Mr. (now Sir) Herbert Morgan to give him a chance in the advertising agency of W. H. Smith & Son, better known as distributors of newspapers and books.

Charles, newly returned to his native England from the States, had further persuaded a tailor to allow him £50 worth of clothes on credit. I took to him immediately.

Then in his early thirties, a little curly of black hair, very vivacious of dark eye and a tremendous talker, Charles yearned to establish his own agency. My new business manager at the factory—a tubby dwarf of a fellow named Philip Cohen—was soon asking me if I objected to a sleeping partnership between them, Cohen putting up the money, £500 I think, and Charles doing the work.

That good man Gundry approving—and consenting to audit the accounts of the new agency—I agreed.

Subsequently Cohen demanded the return of his capital.

Had I been one eighth as intelligent as I thought myself, J. Frankau & Co. Ltd. would have bought Cohen's share in Charles F. Higham Ltd. Instead Charles gave him a series of bills, which we—in order that Cohen could get the cash immediately—discounted with our bank.

As Charles used to say himself, "That put me on velvet, because I knew you couldn't take your advertising to another agency until I had met those bills".

He lived to control an enormous staff, turning over more than a million pounds a year, and advertising, to name only three of many clients, Dunlop Tyres, Bass's Beer and Hillman Cars.

Our friendship lasted until his recent death.

§ 3

Charles placed our first advertisement for the New Sandorides brand, "Lucana", in the *Daily Telegraph* at Easter 1909. About the same time I began to feel the difficulty of living in the West End of London with two children on £1,000 a year.

Main blame for this—my youth was rather good at inventing self-excuses—I laid on the unfortunate Dolly. My decision—my youth adored decisions—was that we must move out of town.

An agent found us a medium-sized house at Bickley, near Chislehurst in Kent, "built by an architect for his own occupation". Twenty years later, lecturing to a London architectural association, I quoted this phrase, and proceeded—solely for the purpose of making points—to criticise various domestic arrangements in my onetime abode.

That part of my speech, I felt, went down particularly well, evoking considerable laughter. Questions to the speaker followed as usual. My first questioner proved to be a bright student who asked whether, by any chance, the house to which I had referred was called Park Riding.

"It was", I admitted.

"And wasn't the architect who built it for his own occupation named Newton?"

"Yes, I believe so."

"My father——" said the questioner; and sat down.

Actually Park Riding was a jolly good little house of red brick and stucco, well-removed from its neighbours, behind the green hedges of Bird-in-Hand Lane. About an acre of garden included a good grass tennis lawn. There was stabling for a couple of horses.

These remained empty until—big dogs for a Big Business man!—I bought a Great Dane bitch.

She died untimely while Dolly and I made holiday in Paris. Bates, our gardener, broke the news on our return. It is a curious commentary on a youth whose pose was now the completely hard-boiled businessman of American fiction, that I can still remember blaming myself for having left that animal when she was ill.

Julia's liberality filled the gap from Mrs. Napier Clavering's kennels at Newcastle-on-Tyne.

By then—note how the lunacy grows always larger—I had terminated the agreements of the two tenants who helped to pay the rent of 30 Gracechurch Street; secured a new lease of the premises (this last, as it turned out, was not quite so foolish); gutted them and refurnished them more after the manner of 111 Fifth Avenue.

The wooden cigar-racks good enough for my father and uncles were now of specially manufactured steel—preserved against rust, in those pre-chromium days, by coating them with shellac. These monopolised most of the ground floor. A crude form of air conditioning, my own invention, made a drying room—which ruined quite a lot of good stock till Pedder learned how to cope with it—of the basement.

On the top floor a perfectly unnecessary telephone exchange, complete with operator, dealt with the scanty internal and external communications.

Visualise an entire floor for the clerical staff, partly occupied in compiling futile statistics; another entire floor for the management—Bishop and Musgrave in a front room with plenty of air, myself solitary in a back room which had no air; one of the first dictaphones bought at the first Business Exhibition to be held in Great Britain; an Elliott-Fisher typewriter which performed its own calculations; and—if you would get a true picture of the megalomaniacal establishment—one mahogany revolving door.

Through this door, folded back for the occasion, there entered—on a spring evening—a kennelman of canny Newcassel, leading Grim Tiger of Axwell on a polished chain.

The ferocious silver-bridled appearance belied a soft nature. Not for nothing does Edric Weldon's caricature show an older Grim legging it in terror before three baby rats.

But five-foot-six of puppyhood dared a taxi with me—and, once again, I loved.

Within a week, Grim must accompany my daily walk to the station; within three, he could time my returning train to a nicety and would leap his stable gate if not loosed. That he performed the same antic to reach up and devour the butter and eggs from the windowsill whereon the early milkman habitually left them; that his sheeps' heads, his raw meat and his sacks of "Carta Carna" (or was it Karta Karna?) cost more than would feed Bates and his wife; that he disgorged an entire day's ration on to the floor of a Bromley teashop; that he would sprawl in full odoriferous length on Dolly's new sofa covers after an hour's walk with me through the wet woods—these and similar canine attributes only endeared him to me the more.

It is only from a psychological angle that I stress the memory of my passion—no other word is suitable—for Grim.

Draw your own conclusions as to the real state of my youthful mind.

§ 4

All this time my brother Jack—though his gentle nature resembled my father's—continued being rather a trial to Julia, who found him more and more difficult to understand.

He would return to Grosvenor Street, unkempt and uncouth, from a season's lambing with a Scottish farmer; hold forth on obstetrical details at the family length—and sally out to do doughty street battle either for or against the militant suffragettes.

My mother held no opinion about that controversy. She contributed an equal guinea to each side—rejoicing enormously in her friend Max Beerbohm's description of the votes-for-women marchers as "The Unemployed". But Jack's love of a row for the row's sake distressed her as much as the state of his fingernails.

"Thank God he wants to go to New Zealand", she told me on a summer's day in 1909.

Jack insisted on going steerage "because it would be more fun". I saw him off in the *Waratah*, then making her maiden voyage. He wrote to us from Capetown, "She rolls a bit and doesn't seem too safe. But I expect we'll get to New Zealand all right".

They did; but the *Waratah* vanished with all hands between Capetown and Durban on her return trip.

On his return trip, some three years later, Jack met a grand girl, Ulica de Burgh Miller, of Te Puke, N.Z.; married her; and went to Rhodesia.

They took up 3,000 acres of government land near Marandellas which Ulica still farms; and had one daughter, Judy, now Mrs. Bagshawe, with two children of her own.

A real sportsman—though his farming venture did not prove

lucky, all his mules dying on him—Jack was to join the Rhodesian Cyclists and reappear to us in khaki very soon after the outbreak of the 1914–1918 war.

CHAPTER TWENTY-SIX

§ 1

THE situation between my wife and my mother—hopeless from the first—was not ameliorated by my move to the suburbs. Very occasionally Julia paid us a duty visit in the Spyker. Very occasionally Dolly, taking the train to town, would pay a duty call at 64 Grosvenor Street. Each told me, privately, her opinion of the other. The family man did his best to hold the balance, to preserve a twofold loyalty, to smooth away exacerbations—but with little result.

Less busy, I might have taken this situation more to heart.

Commerce, however, still enthralled me. A cousinly epigram of the period, "Most men live at home and go to the office, Gilbert lives at the office and goes home", and a motherly one, "How's Gilbert? Oh, he's quite happy this week. He's reorganising both my businesses", held more than a grain of truth.

Routine in my very bones, I caught the 8.55 each morning, worked at the factory till lunch time, worked at Gracechurch Street till six o'clock, and arrived home by seven, still on my toes.

I took up gardening—and wearied of its slow delights. I recaptured my zeal for lawn tennis. I contracted golf mania; imagined myself playing from scratch instead of a fourteen handicap; took three months regular lessons from our local professional; scored a splendid hundred and twenty six by the time I reached the seventeenth hole in a medal competition; broke every club in my bag, threw a box of Black Dots into the pond opposite the club house; and cycled home swearing I would never play again if I lived to be a hundred.

At fifty-five, this oath—unlike various others—is still intact.

Furious Saturday hacking of hired horses about what was still more or less a countryside followed fanatical golfing. I took one toss—my young horse putting its foot in a rabbit hole—that broke a saddle tree, the only occasion I have ever seen this occur. Of a Sunday, Grim and I would walk fifteen, twenty and once thirty-five miles between dawn and dusk.

Local friends were few, but Harold still staunch. He was

always changing cars. One Saturday afternoon he turned up in a new purchase.

"There aren't any gears", he explained. "Just these two leather belts. They slip off their driving wheels if you're not careful. But she's not too bad otherwise; and she's the cheapest thing on the market. Comes from America."

"What's the name of this b. contraption", I asked as my inexpert hand tangled one of those leather driving belts round protesting machinery.

"They're made", said Harold, crawling under to inspect the damage, "by a chap called Ford."

§ 2

Another constant visitor at Park Riding was that slow-spoken Virginian, Edgar Thomas Ware—heaven's own gift at the poker table. "The modern automobile", said he, "is as dependable as the railroad."

In his open Charron, driven by a Charron expert called (I stand open to correction on the spelling) Tiersch, he and I, Dolly and a girl relative of mine dared a trip via Paris to Aix-les-Bains.

Ware, generous even for an American, paid all expenses. In Paris, he put us up at the Ritz. There, he introduced me to that famous connoisseur of the fair sex, Pancho Alvarez, an imposing figure in white spats whom memory paints light-haired, more like a German than a Spaniard, and slightly bald.

Pancho's private brougham, always with a white horse between the shafts, was one of the most famous vehicles on the boulevards. Legend recounted that he need only leave that white-horsed equipage standing outside any young lady's "appartement" for a couple of hours one night—and Paris would acclaim her grande demimondaine next day.

A grande demimondaine of the period, by the way, required more than one millionaire for her support.

Closely associated with Alvarez in the tobacco business was E. D. Laurens, proprietor of the famous Khedive Egyptian cigarettes. Laurens, spry, olive-skinned, below medium height, black of thick hair and moustache, possessed the loveliest young brunette wife.

He allowed her 100,000 francs a year (£4,000) to dress on, out of which he did not expect her to provide herself with furs or jewellery. The smart woman of the Edwardian regime thought £60 moderate for an evening dress, and often gave £20 for a hat.

Julia, this also by the way, bought all her clothes from the celebrated Hiley, who ruled Jay's dress establishment in a frock coat and an Ascot tie invariably pinned with a blue turquoise. There, you could still pay twenty guineas for a pair of silk stockings. Rayon, of course, was unknown.

From Paris we drove to Aix, the ladies swathed in veils and dustcoats, tarmac being also unknown; and covered the three hundred odd miles in two days. One day's run cost Ware seven punctured or blown outer covers (I believe they worked out at £8 apiece) all of which Tiersch and I changed with levers on the rim.

At Aix—for the first and only time in my life—I tried to "buck" the indiarubber ball thrown round the "boule" table. There are nine numbers; and the bank pays you 7 to 1 if you spot the correct one. I paid the bank a thousand francs (£40 in those days) to learn that these simple odds were more in its favour than mine.

Baccara I had learned already at Dieppe. It is a simple card game of even chances. If you get a really good run and leave your winnings up, they double and redouble themselves by mathematical progression. Not knowing this, I was delighted to pocket the single five-franc pieces which the croupier threw me *seventeen times running*. Calculate the possible win for yourself.

Ignorant gamblers are notoriously lucky. On another occasion —an armistice having been tacitly declared between home and mother—Julia took Dolly and myself to Monte Carlo for Christmas. It was the first time I had ever been inside the Sporting Club.

"What number shall I play?" asked Julia; and, closing my eyes, I saw—I can still see those figures, black on a fuscous background—2 2 2 2.

"Two", I said. "And it'll come up four times running."

"Ridiculous", said Julia, backing her favourite 17.

Four times running—with none of her money, or mine, on it— did the croupier call:

"Le deux. Noir, pair et manque".

§ 3

Meanwhile the business gamble on which I was engaged grew daily more dangerous—and my routine mornings at the factory, my routine afternoons in Gracechurch Street left me little time for lunch, except on Friday, when I used to visit our principal West End cigar customers—among them the cadaverous black-bearded Price of the Army & Navy Stores, from whom I heard only recently, the Wilson Brothers of Pall Mall, and "T. B. Carlin" (actually Phillips) of the same street.

Occasionally I would lunch with Hedges, either at his club, the Reform, or at the House of Commons. Usually, however, Friday's midday meal was sacred to Julia—who had painted her dining room sealing-wax red to show off her evergrowing collection of colour prints, and still preferred what I scornfully called "literary people" as co-guests.

There, one day, I met a tall, shy, schoolmasterish man of my own age with two novels, *The Wooden Horse* and *Maradick at Forty*, to his credit.

"I do hope he gets enough to eat", said Julia after this well-mannered young pedagogue left us.

When he and I last met, at the rehearsal of our present King's coronation in Westminster Abbey, the same man confided to me that he was about to become Sir Hugh Walpole. Nobody in those days could have looked less the benign, ready of speech and redolent of prosperity "apple-cheeked Hugh", the most popular literary lecturer England ever sent to the U.S.A.

In that same Georgian dining room, at a larger lunch party, my youthful ears were boomed deaf by the notorious Frank Harris, to whom I took an instantaneous dislike—subsequently justified when, after betraying most of his friends and attempting to betray both the countries to which he owed allegiance, this black-whiskered swashbuckling ex-editor of *Vanity Fair*, the *Fortnightly* and the *Saturday Review* sent me a letter suggesting that I could make a lot of money by writing pornographic novels for him to publish in Paris.

It gave me great pleasure to reply in the third person, using my army title, that he could go to hell.

"He's a scoundrel and a bore", admitted Julia when we were alone. "But he has his redeeming features."

And she told me two stories, one of a furious altercation between Harris and Wilde at the Café Royal, neither the subject nor the matter of which is fit for public print the other of a great reception which Harris gave "with his wife's money".

In the middle of this reception, all coronets and primadonne, his butler whispered a word in Harris's ear. His parents—a working miner and his wife, according to Julia—had arrived.

"Show them up", said Frank Harris; and not only gave them, in their humble best clothes, two places of honour, but insisted on introducing all his carefully collected celebrities to "My father and mother".

So perhaps he is not in that place whereto my letter consigned him after all.

§ 4

My mother's hospitality was so lavish that it would require an appendix to enumerate all the people I met in her company—among them Marie Belloc Lowndes, then a plump young woman with the softest, whitest skin and the sweetest Madonna face, who never sent a novel to her publisher until "dear Julia" had read every line; Reginald Poole, not yet knighted, of Lewis and Lewis the solicitors, who sometimes acted instead of Withers; the beauteous Mrs. Lewisohn, better known as Edna May, for whose second performance of that subsequent furore *The Belle of New York* the house had been so empty that Frank Mendl and I, still schoolboys, secured two front row seats in the dress circle without booking; Violet Hunt, who published one of the world's best short stories in her *Tales of the Uneasy*, and many more.

Julia's friends were legion—among them that celebrated British bank manager who took his British bride to Paris for their honeymoon.

Strolling out to smoke a final cigarette while his wife undressed in Edwardian solitude, the happy bridegroom was accosted by a lady of the town.

"Merci beaucoup", replied he, knowing the language. "Mais j'ai la même chose à la maison, mademoiselle."

Yet my mother always insisted that she preferred things—prints, china, jade—to people; and the arrival of a certain letter of introduction from her New York publishers threw her into quite a pet.

"As you're so fond of Americans", she telephoned, "you'd better come and help me entertain one of them. He wrote *The Jungle*."

"Upton Sinclair", said I—and went.

The man with the pen of a Hercules materialised as a mild selfconscious individual, a little like a thin George Moore. Over lunch Julia led him up the garden as only she could. Soon selfconsciousness gave way to selfexpression.

"Here", I could almost see the future runner-up for the governorship of California thinking, "is the only woman in the world who really understands me." And for once I held my tongue.

We gave him a cigar and escorted him upstairs to Julia's own sitting room. We settled him in an armchair by the fire—and she cooed at him till the last inhibition went.

Alas, that I cannot remember the whole story. But it ended thus:

"Mrs. Frankau, I have the soul of a poet. I wanted only a pure affection. Within a week I knew that I loved a nymphomaniac".

Somehow we kept straight faces—only exploding after he had gone.

CHAPTER TWENTY-SEVEN

§ 1

I HAD been married nearly five years without putting pen to paper except to sign letters or cheques—these last no longer on the Bank of England. Our whole reserve in securities was now pledged to the Midland, and we were beginning to run large over-drafts. The strain told.

Otto, just after my twenty-sixth birthday (April 1910), advised me to "go away for a month and throw stones in the sea".

Interpreting this advice in my own way, I took Dolly, nurse, the two children (and of course Grim) to the farm of one Pile at East Budleigh in Devon, who lent me his old mare of a morning. In the evenings, I fished the Otter for trout.

By the end of a fortnight, accordingly—with no books to read except my father's old Byron—I was bored stiff.

"It would be rather fun", I told Dolly, "to write an up-to-date *Don Juan*." And I sketched out a few stanzas before we went home.

§ 2

Today, social satire is almost taboo in Great Britain, possibly because the newly enriched are too badly educated to understand it; and the newly educated too sensitive to appreciate any criticism of their own shortcomings. The last refuge of the satirist seems to be Hollywood, which can still laugh at itself. Verse, nobody reads except versifiers—for one reason because modern versifiers are such intellectual snobs that their so-called poems are unintelligible to average readers.

From this judgment on living English "poets" I except, among others, Masefield, Alfred Noyes, and Humbert Wolfe, whose masterpiece *X at Oberammergau* must eventually come to its own.

But between 1910 and 1914 the stream which ran pure under

blue skies from Chaucer to lose itself in the dim forest of Auden still bubbled merrily. Not that it carried down much gold, except maybe for Kipling, who sang even as Homer—of "common things".

How far the fashion of the moment, how far a subconscious yearning to be once more the bachelor, how far vanity, ambition, natural aptitude, or mere escape from my domestic and business preoccupations were what moderns call the motivation of the first book that ever won me a hearing, I have no idea.

Only two things are certain—that I did not write a maximum of eight laborious lines a day for money, though I may have done so for fame—and that the writing of verse also became routine, practised for forty minutes twice daily on my journeys to and from London, after dinner on free evenings, and at fixed hours over the weekend.

This activity was superimposed on all my others for the best part of two years . . . during which I began to realise, at first occasionally, later with increasing persistence, the possibility that my business schemes might fail.

I don't think I ever visualised actual failure. Youthful self-confidence, vanity and obstinacy, Julia's magnificent backing and Gundry's courage, alike forbade that. Overwork, too, forbade cool objective judgment. To act, even foolishly, proved easier than to consider wisely. Secretly, nevertheless, I had many moments of fear, and one at least of complete revulsion from business.

That one moment is still vivid, showing me a long-dead self sitting in a room which has long ceased to exist, though I sat at the very same mahogany desk I bought for it, looking at one of those very steel racks with which I furnished our downstairs showroom, only the other day.

"If only I could get out of this and enjoy myself", I remember thinking on that lovely long-ago June afternoon.

I could have. There was nobody to say me nay. Instead I dictated thirty letters asking for business to my dictaphone; and went home to pay the tradespeople. This, I always did myself, analysing out the totals in a book specially manufactured for me by our Gracechurch Street printer, a very nice fellow called Ede.

At school, I had loathed mathematics. Now book-keeping fascinated me. I devised a system of cost accounting for the factory which won even Gundry's approval.

Such a busy, such a selfcentred, such a blind young man!

§ 3

In 1910 Edward the Seventh passed on. As he lay dead in what modern irreverence calls "Buck House", Dolly and I drove past in a taxi.

"That's not like you", she said, as I raised my hat.

I forget my reply; and only record the incident because it is typical of an outlook on life which eschewed all outward displays of sentiment. King and Country meant little to me then; politics nothing at all—unless the Chancellor of the Exchequer raised the tobacco duties. Income tax was an unconsidered trifle; and I never troubled to vote till after the 1914-1918 war.

In 1910, also, I took Ronnie to Berlin, where the advertisements of a flying meeting attracted me. This, to the best of my recollection, was the first time I saw planes in the air.

We hired a taxi from our hotel to the course, an oval of ground some mile long, marked out with wooden pylons, and Teutonically surrounded with eight-foot high boarding, lest non-payers should enjoy the sight.

As we drove up to the entrance, a plane cleared us, roaring and dripping hot oil, by what seemed a few inches. Whenever a machine circled the pylons without crashing, the whole audience cheered. Baron de Caters, an ace pilot of his day, landed without too much damage halfway round—and we clapped him for the feat.

But if flying was still in its infancy, the flights of journalistic fancy carried men far beyond any limit our law permits today.

Among my mother's acquaintances was the notorious Horatio Bottomley, member of Parliament for a Hackney constituency, editor and proprietor of a weekly newspaper, *John Bull*, now controlled by a man I am proud to call my friend—Lord Southwood, formerly J. S. Elias.

Bottomley—Julia once told me—though small and ugly, possessed a fatal fascination for her sex. She went as far as to say, "Much as I pride myself on my virtue, I feel certain he could have had his way with me before I'd known him a quarter of an hour".

The attraction could not have been mutual—for all H. B. asked her to do was to help him in a campaign he had started against unnatural vice. She did this anonymously, pretending to be a man.

By courtesy of the present editor—you cannot consult the files of *John Bull* without permission from its legal department—I re-read those two columns of close print recently.

I dare not quote a line of them. Why no prosecution for criminal libel followed Julia's amazing—and presumably apocryphal—statement, is a mystery.

Even more mysterious, to one who suffers from modern restrictions, did it seem when I read, in the following number, an "Open Letter to Dr. Crippen"—the first murderer to be caught by wireless, already under sentence of death for killing his wife, Belle Elmore, with hyoscin.

This letter suggested to Crippen that he had not told the whole truth because he was not physically strong enough to have dismembered and buried his victim's body in the cellar of his house at Hilldrop Crescent, Camden Town, without assistance.

Next week the condemned murderer—there was no appeal from the capital charge then—replied from his cell; and the week after H. B. addressed his open letter to Ethel Le Neve, who had fled with Crippen, disguised as a boy, on the transatlantic steamer *Montrose*.

She replied too!

A bit of skin less than an inch square and which Crippen could have burned, as he did most of the membranes, in less than a minute, sent him to the scaffold. Sir William Willcox, who analysed this fragment for the prosecution—and who, by the way, saved my brother Ronnie's life in Mesopotamia—told me that it was one of the few parts of a human body in which the presence of hyoscin could possibly have been detected so long after death.

Ethel Le Neve was defended by F. E. Smith. Arthur Newton acted as solicitor for both the accused.

I had known Arthur Newton since my Hawtrey days. One of the handsomest men possible, tall and slightly Kaiserish in appearance with his black moustache, he affected coloured shirts rarely worn in the early 1900's; had a huge criminal practice; and a talent for conversation so extraordinary that he once kept a whole railway compartment in which I happened to be a passenger entertained during a journey between London and Dover that took five solid hours owing to a "peasoup" fog.

According to my mother he possessed the same attraction as H. B.

CHAPTER TWENTY-EIGHT

§ 1

I CANNOT remember exactly when Julia developed a thirst so parching that she would drink as many as a dozen bottles of her favourite beverage, stone ginger beer, during an afternoon's lawn tennis. Equally obscure is the precise year in which she said to me, "I've got a new doctor. Such a nice little man. I've taken a most tremendous fancy to him. His name's Horder and I'm making his wife a quilt for her baby's perambulator".

But it was before this, some time during 1911 I imagine, that I left her in the octagonal room of a Portland Place house built by the Brothers Adam with a bearded specialist named Good-hart.

"Well, what's the verdict?" I asked when we returned to Grosvenor Street. "Have you got the dropsy?"

"I'm as strong as a horse, thank you", she laughed back. "But that idiot told me to put my affairs in order. So I shan't go to him again."

She knew the truth about her condition then—or soon after. A letter to her youngest sister, now dead, proves it. "I'm not going to give up strawberries and cream, sweets, cakes, and all the things I enjoy eating just to live a few months longer", she wrote. "I'd rather be dead than diet like Nellie" (her eldest sister) "was made to."

But of this I knew nothing. I never even worried about her health. Maybe because I had too many worries of my own.

The bank overdraft of Frankaus continued to rise as we poured more and more money into the Sandorides factory. In addition to our securities we had pawned most of our bonded cigar stock. The bank manager suggested we should turn our securities into cash. Fortunately we did so. Otherwise we should have been completely ruined in August 1914.

But Fritz, rightly worried, resigned his directorship—this involving a family quarrel which Julia, who loved him, deplored to the day of her death, and I to the day of his. Pawling took Fritz's place. Every penny of Julia's money was in the business. Remained only the reversion of a legacy. This would not fall in until the death of a lady my bachelor uncle had loved.

Julia mortgaged that reversion to an insurance company (at my request!) misquoting, " 'Tis not in mortals to command success, but we'll do more, my Gilbert, we'll deserve it".

Over-imaginative, over-confident in my abilities, she may have been. But courage she never lacked.

Gundry possessed the same supreme quality. Only one thing worried him—our combined drawings. So how could I increase mine, as that meticulously kept household account-book showed me I must if Dolly and I were to continue living at Bickley?

The house was freehold. More to spend on advertising, if I could sell it. I sold it within a fortnight of my peremptory decision; and put the money back into the business, from which—by the way—it had been borrowed.

Dolly and I moved down several rungs of the suburban ladder. Few women appreciate that.

§ 2

I tried vainly to find my house in St. John's Road, Harrow, the other day. The only impressions left on the mind are that it was semi-detached, that the previous tenant had panelled the dining room (wood being his business) and that the landlord used to collect his modest rent on a bike. Pamela tells me to look for "Heatherton" next time. The garden was just big enough for her Ursula and Grim.

Dolly never liked Heatherton. No domestic war broke out but the French phrase, "Cela ne marchait pas", is not inapposite to the conjugal position.

I continued to work all day and write most evenings. For exercise—horses being no longer affordable—I walked.

As before, we made no friends in the neighbourhood. Visitors from London were fewer than at Bickley, and holidays given up.

Towards Christmas I finished my "novel in verse". Edith Spalding, the best secretary I ever had, typed it. For title I chose *The Nut Errant*.

The operative word can be spelt differently. It has fallen into disuse with the type it stood for. But early in 1914 a young actor, Basil Hallam, was to set all London singing, "I'm Gilbert the filbert, the knut with the K".

Two years later I was to see poor Basil jump from one of our sausage balloons as a Hun plane swooped on it.

His parachute failed to open. His death was publicly regretted in Army Orders—a unique honour. A greater honour, however

heard paid to his memory two days afterwards when I dined
with his squadron commander, Bovill.

"He was sick every time he went up in the damn things",
Bovill told me that evening. "But nothing would make him quit."

§ 3

Julia thought well of my *Nut Errant*. I thought it a masterpiece, worthy of John Murray, Byron's own publisher.

John Murray, with whose red-headed son I had been fairly
friendly at Eton, disagreed. So did some twenty other publishers.
Then suddenly Julia rang up to tell me that Chatto & Windus
would take the risk.

What she did not tell me—I only discovered it after her death—
was that she had guaranteed £50 of that risk. She knew how
fiercely my pride would have protested had I but known.

Head of Chatto's was the benign Percy Spalding, who found my
original title "vulgar". I changed it to *One of Us* for him—and
further removed the adjective "Gutter" from the operative sub-
stantive "George". Lloyd George, older readers will remember,
was celebrated for invective and a certain Down-with-the-Dukes
speech at Limehouse which gave rise to the word "limehousing".

The father of the House of Commons, by the way, has not lost
all his pristine capacity for heaving mud.

Spalding introduced me to the reader without whose approval
£500 would not have made him put his firm's imprint on my
cover, and who materialised in the private office at St. Martin's
Lane as a man of exactly my own age with a merry twinkle in his
eye and a beard which seems red and sacred of cut to the memory.

That reader was to make his own name, Frank Swinnerton,
famous with a book called *Nocturne*, the first "modern" novel in
which the whole action takes place within a few hours, and many
more.

Frank deserves all the happiness and comfort to which he has
now won. He possesses a young wife, a baby daughter, a country-
house with no telephone—and only visits London once a week.

He reviews six novels weekly for the London *Observer* as well as
carrying on with his other work, which includes a penetrating
study of literature from Henry James to P. G. Wodehouse,
entitled *The Georgian Literary Scene*.

Unfortunately he confines his written criticism to contemporary
achievement. Were he to write of personalities as he can talk of
them, he might be acclaimed our greatest living wit.

Though I doubt if he would remain among the living wits fo
long.

§ 4

My *One of Us*—with a little log-rolling from Julia—made it
small stir in this country, and was soon reprinting.

It is an interesting sidelight on the change in British publi
taste that an infinitely better sequel, *More of Us*, also written fc
pleasure and published by Hutchinsons a year or so ago, met wit
no success at all.

The original book was taken by George Doran for America
Doran's printers and proof correctors seem to have been Chocta
Indians. He gave away some fifty press copies of the resultar
crossword puzzle—and sold nearly six.

On an idle man of eight and twenty the effect of the hom
laudations might have been pernicious.

But if the literary man's head swelled a little, the business-man
was bloody and not altogether unbowed.

To be acclaimed the modern Byron, to be guest of honour at th
Poets' Club, with Henry Newbolt in the chair, and Julia, drippir
diamonds, proud at my side, could not compensate for the knov
ledge that the profits on the Gracechurch Street cigars were n
covering the losses on the cigarettes we manufactured at Brixto

That loss, at least, must be covered—or the whole ship
Julia's fortune would founder. Imagination pictured ruin on m
lonely walks with Grim.

We had tried every trick then known to salesmanship. Jul
herself had written us an advertising booklet. We had ev
presented silver cases to every private purchaser of five hundr
cigarettes at our Bond Street shop. But although home sales ro
steadily, they did not rise quickly enough.

Remained one chance—the export. We had an agent in Stoc
holm. I visited him, was treated to a good order, and six Swedi
meals a day—early breakfast at seven, English breakfast at nir
thirty, French déjeuner, complete with Scandinavian hc
d'œuvres at midday, tea at five, dinner at seven, supper at mi
night with the skies still pale, and the punch still flowing. Duri
my visit to Stockholm, our minister there, Sir Cecil Spring-Rice
soon to be appointed our ambassador in Washington—refused
a visa for Helsingfors in Finland, then a Russian town.

"You won't do any business", he said. "And I couldn't
responsible for your safety."

Only Russia demanded to see one's passport in those days. They were plain pieces of paper (mine signed "Curzon") not even worth while forging. Very few travellers bothered with them at all.

Next I appointed an agent in Christiania (now Oslo). There I lived three days in a little wooden hotel at Holmenkollen, where the ski-jumps are in wintertime, to let the frail stomach recover on Norwegian trout and omelettes from its Swedish debauch.

Travelling south from Christiania by the only railway line in the world then civilized enough to provide the lone traveller with a separate sleeping compartment at no extra charge (they are still few!), I received what should have been enlightenment from the German attendant on the through train.

"You're very polite", I chaffed him, remembering gruffer prototypes.

"It is an order", said he. "From the All-Highest himself. We are to be politeness itself to all travellers—but particularly to the English."

German policy, modelled on the old German song, "Sleep, little one, sleep"!

On that same trip, I saw Copenhagen; and Göteborg.

Later, I visited Lisbon; stayed there just long enough to attend a bloodless bullfight, and returned with yet another order.

These helped. Yet not enough.

"If we could open larger export markets", said Gundry at a board meeting, "it might do the trick. Only where's the money to come from? Good export travellers earn big salaries, and need big expense accounts."

"And they don't grow on trees", said Cohen, who had been one of them.

I made my decision while they still talked. The only person to open those export markets was myself.

CHAPTER TWENTY-NINE

§ 1

AT the time, the purpose behind my decision—bound to entail a twelve months' absence—seemed too simple for argument. There was no other way by which the business could be saved.

"You're sure?" asked Julia, when I put my plans before her.

"Positive."

"Then of course you must go. When do you propose breaking this to Dolly?"

"As soon as I get home."

Impetuousness, cocksureness—unkindness if you will, but acquit my youth of that intention—brooked no domestic discussion. The house at Harrow could be given up, the furniture warehoused. Edric Weldon would—and did—take Grim.

Dolly acquiesced—her attitude being sufficiently indicated by the comment she makes on this part of the original manuscript, "Give me credit for understanding you better than you understood yourself. Remember what I used to tell you apropos of your home and family, 'You are like a man keeping up a golf course when he doesn't play'".

Meanwhile Cecil Knox, then a partner in Cox's Bank, undertook to shepherd the chairman of W. Sandorides & Co. Ltd. through India and Burma; Mr. Cook himself to supervise the rest of the world voyage. The Midland Bank supplied a letter of credit which still further increased the firm's overdraft—the Sun and Phoenix Companies two life policies at a limited annual premium for the first five years.

Both companies queried the health of the insured party; and only accepted him at their minimum rates on his threat not to complete the transactions. They kept him covered, however, throughout the war.

I bought fourteen pieces of luggage (a Singapore bullock cart just contained them); a rajah's outfit of suits for all climates, a revolver, a Mannlicher rifle, a travelling medicine-case, and—final touch—one of Mr. Carter's steel-centre tarpon rods.

In December 1912, seven years almost to a day after my marriage, I embarked alone for the East, for Australasia, for South America and the West Indies.

Only these mellower years realise how much the family man— for all his good intentions—revelled in his escape.

§ 2

There are two extant records of sights seen and knowledge acquired during the next fourteen months. One is my first prose novel, *The Woman of the Horizon*. The other is a diary, which I should have burned long ago were there any key to the more cryptic passages except my own memory.

"Pardon, O Lord, my steps aside" at many other places besides "Gay Street in Hong-kong"!

From there, leaving India, Burma, the Malay States and China, each with its trail of cigarettes behind him—I may have stepped aside, but never from my main purpose—the chairman of Sandorides Ltd., valeted by a retired member of the Hong-kong police force, took ship to Australia.

I was writing verse again, a serious poem this time. Having acquired conversational Turkish from an erudite Armenian—Sassoon's chief Oriental correspondent who used to visit me four evenings a week at Gracechurch Street—I further asked the doctor of the Inaba Maru to teach me Japanese. But you cannot acquire even a smattering of that language, which employs different sets of numerals for different objects, in a few weeks.

Between Hong-kong and Manila a typhoon nearly sank us; and I experienced fear of death for the first time. Curiously, I did not pray—as I was to pray on another occasion during war. Perhaps I was too interested in watching the sea through the "starboard doorway, open to the deck".

Forgive one quotation: "The thin useless-looking taffrail slid up and down, rising and falling, nearer and nearer to the water with every roll of the ship. He saw the rails dip, and water rise up over them, a solid wall of it, thick turquoise glass, white-spotted as if by a shower of stones; saw it stand straight up, a smooth opaque window between deck and deck, stand quite still . . . The blue wall tottered, fell back into the yellow slather of sea".

That blue wall—optical illusion when a ship rolls her lee side clean under—rose and fell three times.

In normal human beings, the removal of the death fear is frequently followed by the most intense exhilaration. This, too, I experienced. But your confirmed drunkard does not react normally. We had one such aboard.

I have known various men with a capacity for liquor, but never one to equal his. He drank in the solitude of his cabin—two or three bottles of pre-war whiskey, call it five bottles of post-war whiskey, every twenty-four hours.

Sometimes he would appear at dinner. On one occasion he appeared at tea time; saw a man sitting next to his wife; remarked, "That's a very handsome woman. I hope you can afford her", and retired with alcoholic dignity.

Arrived, after several weeks of this, in Sydney, he took to his room at the Hotel Australia; disdained all food outside a bottle—and utterly refused to accompany his wife on board their homeward boat when their ten days' stay was up.

She sailed. He called on me for comfort; declared himself

hungry; dragged me to a fish restaurant where I watched him eat (this is not fiction) six lobsters, followed by an equal number of dressed crabs; tossed the sporting cabdriver who took us back to the hotel double or quits for the fare until it amounted to a fiver; paid in golden sovereigns; told the hotel valet to pack for him; and took train for Melbourne just in time to catch the ship there.

We were not to meet again until nearly twenty years later . . . at his wife's grave.

§ 3

Successful business kept me in Australia for nearly three months. I also went to Melbourne, where Oscar Asche and Lily Brayton were playing *Kismet*, and saw Obi win the Grand National at Flemington. I visited Brisbane and Adelaide. Both the novel and the diary record a love affair. But neither tells the whole sentimental truth.

I had left England without a qualm. I could hardly bear to leave the Land of the Rainbow Gold, as Dorothea Mackellar calls it in one of the loveliest lyrics ever written—at least to me. I read that poem on my rough way to New Zealand. The last stanza runs:

> "An opal-hearted country,
>   A wilful lavish land—
> All you who have not loved her,
>   You will not understand—
> Though earth holds many splendours,
>   Wherever I may die,
> I know to what brown country
>   My homing thoughts will fly".

Being what I was at nine and twenty, I would not allow myself the luxury of tears.

Yet the words moved me—being so much in love—more than anything I had read since *Baa-baa Black Sheep*. Erroneously, I imagined that my ladylove and I would never meet again.

So the family man determined to forget—and almost succeeded —unaware of the fact that his inborn sensibilities had been sharpening ever since he left home.

Most of my books on that journey, hitherto at any rate, may have been women's looks—but one of them had now taught me to ache for the beauty behind a sunset.

Gradually, too, the many hours of unaccustomed leisure were trying to inculcate another lesson.

This lesson, however, I refused to learn. During the three weeks' run round Cape Horn to Montevideo I must have reasoned —in so far as I was then capable of reasoning—that a man as gifted as myself should easily be able to sell cigars and cigarettes with one hand, write poetry with the other, and kick up his heels in the intervals between.

But a letter from Julia, received with my other mail at Buenos Aires, shattered my egoism. We were "on the verge of bankruptcy"—my own "enormous expenses" a contributory cause.

The last accusation seemed unfair. My expenses, large as they were, had been covered by my orders. A little resentful, but considerably more frightened, I rang for my faithful Macleod, dressed myself in tails, drank a bottle of champagne with my solitary dinner, topped that off with a double brandy, picked up the first piece of French consolation offered by the Royale Music Hall, gave it supper at the adjoining Pigalle . . . and returned to my suite at the Plaza with the jacarandas already showing mauve in the Argentine dawn.

It took me the best part of a day to recover from this antidote against panic. But the panic had gone.

Sentiment followed. I dashed off a curious love letter—there is no other description—to my mother. She was not to worry. She had misjudged the situation. Gundry's letter did not confirm hers. Neither did Cohen's. Several of our new agents had already cabled repeats of their original orders. Everything would be all right. Even if this were not so, we had—we would always have—each other.

She cried when she read that letter—for the first and only time in her life.

§ 4

I had been away the best part of a year by then—but the state of Julia's health was still unknown to me. I found agents in Buenos Aires; and took train across the Andes into Chile, stopping at Santiago de Chile—loveliest of towns peopled by the loveliest of young ladies—on my way to Valparaiso.

Three days there, another trail of cigarettes behind me—and I was racing back to catch the old *Vandyck* for Trinidad. On board that boat, travelling with her parents, was a young American from Dubuque, Iowa, little more than a schoolgirl then, still an attractive woman when my present wife and I took tea with her in Los Angeles this very year.

I had never believed in "revelations". (I am not sure I believe

in them now.) And among my favourite epigrams, at the time,
was Uncle Jimmy's, "Platonic friendship between a young man
and a young woman! I'd as soon believe in platonic jewelry".

But Mary Elizabeth Bradley changed all that, and possibly—to
use the Buchmanism—me. Her encouragement, her enthusiasm,
hammered home the whole lesson my hours of loneliness had been
trying to teach.

There is a short poem to her. The entire incident—fictionalised,
over-dramatised, over-romanticised, but in its essence factual—is
in the novel.

"Your mission", said Mary Elizabeth, "is to write."

She, too, had a problem, which we discussed on the same high
plane, being deadly serious as befitted our youth.

"If you're thinking about this man so much", said I, eleven
years the elder, "you must be in love with him, and it's your duty
to yourself to marry him."

She knew that I was married. So did the girl I had left in
Sydney. Grass husbands who pose as bachelors ought to be
whipped.

Mary Elizabeth decided to take my advice. We parted in Port
of Spain—never a kiss exchanged between us—on a gorgeous day
of December 1913.

The sequel to this tale is curious. On a night in June 1926, I
sat late with the man of whom Mary Elizabeth had spoken
thirteen years previously, the famous Californian surgeon,
Ellis W. Jones—her husband and the father of her two boys.

"She asked me to look after you", he had said, calling on me
the moment I arrived in Hollywood. "She's in the Mayo Clinic at
Rochester. I can't get to her. I'm too busy with my patients."

And that night he said, "I often feel I owe my happiness to the
advice you gave Elizabeth. It may be fate that you're here now.
There's just an outside chance. But I'm not very hopeful. It all
depends on the result of today's operation."

It was a long way from Los Angeles to Rochester, Minnesota, in
those pre-flying times. But the Mayos' telegram bridged the miles
for us.

Before Ellis W. Jones drove me home to the Ambassador Hotel,
we knew that his wife would live.

§ 5

Yet the epilogue—if epilogue it be—to this story is more
curious still.

"I've just had a telegram from Ellis", said the Elizabeth of 1939, as my present wife and I sat at tea with her. "He's had a terrible illness, you know. But now the New York specialist is sure he's going to get well."

CHAPTER THIRTY

§ 1

I HAVE no recollection of regretting—I am sure I had no intention of going back on—the promise I made in a moment of exaltation to Mary Elizabeth Bradley. First, however, I meant to finish my job in the way I had secretly intended it should finish before I left home.

From Trinidad I crossed to Barbados, back to Trinidad again, and down to Georgetown, British Guiana. There I lunched soberly with Sir Walter Egerton, popularly known as Sir Walter Get-it-Done, the Governor, and drank far too many rum swizzles at the club.

The diary further records a voyage to Panama, the canal not yet finished, a walk on the dry concrete bed of what is now Gatun Lock, and a conversation with the Reverend John Taylor Smith, Chaplain General of the Forces, whose "simple faith" I envied, though disputing his theory that venereal disease should not be prevented because it was a scourge sent by God to punish men and women for sexual immorality.

Christmas, and New Year's day 1914, I spent in Jamaica.

There, entertained at King's House, "as they call Government House in Kingston", I sat next to a very lovely woman, popularly known as "Mouse" Dennistoun, now married to a Russian architect, whom I was to meet again. Thence I took ship for Santiago de Cuba, and crossed the island by rail for Havana.

Two young Upmann nephews were in charge of the bank and factory. I called on them; and the years since that day in Hamburg swung full circle. Their uncle had lied to my father. Why should I tell them the truth—or the financial position? We were still solvent—even if we had lost the best part of our capital.

"Our cigarette factory", said I, "is making so much money that I'm seriously thinking of giving up the cigar business altogether."

"But you wouldn't give up our agency? Not after all these years?"

5*

"Why not? It isn't as though it were a sole agency. Leave off supplying our competitors—and I may change my mind."

"We should have to consult our uncle in Hamburg first. Couldn't you go there and ask him personally?"

"I'm not asking. I'm demanding. If the old man will agree to give us a ten-year contract, I don't mind going over to Hamburg to sign it. The rest's up to you."

We settled the terms. They wrote their letter to Germany. Once more I sailed for Key West; and was soon rattling over the coral quays in the new all-steel cars for a New York whose Broadway slogan was "Ich-ka-bibble", meaning "Why should I worry?"

"Ich-ka-bibble", thought I too—with that contract as good as in my pocket, easy enough to finance, and worth a steady £6,000 a year if it was worth a penny. Until I landed from the *Minnewaska* at Tilbury and saw my mother, thin-faced, shrunk to a shadow, supporting her wasted body on Dolly's arm.

§ 2

Memory holds no picture of the short journey from the docks to 64 Grosvenor Street. Julia went back to the bed she should not have left; Dolly and I to a furnished house in Bramham Gardens, Kensington.

The conjugal situation was—to use French again—of an extreme delicacy; but temporarily patched up at my request.

I went to see Julia next day. She was still in bed. We talked business for an hour. Then I told her of the narrative poem I had brought back with me, and my decision to adopt a literary career.

All she said was, "Hadn't you better get the Upmann contract signed first?"

At the cigarette factory I found subdued optimism. At Gracechurch Street—the two managements had not seen eye to eye during my absence—profound gloom, and an unopened letter from Hamburg.

"Cheer up", I told Bishop and Musgrave. "We're not done yet."

Forty-eight hours later I sat in the same room overlooking the Alster where I had once listened to my father talking unintelligible German. That time Heinrich Upmann gave not only his word but his bond.

As thirteen years previously, we lunched at the Rathskeller. Vague rumours were in the air. I asked another merchant at the "Stammtisch" what he thought of the political situation.

"There will be no war", he answered, "as long as our good Kaiser is on the throne."

But a sentry held me up when I left my carriage just before we crossed the frontier into Belgium on my return journey, and grunted, "Weiss nichts. Verboten" ("I know nothing. You can't pass") when I asked him, "What are those new railway lines for?"

There were at least eight extra tracks and sidings, all brand new. If my imagination had not been in Gracechurch Street, fore-tasting commercial triumph, I might have already foreseen disaster.

Maybe I did—subconsciously. Though I couldn't help gloating at the sight of Musgrave's face and Bishop's when I showed them the signed contract neither had believed within the bounds of possibility. Bankruptcy, forsooth—with this monopoly, and the factory almost covering its expenses, advertising included!

Still gloatful, I called a meeting of both boards.

"Are we home?" I asked Gundry.

He told the others that we were—and believed it to the day of his death. His financial judgment was always sounder than mine. So he may have been right.

When we were alone again he said, "With that contract, we could easily raise more capital. Not that we need it. In my opinion there's nothing to be afraid of".

The subconsciousness which has foreseen nearly every political development of these last years must have been already active in me when I answered:

"Nothing except a European war".

CHAPTER THIRTY-ONE

§ 1

BUT that March 1914, hardly a soul in England consciously believed there could be a war. Certainly not the young author of a long narrative poem accepted by Austin Harrison, editor of *The English Review*, which had published Masefield's "Everlasting Mercy" and his "Widow in the Bye-Street", and of which the bookstall man at the Great Central Station used to say, "The poem alone's worth the bob, sir". (Imagine a bookstall man saying that in 1939!)

"You'd better go and see Harrison", advised Julia; and I went.

Memory recalls two figures in a small room, but the faces are unclear. One of these figures, Austin Harrison's own, sat at a cheap desk. Compliments, unusual in modern Fleet Street, were paid to the young poet, who then held forth at the family length on the high purpose behind his poetic tale.

"If you'd been East," he declaimed, "if you'd been to South America, if you'd seen San Ysidro or the Bocca at Buenos Aires you'd feel as strongly about the evils of the white slave traffic as I do." For the original inspiration of my tale had been a personal experience—ending in failure when "French Julie" plumped for Malay Street rather than the Roman Catholic home to which a family man's chivalry had sent her.

Courteously Austin Harrison listened to the rest of my harangue. Then, looking at the other figure in the room, he smiled "Well, you may be right. But I can't feel that the white slave trade is really profitable. Because if it were, my brother would have been in it. He's a great one for making money".

And after this jest, which his brother took in good part, he went on to tell me of the original manuscript of "The Everlasting Mercy", from which he had persuaded the present poet laureate to remove "at least two hundred and sixty-five sanguinaries".

But there the poet laureate's clemency ended. When, in the after years, a clergyman wrote to his publishers suggesting a bowdlerised edition of his works for the schoolroom, he refused on a postcard, adding this couplet:

"The Reverend Septimus then spoke the word:
'Unbloody Masefield for the Lower Third!' ".

The good old English word which derives from "By Our Lady" by the way, was first heard on the stage just before the war Mrs. Patrick Campbell spoke it in *Pygmalion*. And the good old English word for a posterior, which possesses a different meaning (cf. "stumblebum"—a guy who comes home drunk) in America where "bloody" has no significance, never appeared in latter-day print till George Moore fought his historical battle for its use against William Heinemann and Sydney Pawling.

"I will not change it to 'bottom' ", reiterated George Moore using his characteristic gesture. "I abhor and detest the word 'bottom'. The explosive monosyllable is the classic term. The explosive monosyllable is the mot juste. You will either print it—or I take my book elsewhere."

So three letters won the day against six.

§ 2

Ever since my father's death Heinemann's partner, Sydney Pawling, familiarly known as "The Skipper", because he captained the famous Hampstead Cricket Club, had been my mother's best friend. He was still a loyal director of Frankaus, and a joint guarantor of our overdrafts. But he no longer visited Grosvenor Street daily. Why, I don't know.

Julia's illness may have been the cause. It certainly made her rather crotchety. She took a spite to one doctor after the other. On occasions she would even rail to me about "that idiot Horder", who used to sit at her bedside—kindliest, most sympathetic, most understanding of physicians—by the hour.

For those long visits the present Lord Horder, already famous at 141 Harley Street, would accept no payment. He knew, of course, that there was no hope—in those pre-insulin days—for a diabetic who had now developed consumption. I may have guessed this myself.

Anyway, I decided to postpone my literary ambitions—and resumed the old routine, so confident the financial crisis was over that I signed a seven-year lease of a house which took my fancy in Hereford Square.

The London to which I had returned seemed gayer than the London I had left, and Julia's health to improve a little. Eliza and I took her to the play of the moment, *Potash and Perlmutter*—the last she was ever to see.

By June, Horder advised a move to the country. She took a large furnished house at Witley in Surrey, and moved in with her staff, my sister Joan, and my brother Ronnie, just back from Canada, and crazy to go on the stage.

Dolly and I moved into Hereford Square. Ursula was nearly eight years old, Pamela rising seven. I just remember playing with them—not as clearly as Pamela, who maintains that we lit a bonfire in the courtyard and had to extinguish it with water brought in a blue Chinese vase, further threatening a nameless lady who resented these proceedings with my pearlhandled revolver.

This seems pertinent, because—search memory as I may—it is the one and only recollection I have of their existence up to that date.

Sharper is the picture of an evening Dolly and I and Edric Weldon's gunner brother, Geoffrey, spent at a new night club, the

Lotus, where a young woman in oversize gloves sang the hit of the moment, "Oh, oh, oh, oh, where did you get that girl?" and the orchestra played "Alexander's Ragtime Band".

But far sharper—indelible for ever—is the picture of those minutes in Julia's bedroom at Witley, one Saturday of early July

We were spending the weekend with her. That Saturday afternoon, she insisted on playing croquet, wearing slippers and one of the kimonos in which she always worked. She was working still, on the best novel she ever wrote, *Twilight*.

"I don't think I'll come down to dinner," she said that night; and we were still at table when her bedside bell rang.

A few moments later her maid came in to say:

"Mrs. Frankau would like Mr. Gilbert to go up".

I went up. Julia was lying on the bed with a handkerchief to her mouth. I remembered my father's handkerchief at his mouth —as the brougham drove us away from Otto's.

"Ice", she whispered, and pointed to the bowl on the bedside table.

I fed it to her lump by lump. I can still see her eyes; still feel her lips sucking in the ice from between my fingers.

"All right, now", she said, with the bowl half-empty. "Sorry, I'm such a nuisance. I hope you haven't missed your cigar too much."

§ 3

Less than three weeks later Julia was telling me, "McKenna" (Reginald, then Home Secretary) "came to see me this afternoon He says it'll be a short war, over by Christmas. I don't believe him. You'll all have to go. I must see my three sons in khaki"

I have known wiser women. I may have known better women. But no woman more courageous. No woman less selfish. Not one!

Part Three

GENERAL POST

CHAPTER THIRTY-TWO

§ 1

I do not feel that many pictures of its central character as a 1914–1918 soldier are necessary for this tale.

However, since St. John Greer Ervine, the playwright, when temporarily engaged by the *Daily Express* as book critic, once suggested that he was never quite certain whether I or Mr. Lloyd George won the Great War; and since I cannot believe he meant this discourteously, because he had recently accepted lavish fees from me in my temporary capacity as editor of another paper, modesty alone compels me to contradict the sweeping panegyric.

The facts are easily abbreviated thus:

"First commission 9th East Surrey Regiment, 1914; transferred to Royal Field Artillery, 1915; appointed Adjutant to 107th Brigade, R.F.A.; and proceeded overseas in that capacity; at Loos, Ypres and the Somme; promoted Staff Captain for special duty in Italy, Oct., 1916; invalided from the Service and granted rank of Captain, Feb., 1918".

The local colour gathered up to the Battle of the Somme I used in another tale. How *Peter Jackson, Cigar Merchant*, came to be written you will read later. Here, I only add a further disclaimer.

With one solitary exception, all the soldier characters in that book are "composites" and purely fictitious.

The solitary exception, over whom I took particular care, did not fail to recognise his own portrait. He died, as he had lived, peaceably in his unsoiled uniform, before he could bring his threatened libel case.

At the time I regretted his death keenly. Nowadays I am old enough to be grateful to him. Had I not insisted to our Colonel that one of us must go, because I would not obey the orders of a Territorial who had refused to volunteer for active service, I should not have been transferred from the infantry to the artillery.

In all human probability that transfer saved my life—hardly an officer surviving when The Gallants, as my old battalion came to be known, were first thrown into action, starving after forced marches, by Sir John French, whose official despatch glossed over this circumstance.

My old company commander, Lt.-Colonel R. V. G. Brettell, led a battalion of the Bedfords to that same attack. Sheer beef and muscle, of which he possesses some two hundred and fifty solid pounds, saved him from being made prisoner.

Four stout stretcher-bearers in field gray regarded that wounded colossus with awe. Then they shook their heads, and refused the Gargantuan burden.

How many of our stretcher-bearers were needed to carry Brettell to the field dressing-station after a successful counter attack, he has never related at the old comrade meetings where we still applaud him in the chair.

§ 2

The colonel under whose orders I found myself after my transfer to the artillery was another well-known army character —D. R. ("Sleepy") Coates. Of this stout red-headed Belfaster with a grand flow of pre-war language and a peculiar twinkle in his blue eyes, stories in the Royal Regiment are legion. I will only increase the number by one.

Shortly after the Battle of Loos in September 1915, for his conduct at which he might well have been awarded the D.S.O., Sleepy Coates went on leave. My mother, having left Brighton, where she stayed while the 24th Division was in training, had taken a top flat at the corner of Hay Hill, in the very house once occupied by Almack's.

They did not know each other. Julia had been far too ill, even at Brighton, to receive strangers. But the very first call Coates made when he reached London was on her.

He just sent in his card with the message, "This gentleman thought you might like to know how Gilbert's getting on"—and spent a whole precious hour at her bedside. How he managed simultaneously to convey the impressions of my sterling military worth and complete physical safety, I do not know.

Neither did I know of his intention until he returned to a little village called Acquin, where I happened to be occupying the very same billet in which Rudyard Kipling's son, John, had rested before his last spell in the front line.

Our involuntary landlady and her peasant husband had adored John. My brigade wire had been the first to report him missing when the Irish Guards charged Hill 70. Something impelled me to write these things to the man whose genius I had so long worshipped from afar. Rudyard Kipling answered me with his own hand, marking the letter, as was his custom, "Private".

This began a correspondence of which—as you will hear later—only one piece of literary criticism on his part appears to survive.

§ 3

Thanks to Coates I also obtained leave, after less than six months' active service, crossing the Channel on Christmas Eve 1915, in one of its worst storms. A world of thanks is here due to the Hammam Turkish baths in Jermyn Street for taking me in at three o'clock of a morning, washing me, sleeping me, breakfasting me . . . and removing the maritime travelstains from my clothes.

Nelson, if one can believe the legend, was no bad hand at being seasick. That Yuletide I could have given Nelson three Trafalgars —and beaten him to the basin by three groaning lengths.

"It's lucky you didn't volunteer for the navy", said Julia when I reported myself at Hay Hill.

She was almost at the end of her long hopeless battle. But her pluck still held out. We never discussed her health. And, as always, we eschewed sentiment. She made me read her some soldier poems I had brought home with me—and told me to take them to her literary agent, Hughes Massie. Then she spoke about her last novel, its sale killed by the war.

That worried her. But about me, she had no worry except one, which she kept to herself.

"You'll come through all right", she said. "So will Ronnie. Jack's too reckless. He'll be killed." (And so he was to be, most gallantly, leading his platoon of the Rifle Brigade to the attack on Gaza in 1917.)

Of the two businesses, we hardly talked at all. Both were limping along, Frankaus still solvent enough to keep her provided with money. I remember thinking, "She always used to say she would rather be dead than poor. At any rate, she'll never know poverty".

Poverty for myself, I did not then fear; imagination having made up its mind a long while ago that I should not survive. "When it happens", I often caught myself thinking, "there'll be enough to give my sister a small income—and those two life insurance policies plus the pension for Dolly and the children."

Do not mistake this attitude for true courage. Consider it rather an escapist's reaction to failure. I had worked at those two businesses from the time I was seventeen and a half to the time I was thirty. They couldn't last very much longer. But they would last Julia's time. She would never know the worst. Meanwhile, the more fun the better. After all, I was on leave from the front. And I had done the only possible thing in 1914.

That I might have waited to join the army, in the same way my old schoolfellow G. C. B. James, waited, until I had cleared up my affairs, is only a thought of these after-years. I never doubted—doubter though I was born—the cause for which I was fighting. Otherwise I might have reacted differently to a chance conversation that took place within a few hours of my arrival in London.

Dolly was not in town. "Eliza's giving a tea party this afternoon", said Julia after our first chat. "She'd like you to go."

My aunt was living in Fitzroy Square, Bloomsbury. I went there, wearing the only clothes I possessed, to find several people in a blue-walled room with black and gold curtains.

"You know Isidore", began Eliza. "But I don't think you know H. G."

Isidore de Lara, one of the dearest men who ever lived, and so handsome in his youth that a princess left her consort for him, had arrived on a push-bike. He shook me warmly by the hand after detaching his trouser clips. H. G. Wells looked me over as though I were a specimen out of a bottle.

Fortunately I stood in no awe, though I had enjoyed some of his earlier tales, notably *The Time Machine*.

"I see", he piped in his shrill falsetto, "that you're wearing spurs. Why are you wearing spurs? Are they necessary in the trenches?"

"One rides occasionally", said I, pitying his ignorance. *He'd* never kicked an unclipped hairy over a wet ditch under shellfire.

He admitted that gunners sometimes rode, but suggested I had not arrived at Fitzroy Square on horseback. I was tempted to tell him that I had found his *Tono-Bungay* too long, and been bored with his *New Machiavelli*; but refrained.

"How are you chaps getting along with this war?" he continued. "Do you think you're going to win it?"

I believe he added, "Wearing your spurs", but of this I am not quite certain. All I know is that I was not liking him. One did at least expect some decency, some understanding from a civilian.

"You can be certain of one thing", I said. "We shan't stop till we've smashed the German Empire."

"That'll be all right", he piped. "As long as you smash the British Empire at the same time."

My maturity allows that he may have spoken in jest or merely to show his own cleverness. But that H. G. Wells spoke those words is indubitable. I quoted him as saying them, eleven years afterwards, in a speech I made to the Press Club at Washington, and they were printed throughout America without eliciting a denial.

They hurt my youth beyond all anger. After all, I had seen the men of The Gallants begging our gunners for a mouthful of bread as they marched by the pits into action beyond Lone Tree.

My memory of this conversation with Wells is all the clearer because it was at this same party that I first met the lady who became my second wife.

§ 4

Within ten days I had to bid my mother goodbye. There was little hope that we should see each other again in this world—and neither of us possessed a sure faith in the next. We made no fuss. We wore, to the very last, those breastplates of insouciance behind which beat two hearts that had loved each other and trusted each other more than most.

One kiss, one casual, "See you the next time I get leave, Julia", and I was going from the room.

I remember turning at the doorway. I remember how frail, how wasted she looked by the light of that one lamp burning at the bedside. I remember her eyes suffusing, and how I told myself, "She wouldn't want me to see her blub. And she mustn't see that I'm blubbing either".

I thought of her as already gone.

But many more weeks were to elapse before Coates, who had been on leave again, came riding from Poperinghe to those dug-outs by the Ypres Canal; and I knew, seconds before he told me, that she was dead.

Her high courage endured to the very end. Only a night or two before she passed on, there was an air raid. She insisted on being carried from bed to a chair by the window. She commanded her two nurses, her staff, her sister and my sister, to leave her.

"You'll be safe enough in the basement", she told them. "Go there." And, not daring to disobey, they went.

Before that, her keen brain had divined most of the financial position. She sent for a relative, a solicitor.

"Draw me a new will", she ordered—and dictated every term.

No testament could have been more fair. Eliza's allowance must continue while Eliza lived, Joan's portion never be in jeopardy, the residue go into trust for her sons.

"The only one of them I'm really troubled about", she said, "is Gilbert. If the businesses are sold, how will he earn his living? He wants to be a writer. But I can't see him ever making even a competence with his pen."

That was why she sent, very secretly, for John Withers, whose letter reached me in Ypres forty-eight hours after her death.

§ 5

That letter, typed almost in official language, endeared Withers to me for life. I think of it whenever my faith in human nature is apt to wane.

Briefly, he put his experience and his whole organisation at my service *free*.

"That's the least chaps like myself can do for the men who are fighting", he said when I saw him in London about a month after Julia's funeral, for which I could not return.

He wore uniform himself, with a G.R. band round his right arm. (Wartime slang called that corps the Gorgeous Wrecks; but Withers had been up all the previous night, manning an anti-aircraft machine gun in Hyde Park; and he was fifty-three then.)

"Your mother gave me a sealed envelope for you. Here it is. You'd better open it alone", he went on, and left me in that Arundel Street room I was to know so well.

I opened Julia's monogrammed envelope. Inside were five £100 Bank of England notes, and a letter, the first half in ink, the second in pencil—scrawled with her final strength.

"Do not grieve for me," she ended, "but think kindly of me sometimes."

If there be any survival of personal consciousness—if, indeed, as some believe, the dead are still aware of the living—what you have read so far will prove to her that I have not disregarded her last wish.

CHAPTER THIRTY-THREE

§ I

WITHERS made no bones about my financial position. The businesses would have to be sold and the capital invested in trustee securities. It might be twenty years, "according to the tables", before I could expect a shilling from my mother's estate. Meanwhile my private liabilities—of which I gave him a list—amounted to about six years' pay. Over and above this I already owed two years' rent on the house in Hereford Square—the solicitor acting for my landlady having refused to take back the key.

We agreed that I might eventually have to file my petition in bankruptcy; but decided to wait.

He wrote a round-robin letter to my creditors; I—returning to the front—continued to write poetry for a weekly home paper called *Land and Water*, and our divisional trench journal, *The Wipers Times*.

The origin of this peculiar sheet, which changed its title whenever we were shifted to a new part of the line, had been the discovery by an enterprising Sherwood Forester, F. J. Roberts, who afterwards commanded the battalion and is still among my best friends, of an "old printing house just off the Square at Wipers".

You can read the rest in his preface to the facsimile edition published by Herbert Jenkins in 1918 and beautifully printed on a copy of the original paper by William Brendon & Son, Ltd., of Plymouth.

The "advertisements" are still a joy to those of us who can solve their riddles, and one of Roberts' couplets deserves immortality.

> "Would you as a decent cove ack-
> nowledge yourself a Czechoslovak?"

he wrote while we were still mystified as to the whereabouts of that country.

I hope a little nation of great fighters, treacherously delivered over to the enemies of civilisation, will forgive the old jest. There can be no real peace in Europe until their independence is fully restored.

§ 2

"Characters", my mother always maintained, "do not alter. They only develop." But the development, surely, depends on circumstance. Two wartime circumstances at least must have influenced mine.

One was concerned with religion. It is succinctly set forth in a subsequent letter to Lord Northcliffe's *Daily Mail*, which I reprint by courtesy of its present editor.

The Church Militant

SIR—At the Christmas service for my brigade in France in 1915, the following *official* prayer was duly intoned by the chaplain: "And we pray that our enemies may be healed of their *bodily* hurts".

This to gunners who had been trained, equipped, and paid by the State for the express purpose of "hurting" said enemies!

To wound your foe one day and pray that he may be well enough to kill you the next seems to me the last word in— Ely-ism.

"Ely-ism", it must be explained, is a reference to the then Bishop of Ely whom Northcliffe had accused of lukewarmness to the cause for which we were fighting.

This circumstance had such an effect on me that I never willingly attended church parade again.

The other circumstance, I used in fiction; but the central fact of that tale is true. The idiot girl who sat dribbling by her mother's stove in Bailleul while our interpreter and I drank coffee had been raped at the age of sixteen in the open street by more than a dozen drunken Hun infantrymen *while their officers looked on.*

People with less prejudiced minds than my own may suggest that such behaviour is possible in all warring armies. I maintain that it would have been utterly impossible in ours.

For one lesson my fourteen months at the front did teach me: that the world's finest gentleman is "poor bloody Tommy".

A further lesson, that the finest gentleman in the world needs his officers and his non-commissioned officers, on whom lies the ultimate responsibility for his welfare, as much as they need him, I learned mainly from Coates.

§ 3

Nevertheless there came a day, a night rather, when I parted brass rags (as they say of friends who quarrel in the navy) from Coates, who could occasionally be difficult—standing on my silly dignity as a man, where I should have apologised as a subordinate.

We were just going into action on the Somme. "Corps" had demanded one officer from each brigade for anti-aircraft training. A vindictive superior would not have recommended his ex-adjutant for that safeish job. Coates did.

At home in the meantime one J. C. Faunthorpe, the famous Anglo-Indian big-game shot, temporarily at the War Office, had fortuitously encountered my Aunt Esther—Jimmy Davis' widow —who worked at the Admiralty throughout the war.

It is just possible that she remembered a long-ago night when I and my adored Elvira vacated a brougham to make room for her and Julia. Anyway, when Faunthorpe told her that he was looking high and low for an officer who had seen active service, possessed some commercial knowledge, and spoke Italian with sufficient fluency to undertake a particular mission, she mentioned me.

How I knew about this, or how much I knew about it, when I reported to those old-fashioned "Archies" near Montauban cross-roads, memory cannot recall.

My new superior was that grand chap, A. R. F. Kingscote, who reached the final of the All-Comers' Singles at Wimbledon in 1919, and ran Tilden to five sets in 1920. On a day early in August 1916, he lent me his car, and I drove to "Advanced General Headquarters", some twenty miles behind us, where I demanded to see "General Charteris".

Remark that it was a slightly unusual procedure for un-summoned subalterns to demand interviews with the "B.G.I."— the brigadier in charge of all military intelligence on the Western Front. Remark further, in mitigation of my deliberate intent to get that cushy Italian job if humanly possible, (a) that I needed the extra money and (b) the loss of my adjutancy.

I was sore. I was growing excitable. And a tooth or two were already giving me gyp.

As a staff officer, I knew my own capabilities. As a regimental officer, I doubted them. My job, from the very beginning at Brighton, had been organisation. Only once, at practice camp, had I directed the fire of a gun.

Charteris must have liked my cheek. He saw me at once.

"You're the man they want", he said. "And I'm quite willing. The trouble is that Delme-Radcliffe won't let a single trained gunner go."

Delme-Radcliffe, it transpired, was the ultimate authority on the employment of gunners in the British Expeditionary Force.

Having memorised his name, I pointed out to Charteris that I was rather far from being a trained gunner, and returned to Montauban via Amiens, being hospitably entertained there by Philip Gibbs, Beach Thomas, Russell and others of my present craft at war-correspondents' headquarters.

How I originally gate-crashed that threshold is another detail memory cannot recall. But I have the clearest recollection of one thought, "This job is telling on Gibbs". He looked so worn.

Followed a few more safeish days with Kingscote, my one and only lunch at the famous Restaurant Godbert in Amiens, more drillings by a Canadian dentist, and a visit to Querrieux, where I found Edric Weldon with the 8th Hussars.

My anti-aircraft training over, I returned to duty with one of our own 107th batteries, Major Galloway's, then in rather a nasty position just behind Bernafay Wood.

Remark here, the peculiar fortune of war.

Some half a mile to our left was Geoffrey Weldon's "regular" battery. On a quiet afternoon I walked over to have tea with him. Returning to the coffin-shaped hole where I spent my nights I found a man-deep shell crater just outside it, in the exact place where I should have been sitting had I stayed "at home". Within a few hours another shell, falling on his battery position, wounded Geoffrey to the death.

The worse soldier was to write the better's epitaph. Edric and I still stop to read, as we walk—more slowly than we three used to—up the hill behind his Devonshire home:

"Brother, take heart! God's world is clean and wide for you.
 Regret not one whose pride is that he died for you.
 He would not have you weep nor idly pray for him
 Who gave this life while yet young life was gay for him,
 That you and yours might sturdily possess
 This land he served in utter faithfulness".

For, on that very September day when the world's first fighting tanks lumbered for the front line from Carnoy siding, I was ordered home.

§ 4

At Loos, Coates acted as brigadier and I as his brigade major. On the Somme, one more fortune of war—the death of two comrades, killed by the same shell at the Briqueterie—had brought us together again, in the very same capacities, a day or so before the order for my return to England arrived from G.H.Q.

Acting staff captain was an Irish pal of mine, Bellingham. It is not easy for an acting staff captain to refuse an acting brigade major's orders.

Coates' blue eyes twinkled when he heard me tell Bellingham to sign two railway warrants—one for myself and one for my batman, an apple-cheeked Yorkshire boy named Wilson. He queried my authority for this procedure. I referred him to King's Regulations (for home service!) by which an officer proceeding to a staff appointment was entitled to take two horses, his servant and his groom.

"Spare the horses", laughed Coates—and let the regulation breaker go.

Some weeks later Driver Wilson, stationed to guard his master's cabin on the Dover-Calais staff boat, left his post to announce, "There's a general outside, sir. He wondered if you'd mind his coming in for a bit".

Whereupon a temporary captain who now wore the green tabs and hatband of the Intelligence Corps with his artillery badges, rose, went to the door, saluted, and told a red-tabbed general with a handsome humorous face, "I expect it'll be all right, sir. Anyway, I'll risk it".

"King's Messenger, eh?" said the general, regarding some dozen tin boxes. Having posed as such to secure my cabin—and pinched the regular messenger's reserved compartment on the train into the bargain—I did not deny the honour.

"What have you got in there?" he went on.

"Cinematograph films, sir."

"Really."

"Yes. I'm taking them to Rome."

The general sat down, lit a cigarette, and inspected my badges.

"You're actually a gunner, I see."

"Well, I was. Now I've been seconded to the Foreign Office for special work in Italy."

"Rather a good job. How did you manage to get it?"

Whereupon Captain (temporary) G. Frankau waxed confidential.

"I damn nearly didn't", said he. "The B.G.I., that's General Charteris, had to write Lloyd George personally before G.H.Q would let me go. There's an adjectival brass hat there called Delme-Radcliffe who simply kicked up hell about it."

The language of the period had not bowdlerised the single word which is supposed to be used as a term of endearment among sailors into "adjectival brass hat". The general who was sharing my cabin smiled.

"I am afraid I am that b——- Delme-Radcliffe", he said. "Let's have a drink."

Add to this episode Edric's recollection of my first public greeting to him at Querrieux, "You're a nice kind of pal. Why didn't you warn me that the infantry is sheer suicide; and that it's almost as dangerous to be a gunner?" and the roars of laughter this evoked among his attendant cavalrymen, before you determine that the muckraking of these latter days is the entire truth about the 1914–1918 war.

CHAPTER THIRTY-FOUR

§ 1

IT is possible that a certain shell which had decapitated the infantryman at my side, knocking me flat, and embedding three tiny pieces of grit behind my left ear, was already affecting me before my undiplomatic behaviour on the staff boat.

Otherwise I should hardly have replied to the Right Honourable Charles Frederick Gurney Masterman, P.C., ex-Financial Secretary to the Treasury and Director of the Wellington House Propaganda Department, when he greeted me jocularly on my return from the front, "Well, we seem to have saved your life for you, Frankau", with a dignified:

"You can certainly flatter yourself that you've rendered a supreme service to English literature".

But to myself, throughout the many months I laboured in Italy, I seemed normal enough.

With Masterman, at that first interview, sat a charming clean-shaven barristerish Civil Servant, four years my senior, who is now Sir Ernest Gowers. He told me, when Masterman left us, "I'm feeling a bit harassed this morning", but consented to a new kit allowance, and, all preliminary staff work accomplished, sent me to the present Sir Godfrey Thomas (afterwards King Edward VIII's secretary), whose father had been my first gunner general, and of whom I craved two red diplomatic passports.

Vainly Wilson, wandering about Paris where we sojourned for a day or so, showed his token of diplomatic immunity to an ignorant British military policeman—on the lookout for soldiers who had overstayed their leave.

An appeal to Zena Dare's husband, Maurice Brett, the Provost Marshal—there is no old school tie to compare with Eton's—drew a rebuke on that policeman's ignorance; and Wilson and I proceeded, in another reserved compartment, to Rome.

With us went one Chambers, a civilian expert in the showing of films.

"I think we ought to see his nibs together", remonstrated Chambers when we reached our destination. But I insisted on interviewing Sir Rennell Rodd alone.

Courtesy itself, he at once took pains to inform me that—while he would do everything possible to make my mission successful—I must consider myself "nobody's child".

"You're not attached to the Embassy", he explained. "And you're not under the orders of the Military Mission. Though you'd better make yourself known to General Delme-Radcliffe."

The official Secrets Act, though it will slightly handicap this part of my story, cannot prevent me from stating that the chief of the British Military Mission was not the Delme-Radcliffe who stood me a drink after my gaffe on the boat.

§ 2

In the fullness of time Chambers departed, leaving me and Wilson in dual glory at the Grand Hotel, Rome. My main mission was to convince the Italians that we had several men fighting in France and Flanders—the Hun propaganda machine denying this daily, through a secretly subsidised press. "No War Here", said a Welsh miners' leader addressing a home audience—and the headline appeared in a Naples paper next day.

The battle films with which I had been supplied might have proved convincing. But Chambers hadn't been able to sell them; and I could hardly persuade invited audiences to sit through them in free seats.

After some four fruitless weeks of travel I again took counsel with our ambassador; and dashed back to London.

There, I looted every scrap of official film I could find, including several priceless feet of General Cadorna, then generalissimo of the Italian armies, Lord Kitchener, and a sausage balloon taking the air at Queen's Club.

With these, Muirhead Bone's etching of a tank in action and complete orchestra scores for "The British Grenadiers", "Tipperary" and other martial music, I returned to Italy, and took up my headquarters at the Hotel Cavour, Milan.

What Luca Comerio, the Italian cinema man, and I did to the official British war films in the solitude of his studio is nobody's business but our own.

The very first caption thrown on the screen over the facsimile signature of "Capitano Gilbert Frankau, Stato Maggiore Inglese" (English General Staff) guaranteed the story of "La Battaglia dei Tanks" completely authentic.

And what a story! We printed twelve copies. Within ten minutes of the private preview we sold them all—my instructions were to make the thing pay if I could—to five renters whose theatres covered the whole of Italy.

Tears blinded even those hardboiled renters when a shell burst obscured the entire screen, and the film seemed to break and that most telling of all our captions read, "Alas—alas, for the too-intrepid cameraman". With muted music the effect on large audiences had to be seen to be believed.

Among the believers in the death of that mythical cameraman —for I never had the heart to disillusion Her Excellency—was Lady Rodd.

§ 3

Rudyard Kipling arrived at the Grand Hotel, Rome, at the very moment of my movie triumph—to see queues waiting for admission to the theatre on the Corso. I had plastered every available wall with enormous posters of Muirhead Bone's tank; and played the press for columns upon columns of free publicity.

But of my master in letters, my friends on the Roman press knew naught.

"Keepling", they had said, when I advised them of his coming "But who is this Keepling? Is he a great poet like yourself? Is he like yourself, a great student of our Dante?" From which i should be clear that the free film publicity—as is still the habit— had not excluded some mention of the producer's titles to fame

Accordingly I wrote more columns, of advance notices about my master, which duly appeared after my colleagues had corrected my Italian, and were slightly more accurate than the information I had given them about myself.

Whereafter I awaited Kipling's coming in that bar with a revolving door.

He appeared, punctual to the second for our appointment—nut-brown; of medium height; shaggy of dark brow, under which the piercing eyes were kindly; well-kempt of thick moustaches; wearing his perfectly cut dinner clothes as only your man of the world may.

But to me he had always been something more than man.

For the first, last and only time in my whole life, I felt shy. I blushed. I stammered. Words nearly failed me—but not quite.

Afterwards, when he had put me at my ease as only he could, I said, "You didn't mind my writing to you from Acquin. I simply had to. You see, I know every line you've ever had printed. I believe that if every one of your poems were destroyed, I could rewrite them by heart".

Kipling said, "what evidence of a misspent youth". Secretly, I could not help comparing him with Wells.

Twenty years later I was to meet another who had made similar comparisons.

"Kipling was here once", said the curator of the Alhambra at Granada. "I showed him round, too. Also your H. G. Wells and your Bernard Shaw."

"And what did you think of them?"

"Dos gran commerciantes y un hombre de genio", replied the curator instantly.

And it seemed unnecessary to inquire who might be "the man of genius" and who the "two big businessmen" his lisping Spanish so graphically portrayed.

§ 4

That night in 1917 I took Rudyard Kipling—and two charming American women whose names escape the memory—to the theatre where my film had been showing since noon. Gerald Tyrrwhit, unpaid attaché at the Embassy, now Lord Berners, had trained the orchestra for me. They struck up "Rule, Britannia"—by pure coincidence—as we seated ourselves in the box.

Kipling watched the screen. I watched Kipling.

The tunes and that first captional guarantee of authenticity surprised him a little. But he did not even blink when he saw Marconi inventing the tank, or General Cadorna arriving for a conference with Lord Kitchener at which it was decided that the English army should attack on the Somme.

"Good work", whispered my master. "How did you come to think of that fiction?"

Modesty kept silence. Our troops, tinted blue and brown, massed by night. The London Scottish appeared complete with band to "Auld lang syne" and "A wee doch and doris". Then "Came the dawn of battle"; and my Queen's Club sausage balloon rose to survey the German trenches.

Promptly the enemy planes—ours from Salisbury Plain—swooped to the attack, their machine guns chattering. (Tyrrwhit managed that rather well with his drums.) Down fell the balloon (tinted red, and two out of every three pictures excised, to say nothing of the men on the ropes, giving the effect of speed) in real flames.

"Gorgeous", whispered Kipling. "Cost you a truss of hay, I expect."

Our planes counter-attacked. A German Fokker, which looked a little like one of our own B.E.2C's to Kingscote's pupil in anti-aircraft gunnery, also fell in flames.

The crashed plane, I think, was a real picture. Item, it had no British circles under its wings. If anyone faked the Iron Crosses there, it was not done in Milan.

"But where are the tanks?" whispered Kipling. "We must live up to our titles."

Again his fan kept silence while superimposed shell-bursts—the damn things never looked quite real, they waggled about too much—rained on our advancing infantry.

"Meanwhile . . ." read the next caption; and suddenly Kipling chuckled:

"Tanks to the rescue. The Devastating Blinders, eh! Grand"

They were my own words, my very own dictionary-dredged Italian words; and I could not refrain from displaying my erudition.

"Blindati Devastatori means armoured devastators", I corrected, as the tank-noses reared high to crush walls I could have sworn built in England, and swept on to the apocryphal attack

But Kipling preferred his own translation, repeating to himself "devastating blinders", till that thrilling moment when the mine blew, and spotless Highlanders stormed forward, bayonets flashing, at no double ever seen in France or Flanders to victory or

eath. We faded out on coloured flags and "Long Live the
lllies" to a complete symphony of national anthems.

"What do you think of it?" I asked, as we walked the un-
.arkened streets. (Even the Huns of 1914–1918 never dared to
•omb the Eternal City.)

"Superb", chuckled Kipling. "But you will be slain for this,
ny friend. Most indubitably you will be slain."

§ 5

Within six months Kipling's prophecy came true.

One man alone saved me from slaughter when I wrote the truth,
he whole truth, and (with one trifling inaccuracy) nothing but
he truth in a report which only that infernal Act prevents me
rom reproducing here.

The present Lord Rennell corrected my one trifling inaccuracy
iimself; and approved the rest of that long typewritten document
)efore it was forwarded to the Foreign Office.

Only those of you who have been "nobody's children" playing
one hands to successful issues with authority looking the other
vay lest you should fail it, will understand the debt I owe him.

Hereby, I hope, repaid.

CHAPTER THIRTY-FIVE

§ 1

)UR Military Mission, its headquarters at Udine, did not alto-
;ether approve of my ten months' single-handed effort to educate
he Italian civil population by films, by press propaganda, and by
)ersonal appearances complete with artillery sword and white
;loves—one of these appearances before the Queen at the
)uirinale, where I gave a special command performance and got
;tuck in the lift with one of the young princesses, to Driver
Nilson's supreme joy.

Memory recalls being asked, via the F.O. and the Embassy, for
in explanation of why I "consorted with well-known pro-
;ermans". Incipient neurasthenia had the honour to retort
(a) that I was not under military orders and (b) that any fool
:ould preach to the converted.

But Driver Wilson, R.F.A.—missing from the British Expedi-

tionary Force since Bellingham signed that railway warrant—wa
G.H.Q.'s own pigeon. Their chit reached me direct; and to then
I quoted King's Regulations as my authority for kidnapping in vair

"Passed to you." "Passed to you." "Passed to you."

The fat dossier piled up and up. Authority after authorit
demanded, "Send Driver Wilson, R.F.A., back to France or tak
the consequences".

Between "The Battle of the Tanks" and "Tanks Triumphant'
(humanly, our renters asked for a second moneymaker to follov
the first) I sneaked my friend and batman back across the Channe
and hid him far from prying eyes.

Then I called at the War Office and reported to "A.G.6", b·
that time in possession of the whole dossier.

"But where *is* Driver Wilson?" fumed a lamed field officer.

As one seconded to the Foreign Office, I refused to say mor
than, "Somewhere in England".

"You brought him home with you—through France?"

"I did, sir."

"And you intend to take him back to Italy?"

"That was rather my idea, sir."

"Through all the controls?"

"Yes, sir."

My lame field officer inspected me for a moment.

"Try it on", he dared. "And if you bring it off, you can kee|
the young gentleman" (only he did not say gentleman) "with m·
compliments."

It hardly seemed advisable to mention red passports or dip
lomatic immunity. I said, "Thank you very much, sir"; clicke·
my spurred heels; saluted, and left again for Rome.

Not until four months later did I have the honour to report tha
I had granted Driver Wilson, R.F.A., leave to pass a fortnigh
with his mother in Hull, whence A.G.6 could fetch him if the
needed his services.

They did so promptly; and returned him to the British Ex
peditionary Force with more compliments.

He survived the rest of the war and still flourishes. Almost th·
last thing he did for me was to punch three more holes throug
my Sam Browne belt.

In October 1914, Temporary 2nd Lieutenant G. Frankau of th·
9th East Surreys had tipped the scales at 148 lbs. exactly. By th·
end of his Italian adventure, the temporary captain seconded fo
special duty with the Foreign Office weighed 97 lbs., one ounc
under seven stone.

Add that I still considered myself in every way normal and the victim of the most damnable injustice, if you would have some idea of the peculiar individual whom John Buchan, now Lord Tweedsmuir, C. F. G. Masterman's successor in the Propaganda Department, had to handle on a morning in the late summer of 1917.

§ 2

John Buchan received me in a big room at the Foreign Office. His emissary to Rome, one Heron—proprietor of a cinema paper, I think—had been kind, clever and tactful. But I had lost my job; and was in my very best be-sugared-if-I'll-be-sugared-about temper with more than a touch of persecution mania underlying the potential volcano.

Officially slain, I might be—but still very far from dead.

Realise why Canada wishes Lord Tweedsmuir to stay on for another term of office from the fact that he began the interview with a compliment on my war poems, and went on to apologise:

"The other committee forgot to tell us about you when we took over. That's the only reason you haven't had any pay for the last three months".

It is just possible—my films had shown to paying audiences throughout Italy—that some kind friend may have queried my financial probity. But Heron had already seen my accounts, and that I only possessed a credit balance of seven lire at the Banca Commerciale, Milan.

At Cox's in London I was overdrawn several hundred pounds. "And what about my allowances?" I asked. "They haven't been paid either."

An interview with Lever, Honeyman & Co., the chartered accountants, was suggested. Hugh Walpole lounged in. He asked if I'd seen "Monty" Mackenzie while I was in Rome. Memory recalls him in naval uniform—but may be wrong.

"Rather", said I. "On his way to Greece."

Walpole lounged out again. I asked Buchan whether there would be another job for me. His answer didn't sound too hopeful. Next day the accountant—Mr. Honeyman himself, I think—discovered that I was attempting to embezzle a vast sum, nearly two shillings and sevenpence, from the British Government.

This, he surcharged with a honeyed smile. Soon, I was a few pounds in credit at Cox's. From first to last my Italian propaganda had cost the country only £200 over and above my pay and allow-

6

ances—that sum being for a special purpose which I cannot disclose.

Algar Thorold, who so closely resembled that famous actor Sir George Alexander, that he doubled for him in Mr. and Mrs. Temple Thurston's play *John Chilcote, M.P.*, had come out with Heron.

I believe he carried on, using slightly less economical methods with the good work.

§ 3

Mental pictures of this period are slightly confused. Presumably Buchan told me that I should be returned to the army. For I certainly gatecrashed my way to the Military Secretary at the War Office, demanding of him personally my promotion to major and a battery at the front.

The unhappy gentleman, harangued at high speed for a good ten minutes, eventually rid himself of me by promising that my merits should receive their deserts.

I left in good spirits; and was demoted to lieutenant in the artillery within three weeks.

Written orders told me to report to the reserve brigade in St. John's Wood, London. Persecution mania decided that I should be sent to the front speedily—an outraged government craving for my death in action owing to certain paragraphs in my report, notably the last one, which requested official permission to communicate the entire document to the press.

The prospect of death in command of six guns, I seem to remember, would have been tolerable. It was the demotion that set me blaspheming till a Baron's Court flat rang with my oaths.

"But I'll go", I swore. "I'll go right away and show the adjectival sons of lady foxhounds——"

A dulcet voice suggested that it might be advisable to see a doctor first.

I consigned the Royal Army Medical Corps to the nether regions—but finally consented to ask Horder for an appointment, finding him in a Territorial major's uniform at 141 Harley Street.

"And what have you been doing with yourself all this time?" he asked.

Given a resumé, he said, "I shouldn't have liked to pass you mentally fit for active service in 1914. Take your clothes off, please".

Then he did a few tests; and weighed me, with the result you know.

"Ever heard of shellshock?" he went on when I had dressed again. Believe it or not, I never had.

Horder meditated—and explained.

"I've had some pretty bad cases through my hands", he said next. "But you're the worst so far. And you think you're·fit to command a battery in action."

I protested stoutly that I was. Few other men—it seems to me—would have found an argument as convincing as Horder's:

"Possibly you're right. But have you thought of the men you'd be commanding? You'd be responsible for their lives as well as your own. If you got in a tight corner, one of two things would be bound to happen. Either you'd lose your head completely or else you'd sacrifice the lot of them on the chance of earning a decoration for yourself. That's my opinion—for what it's worth".

There is a mental condition now called "schizophrenia", or "split personality". I experienced a slightly similar condition for the first time then, and constantly for the next year or so. One of my personalities was suggesting, "By jove, I'm not going to be killed after all. This *is* good news"; and the other, "I don't care what he says. I'm going out to the front again".

The first personality found no words; the second plenty.

When I paused for breath, Horder said, "Have it your own way and report for duty if you insist. You'll never be sent to the front; but you will eventually be sent to the shellshock hospital at Craigellachie. It's a nice place—if you like fellows jumping head first from the top storey on to the terrace just while you're having your after-breakfast stroll there".

He gave me full details of that actual happening—and eventually a chit which stated that, in his opinion, I should be granted three months' home leave.

For a consultation which must have lasted at least an hour, and indubitably saved my reason, he refused even to consider a fee.

§ 4

Horder's word on "shellshock and neurasthenia" must already have been law. I forwarded his chit to the competent authority—and was granted leave almost by return of post. My creditors, however, proved less complacent.

"You can't blame them", said Withers, interviewed about the same time. "After all, they've been waiting three years."

You will remember that Julia's envelope contained five £100 notes. But they were locked away in the deposit vaults at

Chancery Lane. (What would have happened to that money had I been killed in action between April and August of the previous year, the damaged film of memory does not show. I certainly deposited it under a false name.)

"How about your furniture?" went on Withers. "That ought to fetch a hundred or two."

From him I went to Maples, where the Hereford Square furniture had been warehoused. They made me an offer. I took it without haggling. That came to 2s. 6d. in the £ on my liabilities; but Withers had suggested 5s. as a preliminary payment. So some publisher would have to find the balance.

Under pressure, Percy Spalding of Chatto & Windus gave me an unusual advance on my first prose novel—scribbled in exercise books while we trained at Shoreham and Brighton, its opening chapters redrafted on the Somme while I was under Kingscote, the whole rewritten during those months between Milan, Rome, Florence and Venice. (Memory does recall how acutely conscious I became, from 1916 onwards, of the need for earning a competence now that I had a chance to survive.)

As a tribute to the good influence of Mary Elizabeth Bradley, thinly disguised as "Beatrice Cochrane", this *Romance of* 1913—to which I have already referred—might have been worse, though a certain cynic described it as "the immoralist Baedeker". It ends, curiously enough, with a plea for Anglo-American cooperation in world politics; and also made its little stir.

Even more curiously, it failed—on the grounds of "moral turpitude"—to find an American publisher. At least for some years!

Long before it was published, lying exhausted on a sofa in that Baron's Court flat, I had dictated the wartime sequel—a hundred and fifty thousand words, if you please, in ten nights.

§ 5

What happened during the next weeks is a blur. I believe I gave evidence in a law case—the only one I ever lost—brought by a dismissed traveller against J. Frankau & Co. Ltd. and postponed owing to the absence of the principal witness, myself. There must have been meetings with the co-executors of my mother's estate, who had—I think—disposed of the cigarette factory and all her effects while I was in Italy. Shortly afterwards they received an offer for the Frankau business—and that went, too.

Positively, I remember an air raid which the shellshocked mind found more terrifying than all its previous experiences, though no bomb dropped within a mile of me; and a night (possibly the same one) at Murray's Club during which, supping alone, I fell into conversation with a party of four and told them my name.

Flat disbelief from a lovely lady greeted the statement.

"There can't be two Gilbert Frankaus", she said. "You'll be telling us you wrote *One of Us* next."

"But I did."

"You're a lovely liar, aren't you? Poor Gilbert was killed on the Western Front a few days ago. Flying. I read all about it in an American paper."

How I proved my identity, I forget; but an English newspaper confirmed me living next day. I telephoned both items of news myself. Not for nothing had I taught myself to be a propagandist in green tabs.

Positive, too, is the recollection of a cheery meeting at Chatto's office with Robert Nichols, another war poet, and my gentle friend Cecil Roberts, who has since won himself much fame as a novelist, and Frank Swinnerton, and Geoffrey Whitworth, now of the Drama League—and how I wrote to Charles Higham, "I've got a novel coming out. Could you help me get some publicity?"

Charles replied by return of post, and introduced me, over lunch at the Savoy, to a tall, emaciated cross between an actor of the old school and a priest of the Spanish Inquisition.

"Meet Hannen Swaffer", boomed Charles in that hearty voice of his. "He's editing the *Weekly Dispatch* for Northcliffe, and he may be able to do something for you."

I fancy Charles must have told Swaff privately of my financial position. For although Swaff's tongue is of the sharpest, and nobody wields a more caustic, or a more truthful pen—actually he dictates, sometimes as many as four articles daily—nobody is kindlier to his less successful colleagues.

"Tell you what I'll do, Gilbert", he said. "You write a review of your own book over your own name—and I'll print it."

He did, too, half a column at the top of a news page. And this at the height of the paper shortage.

§ 6

Just before that self-laudatory review appeared, or it may have been just afterwards, heavyweight misfortune landed a neat upper cut, nearly giving me the count.

CHAPTER THIRTY-SIX

§ 1

THE psychological effects of "shellshock and neurasthenia" are intrinsic to the mind and character of the individual patient. That is what makes the condition so difficult to cure.

Foolishly I had told Horder nothing about my domestic and financial conditions, both extremely complex. Too proud to take further advantage of his generosity, I put my own interpretation on the treatment he had advised at our one and only interview, which can be summed up in the single word, "Rest!"

A real rest, the financial and the domestic conditions alike forbade. I needed money—and the only way I could earn it was with my pen. A resting place, nevertheless, had been provided for me.

And there, five Berkshire miles from the nearest railway station, I awaited the coming of those hundred and fifty thousand words dictated in London, all typed and ready for a modicum of rewriting.

Instead, late on an autumn afternoon, came a parcel containing the first few chapters, and a letter from the stenographer. She was awfully sorry—but a "foolish maidservant" had thrown all her notebooks except the first one into the fire.

Prior to the war, my temper had been of the gentlest. Now there was a devil in me—which I still find difficult to control when I am overworked.

I remember, and regret, one of the hot phrases—"you have done me the greatest wrong one human being can do another"—which I dashed off in reply.

And here, if anywhere, it seems fitting that I should pay tribute to a lady, resident in the same Berkshire village, without whose comfort I think I should have gone crazy that night . . .

§ 2

Once again, memory's damaged film flashes pictures with no sequence. All I know for certain is that nothing would induce me even to read those few chapters of my burned novel. I just put them away. There was an incomplete poem begun in Ypres. I finished that off and sold it. More poems must have been laid on me; because I have a clear recollection of waking towards six o'clock of a morning in the Curzon Hotel, London; and lines flowing to paper of their own volition.

And into that same hotel—could it have been on that same afternoon?—there walked temporary salvation, personified by a smart clean-shaven editor named Edward Huskinson. Would I consider—asked Huskinson—writing a novel in verse on the lines of *One of Us* to appear in his paper, *The Tatler*?

Would I, up to my eyes in debt, with only a subaltern's pay on which to keep a wife and two children besides carrying other responsibilities, *consider* a firm commission at eight guineas a week for twenty-six weeks certain? Ye gods!

The writing of verse still comes more easily to me—and appeals a thousand times more—than the writing of prose. I returned to Berkshire; went for the thing bald-headed—and was ordered into a Reading hospital, under new regulations which denied shellshock patients the refuge of their own homes, while the rhymes still poured.

Nurses and doctors were as kind as circumstances permitted. But to wake a patient whose sleeping hours are only intermittent nightmare at six in the morning may produce strange results.

I sent for the matron that first morning; and told her—in the presence of four others who shared the room—that I would rather submit my seven stone of shrunken manhood to sanguinary and perverted indignities than go down to breakfast. Apologies herewith.

Long-suffering benevolence kept me and my tantrums in hospital for a whole week. Then I went before a medical board at Oxford—and received permission to return home.

Followed a communication from the War Office, granting me captain's rank for my three and a half years of service, the right to wear uniform on "ceremonial occasions" . . . and a first lieutenant's gratuity.

Temporarily awarded an "eighty per cent. disability" pension (not at captain's rate!), I was ordered to report regularly at a huge house in Lancaster Gate, London, for inspection and treatment.

That it might be advisable for shellshock patients to be inspected and treated by the same doctor on each visit did not, apparently, cross the authoritarian mind.

Chronicle of the ensuing consultations may be summed up thus.

Shellshock Specialist A.: "Living in the country, are you? I should hardly have thought that advisable. You need cheering up. London's the place for you, my boy."

Shellshock Specialist B.: "So you're up in town for a few days. Why not go back to the country? A quiet life, fresh air and plenty of physical exercise. That's what you need."

Shellshock Specialist C.: "Now, remember, no alcohol!"

Shellshock Specialist D.: "Plenty of good beer and a couple of glasses of port after dinner. Avoid hard exercise like the plague. You're not up to it. Just gentle walks."

Shellshock Specialist E.: "Let's see. You're the writer, I believe. I'd chuck that for a bit if I were you."

Shellshock Specialist F.: "Ah, of course. You write. That's splendid. Go on writing. It'll take you out of yourself."

Shellshock Specialist G.: "About this writing. I wonder! Of course if you must, you must. But couldn't you just write for fun? Something easy, you know. Like a detective story."

Pyschiatry—you will observe—was still in the teething stage. So was dental radiology.

Wearying of the fortnightly comedies at Lancaster Gate, and still foolishly abstaining from Horder, I heard of one Kenneth Goadby, reputedly a worker of miracles, and palpably a presence in what memory suggests to have been a frock coat and an Ascot tie fastened with a scarab.

Let me confess here that I considered Sir Kenneth an expensive charlatan when, after the usual tests, he led me to a curtained alcove and put an electric light bulb in my mouth.

"The b.f. says I ought to have half my teeth out", I reported in Berkshire. "And there isn't one with a hole in it. He charged me five guineas, too."

More, and more profuse, apologies. That advice—had I taken it—would have saved me a whole year of pain.

§3

Working six, seven and sometimes eight hours a day, I finished my job for Huskinson, who had started publication in the March, by the beginning of June 1918.

"When you're next in town", wrote my agent, Hughes Massie, "I want to introduce you to Sir George Hutchinson's son, Walter."

So Walter Hutchinson and I met, for the first time, just outside some government office in which he was working—and have not parted brass rags since.

Walter made me an immediate offer for three books, including Husky's "novel in verse". Staggered by his liberality, I managed to conceal my delight; returned to my rural hideout, and riffled through my mother's literary papers, finding memory not at fault.

It was to Hutchinsons' office in Paternoster Row that I had escorted Julia nine years previously. It was of Sir George's offer for the story whose plot she bought from her brother Jimmy that William Heinemann had written, in effect, "She's a liar. He hasn't promised her that amount in advance, and if he has he's crazy".

But Sir George's sanity proved itself before my mother's *The Heart of a Child* had been on the bookstalls a fortnight; and it earns royalties to this day.

Then as now Walter's word was as good as his bond. A signed contract reached me within the week—and I took three off, holidaymaking (in a racing punt upriver) and completely idle for the first time in many years.

Goadby's warning forgotten, it never struck me as peculiar that my mouth—after any undue exertion—ached more than my arms. And, home again, I at last summoned up enough courage to re-read those few typed chapters of my burned sequel to *The Woman of the Horizon*, to grub out my old field notebook, my little red *Infantry Training* and *Artillery Training*, and my soiled maps, on one of which General Wardrop's pencil had indicated our artillery zone at Loos.

A few days later I wrote the words, "Peter Jackson, Cigar Merchant, A Romance of Love, War and Business" on a clean sheet of white foolscap—and was lost to mundane affairs.

§ 4

Yet still, poetry—verse if you will—was being laid on me. In October 1918, I broke off from my novel and told Massie to submit the resultant work to the *Daily Mail*, then the only paper with a mass circulation in Great Britain. Thrillingly, with my poem already in print on the leader page, came a letter signed "Lewis Rose Macleod. Literary Editor".

Lord Northcliffe himself wanted more. The hot wine of a great man's praise, of nation-wide publicity, and the sheer joy of selfexpression in the only form of literary craftsmanship which I have ever really loved, wrenched me from cold prose for a whole week.

Forgive a quotation from "The Reason", published on the 2nd of November, 1918.

> "You ask me why I loathe these German beasts
> So much that I have dedicated self—
> Brains, heart and soul—to one black creed of hate,
> Now and hereafter, both in war and peace.
> You say I had a sense of humour once,
> And kindliness, and Christian charity . . .
> Perhaps I had—*before my pal came back.*
> To-night he sleeps (thank God for morphia!)
> And I shan't wake to hear him screaming out,
> 'Don't. I *will* work. Don't tie me up again.
> Gilbert, for Christ's sake, keep these fiends away'."

Among the last lines are:

> "Sometimes I wish they hadn't sent him back,
> Sometimes I feel he would be happier dead—
> Cold-butchered by some Unteroffizier
> In those latrines which they call prison camps".

Substitute "concentration camps" for "prison camps"—and how has the Hun changed?

But the 11th of November found me at my novel *Peter Jackson* again; and when, shortly after eleven o'clock, a hunting horn sounded beneath my study window, I ran to it, shouting down.

"I'm working. Go blow your blasted musical instruments somewhere else. What the hell do you think you're making all that ruddy row for?"

The voice of an unknown horseman called up, "Because the war's over, you idiot", and the tiny field of the local hunt rode on.

§ 5

Queerly, I have not yet spent an Armistice Day morning away from my desk.

CHAPTER THIRTY-SEVEN

§ 1

I SEEM to remember that the price of new-laid eggs—for which the comforting lady to whom I have referred could charge her sixpence halfpenny apiece without profiteering while the war lasted

—dropped a little after that first Armistice Day, which should have been called Victory Day. But otherwise the coming of peace made little change in Berkshire.

An uncanny child of seven, sent for at need, still exercised his supreme authority in determining the sex of table rabbits. The pigs still gobbled expensive food. My octogenarian farmer neighbour continued to talk about four sheep I had bought from him as "they tegs". The vegetarian doctor continued to preach a very mild form of socialism; and the lawfully married clergyman to drop in for a cup of tea.

I continued working—on twenty grains of aspirin and thirty-five fat Turkish cigarettes a day.

The Hereford Square lease was off my shoulders by then, though an attempt to take advantage of legislation passed by Parliament to free fighting men of similar liabilities had failed.

"This act under which you're seeking relief", the county court judge had told Withers' partner, Covell, when we applied for relief, "only applies in the case of soldiers who are conscripted. Your client, having volunteered to serve his country, cannot take advantage of it."

And he added, mindful of the Almack Case, "Perhaps he will be able to win enough at bridge to satisfy his landlady."

Why I was not arrested for contempt of court when I heard that judgment, I shall never know. But mere language could not avail.

"It's neck or nothing this time", said Withers; and he made me sign a blank petition in bankruptcy. When he saw that it was no bluff, the solicitor for the other side very wisely advised his client to settle for the amount we offered.

Half my debts, however, were still unpaid, and local liabilities accumulating, and three of those notes from the safe deposit vault melted, by the time Reginald Poole, acting for Dolly, wrote to ask Withers if "our mutual friend has sufficiently recovered from his war experiences to stand the strain of a divorce case".

That process, experto crede, is not always cheap.

But a hotel bill, and a covering letter which began with the dramatic fiction, "Dear Dolly, As I am tired of being pursued by your inefficient detectives——", initiated the amicable proceedings, and no further evidence was subsequently required.

Meanwhile a young official summoned me to Somerset House, and demanded income tax on my 1914 director's fees from J. Frankau & Co. Ltd. This was the company's liability. I told him so with considerable picturesqueness, but he refused credence, stuck to it that the debt was personal, and told me that I must "make an offer" if I couldn't pay in full.

Eventually—the new proprietors of the business having paid me in full—I made yet another offer. My official took off a tenner like the lamb he was.

Shortly after this interesting transaction the post-war influenza epidemic laid me flat.

§ 2

I am still violently affected by misprints of my own words—even in a newspaper article. Hutchinsons had made several in the book version of *The Tatler* verse novel which reached me on my bed of sickness. It is just possible that this drove the mercury in Doctor Gandy's thermometer to 106 degrees.

He, and devoted nursing, pulled me through. One day I staggered up the little hill that leads to Sonning Common; the next I was back at my writing table, with my teeth giving me such hades that a bottle of aspirins barely lasted one day and a box of a hundred cigarettes two.

Tribute is here paid to one Chapman, tobacconist of Reading, who trusted me when I most had need, to various other tradesmen of the locality for similar courtesies, and to a cousin who lent me some money against a post-dated cheque.

I forgot all about that post-dated cheque, proudly sending a second one a week before it fell due. That my mental state at this period of my life was hardly normal is further proved by a multitude of recollections—notably one of a determination, secretly reiterated to myself every morning before I sat down to work, "If I don't make a success this time, I'll b. well commit suicide".

The amateur psychiatrists of Lancaster Gate, nevertheless, had taught me one lesson. Only my own mind could heal its own lesion. Instinctively—for as yet I was quite incapable of reason—I set about psychoanalysing myself.

Here, the split personality proved of definite value. I discovered —how, I don't know, that one side of my mind could stand coolly apart while the other experienced a series of phobias.

"Investigate the sources of all these phobias", I must have said to myself, "and they'll be as good as cured."

Memories of my father helped—one of them considerably. I grubbed out a story he had told me, when he gave me my first money box, about a little boy who looked into his money box and found that all the golden sovereigns had turned to pennies.

"The pater", I said to myself, "must have had a money phobia. This fear's hereditary."

Another fear—I found—had been early experienced at Hawtrey's, when trying to struggle out of the tight jerseys in which we played football. Psychiatrists call it claustrophobia.

Continuing my process while I continued my novel, I decided to give its imaginary hero my own very real symptoms. The reaction of a different character, differently situated, to a condition identical with my own, helped a little—but effected no real cure.

In March, when I finished my book, I was still in such a state of what are now called jitters that I could not hold a live chick in my hand because my fingers wanted to kill it rather than have it flutter under them. And—had it not been for sheer vanity—I could have screamed as loudly as the pet bacon pig on which I was sitting just before the summoned expert slit its throat.

For the one thing I had not discovered—and of this discovery I still feel fairly confident—is that the first cause of all so-called psychic disorders is physical.

Goadby's snap diagnosis was confirmed later—by Horder himself.

§ 3

Among my friends, the Reading tradesmen, was the manager of W. H. Smith's bookshop there, named F. S. Bradley, who subsequently retired under that firm's excellent pension scheme and died only the other day.

From him then—and subsequently from many other booksellers—I learned much about my new profession. One day Bradley told me how the girls at Huntley & Palmer's biscuit factory clubbed together to buy the novels of Ethel M. Dell, then at the height of her vogue.

"But she's not a really first-class novelist", protested my still-highbrow self.

"She's a first-class storyteller", said Bradley. "So is Charles Garvice. That's why they sell."

It is possible that I suggested:

"So the public likes tripe".

"Would you say Kipling writes tripe?" asked Bradley.

He had me there, and continued his lesson.

"Kipling, Dell, and Garvice", he went on, "have one thing in common. They tell good stories. Has this novel you're always telling me about got a good story?"

"Yes. I think so."

"Then try to sell it as a serial before it's published in book form. Ethel M. Dell's always in the magazines. They help enormously to keep her name before the public."

I cycled home, the last of my typed manuscript tied to the carrier, thinking my hardest; and telephoned to Massie—it took the best part of an hour to get on to London from the local post-office-cum-grocery—next day.

Some fortnight later I was talking to J. C. (now Sir John) Squire and a young poet, ex-editor of the Cambridge *Granta*, with a fine war record, Edward Shanks.

They were editing that old home of my poetry, *Land and Water*, which had attained a big circulation during the war years, largely on account of ar*t*les proving that the Central Powers must collapse through lack of manpower, by Hilaire Belloc, affectionately known to the front line as "Hilarious Bolux".

You may remember that "all right" was correctly spelled by the Hawtrey boy "learning to play chess a little". Shanks had already corrected some hundred "alrights" in my manuscript with his own hand, and altered my commercial "*e*nquiries" to the literary "*i*nquiries" with a similar fervour.

But they were taking my book. Gilbert Holiday—also a gunner —would illustrate the instalments. They would pay half the liberal price at once.

Actually, they paid the other half before it was due. I often wonder whether Shanks knew the extent of my need when I asked that favour.

Him, I have not encountered for many years. Squire I last met when he took the chair at a fascist dinner party, where a young Boche (this must have been in '33, I imagine) talked with some pride of his leader's new treaty of peace with Poland.

Squire asked me to speak—but I could not have done so without referring to a certain "scrap of paper".

Needless to say that Sir John is no fascist these days.

§ 4

If, for your taste, there is too much about money in this part or any other part of my tale, I can only plead that a knowledge of material facts is necessary for psychological investigation—and that Galsworthy laid down the maxim, "Men only write for bread or praise".

Presumably Galsworthy intended the word "praise" to include "ambition". That was certainly one of my spurs.

If, on the other hand, you demand a more romantic spur for your central character during this period of his mortal existence, I can only refer you back to the last sentence of my "Foreword"; and ask you to use your imagination. Chivalry, also, rowelled me at my desk.

If, finally, you feel that this part of the tale is beginning to read too much like a conventional success story, I make no extenuating plea whatsoever. For that was the precise feeling I began to have after my first interview with Squire and Shanks.

Months previously, pining for just one night in town, I had attended a dinner of the Printers' Readers Pension Fund, where chance put me next to an old friend of my mother's, a cheery soul, once a boot-factor, better known as a master storyteller under the name of Phillips Oppenheim.

"How's the world treating you?" he asked.

"Not too well. I'd sell myself body and soul for a thousand a year."

"Rubbish, my boy", Oppy had said. "You keep your pecker up. And you'll make lots more than that by your writing before you've done."

And now those cheery words—he'll know, if he happens to read this, how much they meant to me—looked like coming true.

Already, I had another novel in my mind. I fled to my hide-out; and flung myself at the job. Somewhere about this time, I must have seen Horder again. But the date is vague.

Vague, also, is another date: when I asked a stocky intelligent-looking clean-shaven businessman, with something of the seafarer about him, to whom I had been introduced by an acquaintance on the journey from Reading to London:

"Tell me, Mr. Morris—as you seem to know something about motorcars—what are we going to have to pay for them now that the war's over?"

"I haven't the slightest idea", answered the present Lord Nuffield, who has given away more in one day than I shall make in my lifetime.

But a motorcar was still beyond my means.

§ 5

The new novel waxed apace; but money was still such a problem that when Massie wrote, "There's an American publisher named Knopf who'll take your *Peter Jackson, Cigar Merchant*. Only he won't have your title, and he won't give you more than a two hundred and fifty dollar advance, unless you cut twenty thousand words out. If you'll do that, he'll raise his advance to five hundred dollars", I had no option but to accept.

Needs must when finance drives.

Dolly's decree nisi was granted in the February. By June 1919, I finished my third prose novel; paid a third instalment of 5s. in the £ to our creditors; told Withers I should insist on paying his costs to the last farthing, and was at my mother's papers again.

Once before, these had provided treasure—a posthumous volume of short stories, published early in 1918 by Collins, under the title of *Mothers and Children*.

Now I found a letter to my mother from the American theatrical producer, David Belasco.

"Nobody", he wrote, "could possibly make a stage play out of your *Heart of a Child*."

There is no selfconfidence like the amateur's. Instantaneously I decided that Belasco—and the present Sir Seymour Hicks, who had also flirted with the dramatic rights of Julia's very-best seller—didn't know their own business.

Chivalry also impelled me to take up the challenge. The lady who had been so kind to me, and who still lived in the same village, was an actress. I asked her to collaborate, and promised her a good part.

Before *Peter Jackson* had run his serial course, my third novel, *The Seeds of Enchantment*, and the play were done. Miraculously —this was to be the only time it ever happened—*The Seeds of Enchantment* sold itself to an American magazine.

CHAPTER THIRTY-EIGHT

§ 1

HUGHES MASSIE was a dying man when he sold my play to a tall, blonde, beautiful star of the period named Renée Kelly—who took wartime London by storm with a play called *Daddy Longlegs*— and her husband, Hylton Allen. Flushed with the anticipation of a fortune, proud of those letters of thanks from my grateful ex-creditors, at last paid in full, I abandoned my rural hide-out for a maisonette at the top end of Westbourne Terrace, near Paddington Station. Various motives underlay the move.

A molehill of literary success was actually mine. But of this imagination soon began to make a mountain. I must have a private secretary—no recognised author being complete without.

Fortune sent me a capable red-headed Australian girl, Margery Sadleir. The telephone began to tinkle out commissions. William Lees, working for my mother's old friend, Edward Hulton, ordered a series of articles for a Sunday paper; and chose the then original title "Has the World Gone Mad?" F. E. Baily, then editing a magazine called the *Royal*, thought I might be able to write him a short story, commissioned and approved it.

But Renée Kelly did not altogether approve of her part, and there were other difficulties. Summer came before we began to select our company for the preliminary run in the provinces.

Very courteously, I was consulted about the cast, and particularly about the leading juvenile, "Lord Kidderminster".

Various actors, accordingly, climbed the steep stairs to the maisonette for interviews—and a potential tenner or so a week.

"I think I've got the right chap this time", phoned Allen after my inexperience had turned down three applicants—and that afternoon there appeared a shy, gentlemanly, moustached youth of the ex-officer type, complete in trench coat and a cheap soft hat, with rather appealing eyes.

Relieved of these, he seated himself diffidently on the edge of an armchair; and listened to the famous young author with quiet patience for a good half-hour.

The famous young author, who esteemed himself no poor judge of a man into the bargain, dismissed his suitor with the usual promise to consider his suitability.

This done I stepped to the telephone (Margery was not there, otherwise my rising self-importance would hardly have demeaned itself to so menial an office) and called up Allen.

"Quite a nice chap", I said. "And he's not bad-looking in a way. But he doesn't seem to have had much experience. And, if you want my candid opinion, I can't see him ever making a romantic actor. He's got no presence, if you know what I mean. No personality. I'm sure he'd be hopeless for Lord Kidderminster."

"Now let's see", answered Allen. "Who did I send you? Wasn't it that young fellow, Ronald Colman?"

It was!

§ 2

About this time there drifted into my growing circle of acquaintances a slim, dark, attractive, Oriental-looking young woman, newly married to another shellshock case, whose history seems worth relating, because he had contracted the complaint as an officer while still training in England . . . and cured himself, after being invalided from commissioned service, by enlisting as a private soldier with the New Zealand Forces, in whose ranks he fought gallantly at the front.

Responsibility—I have always presumed—must have had that peculiar effect on Geoffrey Holdsworth. The experience, however, had not impaired his memory.

He and his wife arrived punctually as invited—for the very first time—a few minutes before eight. Fortunately I could not yet afford a cigar after dinner and was only smoking a cigarette. Even more fortunately the principal ingredient of an already consumed meal had been Irish stew, and the dining room was on the upper floor of the maisonette.

Panic ensued; but orders reached the staff. Swiftly she, my single-handed domestic, relaid the table while a party of four chatted—my coffee cup behind a photograph frame—about this and that. Presently we returned upstairs. Soup from a tin preluded the warmed-up remnants of the stew; the fruit "shape" which concluded the banquet had been reshaped, and more coffee followed.

Over the years I have entertained many a lovely lady; but only for that one have I ever eaten a brace of dinners within two hours. You probably know her as G. B. Stern, novelist and playwright. I still call her "Peter"—and agree with my daughter Pamela that she's a "good chap".

Through her, I believe, I made the acquaintance of a couple of crazy kids, up to any pranks going, and then some more. The girl was dark-haired, the boy fairer, with a queer puckered face. She had already won some success on the stage—as a Co-optimist, I think—under the name of Betty Chester. He also yearned for fame; and gave us a box for the first performance of that old comedy, *The Knight of the Burning Pestle*, in which he was to play the part of Ralph Roister-Doister, at the Kingsway Theatre.

As we drank together afterwards, I said, "If you only persevere and don't fool about so much, you might make quite a name for yourself".

Noel Coward, the kid in question, certainly has; though it was to be December 1924, before another youngster I met in my Westbourne Terrace days put up some of the money which produced his first success, *The Vortex*.

Sleek, suave, just the tiniest mite too well-mannered and too well-groomed, was that other youngster of whom the lady he called Shelmerdine in his first slim volume wrote to me:

"I want you to read a book by a friend of mine. He's an Armenian with the impossible name of Dikran Kouyoumdjian".

I recognised the original of the "Shelmerdine" in that slim volume, entitled *The London Venture*, from the moment she was reported as saying, "Oh, my dear, my dear". Had she not said the same to me when she spurned my pre-war passion?

"Tell your friend I like his book because it revives such painful memories", I wrote back. "But if you've any influence with him—I gather you've quite a lot—make him change his name."

He did—by deed poll. Time and early successes—of which he was wise enough to invest the golden fruits—have mellowed him beyond all measure.

Married to a young woman he himself might have created—beautiful beyond flaw, not entirely unendowered and of considerable social precedence—he is the only man I have ever heard admit freely, "But of course I'm a snob".

Against which set the facts that he is completely at his ease in any company, that he can make the stickiest party "go" by a combination of wit and sheer kindheartedness—and that he is the only member of my craft who ever took the trouble to write to me, after reading an undeservedly good notice: "I'm so glad, old chap. How pleased your Aunt Eliza would have been".

To Eliza Aria, while she lived, he wrote constantly; and he never came to London from his home on the Riviera without calling on her, and sending her flowers.

Whether Adolphe Menjou used to be his double or he Adolphe Menjou's remains a problem in relativity worthy of Einstein.

And just one more fact, that he is infinitely more intelligent than his heroes or heroines—and the picture of Michael Arlen is fairly complete.

§ 3

Towards the end of May 1920, Renée Kelly's husband was at last satisfied that potential audiences could not consider her a woman of easy virtue when she ran away to Paris with my Lord Kidderminster, personated by a charming fellow named Peter

Pusey, in my last act. That the rewriting of this act wrecked the entire characterisation of "Sally Snape", and deleted the key line, "Must we?" spoken by her to the hero just before she was due to be saved from a fate worse than death, worried me a little.

Neither did I appreciate being wrenched from Margery and her notebook to attend rehearsals. Nevertheless I went on tour with the company. Not only to hear my own lines.

We were to open in Huddersfield at the Theatre Royal, managed by a dear fellow, Alfred Wareing, once literary assistant to William Ernest Henley, the poet. He met me at the station with an invitation to a man's dinner at the Huddersfield Club.

No county in all England cooks better than Yorkshire. Grouse were in season. Lashings of port followed copious draughts of Burgundy. By ten o'clock my experience of army messes, of a naval wardroom in Venice, and of the Long Bar at Shanghai, began to perceive that Huddersfield had expected an author to be a pallid highbrow, unused to the ways of ordinary alcoholic men.

Toast succeeding toast—and who was I to refuse?—knowledge demanded vintage's best antidote, bread, of which eat only the crumb if you wish to survive.

Relics of that roystering crew fared home atop of a tram. 'Twas not the presumedly guileless highbrow who slithered from roof to pavement, and there lay semi-senseless. Neither was that what became of Wareing. Memory suggests a municipal personage for the succumber. But tact draws a veil.

There were war comrades in Huddersfield; and they took Renée Kelly to their warm hearts. She broke all records for the theatre with £2,500 in one week. But another lady of the company put her foot well in the plate when entertained by the famous Joe Lumb, whose wife was rather proud of her gardens, beyond which lay her husband's mills.

"It's a pity about those factory chimneys", said that dignified lady. "They do spoil the view so."

"Lass", interrupted Joe Lumb, "if there were no chimneys, there'd be no gardens."

Lumb also collected pictures. In his dining room hung the well-known Academy canvas by Clausen—a nameless blonde model, seated and nude to the waist.

Said a less aesthetic crony, placed opposite the newly hung acquisition at that hospitable board:

"Shame on thee, Joe, to have had thy own daughter took in oils that way".

§ 4

When the time came to leave Huddersfield, I took with me a roll of good blue serge cloth presented by Martin's Mills, subsequently fashioned into a suit that defied wear—and the certainty of a fortune from my genius as a playwright.

Ensued Blackpool, and more huge takings. Imagination envisaged motorcars and mansions . . . till Manchester refused even free seats.

CHAPTER THIRTY-NINE

§ 1

THE lesson of Manchester, however, went unlearned. Returning health had brought a return of superfluous energy. The prospects of a play to be produced in the West End, the dictation of yet another novel, of more short stories and more journalism, did not suffice my furious needs.

It may have been just vanity that fired the spark of a new ambition, laudable if rather foolhardy. It may have been the memory of that talk with Wells. It may have been the inspiration of Kipling who wrote to me about my *Seeds of Enchantment*, "You've overlaid the forest with the orchids in my opinion—and this is a time when, at the risk of being monotonous, one ought to hammer away at the 'ultimate decency of things' ".

Anyway, however, there the ambition was, urging the mere writer to play at politics. A dangerous game!

From the age of thirteen, when a little red-headed girl's father challenged me—never imagining I would accept his challenge—to propose her health at a birthday party, I had known myself possessed by that most fatal of human facilities, the gift of the gab.

The League of Youth, therefore, for me!

What this short-lived organisation stood for, or who founded it, I have no idea. It must have been, however, on the night of October 25th, 1920, that I first mounted its platform. For Alderman MacSwiney of Cork had just died at Brixton Prison after seventy-three days' hunger strike.

In my pocket were three threats of murder, the result of an article—for the *Sunday Pictorial*, I seem to remember—on the Irish situation. By my side sat Philip Gibbs, whispering, "I've just heard that you and I, Churchill and Birkenhead are to be the first on the lamp-posts when the revolution starts". Below us sat a mixed audience, not altogether hostile—which included several Indian students.

Gibbs spoke wisely, kindly, humanely. He, I imagine, had prepared his speech. Our chairman said, "Your turn next. I wouldn't be too violent, if I were you".

The year before, Brigadier-General Reginald Dyer had adopted stern measures to quell riots at Amritsar. I still believe he saved India from another mutiny and wish that the editors of my constant desk companion, *Everyman's Encyclopædia*, would delete the words with which some otherminded scribe attempts to sully the memory of one who only did his duty as he saw it by an ungrateful state.

I was not the only holder of this belief even in 1920. But to voice it and still more violent opinions from such a platform scarcely made for harmony. Only Coates' system of voice training —he would make us drill the batteries by word of mouth at two hundred yards—saved me from being howled down.

I got a real kick out of riling that audience. And the lust to hear my own voice grew.

§ 2

Some time later, Mr. Edward Iliffe, as he was then, entertained the League of Youth to a champagne dinner. Up rose I, as always without preparation. That evening my plea for no more disarmament won applause.

This may have aroused professional jealousy. For, afterwards, a tall, dark, handsome young member of parliament, also among the speakers, having presented me to a typically beautiful young Englishwoman, his wife, pronounced:

"It's all very well for you to demand a strong navy. But I can't I'm in the House; and as a good conservative I'm bound to support the League of Nations".

Thus Mr., as he was then, Oswald Mosley—newly married to the Lady Cynthia Curzon—who afterwards went over to Labour and is now leader of British fascism. Is the love of lost causes hereditary? His John Bull of a father tried to make us all eat whole-meal bread.

My tirades against disarmament were not so popular at another meeting, to which I was invited—with E. T. Raymond, the novelist, then in holy orders—by "Tubby" Clayton, whose predecessor in office once gave me a bed at the original Talbot House in Poperinghe.

The flannel-trousered young men of the civilian Talbot Houses —I discovered to my discomfiture, because I would not have offended that great soul Tubby for a fortune—were being nourished on more pacific ideals.

Mixed with these and many more political orations I gave literary lectures, also without preparation, and also unpaid. Mrs. Dawson Scott had just founded the Tomorrow Club. There I crossed verbal swords with Frank Swinnerton, who pinked me several times before we adjourned for coffee and sandwiches.

Today my daughter Pamela gets the same fun out of the same sort of functions. She is much wittier than her father used to be, but lacks the cool, deadly attack of Philip Guedalla.

Perorated Philip, on a later occasion, when the subject of debate was Aldous Huxley's new book, *Antic Hay*:

"Little boys must have scribbled naughty words on lavatory doors since such conveniences were first invented. But Mr. Huxley's publishers are the first to succeed in commercialising the door".

I hope the publishers in question—my old friends, Chatto & Windus—will forgive this tale out of school.

No house in the publishing trade bears a higher reputation. While as for that of Aldous Huxley, it needs no soft soap from a romanticist like myself.

Why he should be so averse to the romantic outlook, nevertheless, puzzles me—if the story I heard from one of his old pupils is true.

"Didn't you know", said that old pupil, "that he lost his sight during his last half at Eton; stayed blind for the next two years— and still managed to get a double first at Balliol?"

For less heroism men wear the Victoria Cross.

§ 3

Nineteen-twenty was a boom year in the theatre. Robert Loraine, Fay Compton and her future husband, that fine actor, Leon Quartermaine, drew all London to J. M. Barrie's *Mary Rose* at the Haymarket. At Drury Lane—still under the sway of my cousin-by-marriage, Arthur Collins—Godfrey Tearle and Quartermaine's sister-in law, Madge Titheradge, co-starred in Hichens' *Garden of Allah*. Ethel Irving played Sardou's *La Tosca* at the Aldwych. Way down on the programme of *Mr. Pim Passes By* at the New, one read the comparatively unknown name of Leslie Howard.

In Galsworthy's *Skin Game* at the St. Martin's, you could see "the most promising and the loveliest of all our young actresses", Meggie Albanesi, who died untimely. A boyish Jack Hulbert was dancing in *A Little Dutch Girl* at the Lyric; and Ethel Levey was singing in *Oh, Julie*, at the Shaftesbury.

Add Leslie Henson at the Winter Garden, and Peggy O'Neil— of whom more anon—with a crashing success called *Paddy the Next Best Thing* at the Savoy, and you will realise why Renée Kelly and Hylton Allen couldn't find a home for my *Heart of a Child*.

Christmas came and went. My sister Joan, after a mild attack of defeatist socialism at Girton (she is now on the establishment there) and a short convalescence on good works in an East End hostel, had fallen in love with a wounded soldier, one Stanley Bennett, now Fellow of Emmanuel College, Cambridge, and known wherever men and women study the history of the Middle Ages for the exhaustive scholarship and the fine prose of his two great works *The Pastons and their England* and *Life on the English Manor* 1150–1400.

January came and went, with my mother's old friend, Rufus Isaacs, created first Earl of Reading in 1917, accepting the vice-royalty of India. Yet another coal strike threatened.

But still the Allens could not secure a "West End theatre" as called for under the contract—and if they had secured one it would have cost, in those days, £500 a week.

I was still forgetting the lesson of Manchester. Like all young playwrights in a similar position I imagined myself being robbed of a fortune. And when the Kingsway Theatre, which is barely in the West End, then under Herbert Jay's management, was suggested, I behaved much in the same I had behaved to the matron of Reading hospital three years previously.

Fortunately Herbert Jay possessed tact.

He engaged one of our best producers, Fisher White. C. V. France—the only actor for whom Somerset Maugham finds a crumb of praise in his disingenuous autobiographical sketch *The Summing Up*—accepted a minor part. Enthusiasm ran high as is the custom at rehearsals; during which, superstition—this being also the custom—forbade the speaking of the final line.

o why shouldn't I take my due ovation to repeated calls of Author. Author" after the triumph of our first night?

A lady member of the cast and a curious coincidental happening, rather than any access of nerves, dissuaded me. Those fateful rst-night hours I spent dining and dancing at Ciro's with that ery companion for whose sweet sake I had hardly borne to leave ydney.

We had a sofa table. Close by sat another couple. The four of s falling into conversation, the other man said, introducing his irl, whom memory recalls as a mere flapper, slim, and considerbly charming, "This is Gertrude Lawrence".

My companion was to say, almost exactly five years later, It didn't seem like you at all. You never even kissed me on the ay back to that flat of yours".

At the flat we found the usual first-night party—all champagne nd, "I thought you were simply too marvellous, darling", and You mark my words, it'll run for at least a year".

§ 4

The Heart of a Child ran some thirty-five performances, mostly o those seats theatrical slang calls "paper".

Waning youth—how I used to hate passing Wyndham's, where erald du Maurier was starring in *Bulldog Drummond* to capacity ouses—apportioned blame for the fiasco between lack of advervising, the location of the theatre, Renée's alteration of the riginal script, the cast and the opening weeks of yet another oal strike.

Experience realises that David Belasco and Seymour Hicks ere both right—and the play itself beneath all contempt.

A different dog might have returned to its vomit. I swore, as ormerly on a golf course, "Never again". That oath I have only roken once.

The only other play I was ever moved to write is still unprouced on stage or screen, though my good friend Sydney Carroll ook an option on it, and a cinema company bought the film ights.

The reasons for this may be inherent in the plot, already used or a short story.

Asked a friend in the Secret Service, having read my story: "Where the blazes did you get that idea from?"

"From a German book on spying. It's banned now."

My friend was the soul of reticence. But I could not help

gathering that my tale of the German naval officer who sold u their battle code contained more than a grain of truth.

CHAPTER FORTY

§ 1

MEMORY insists on a few more flashbacks from those eighteer months during which I occupied two top floors near Paddingtor Station.

Piebald rodents complicated existence; and presented biological problem, imaginatively solved by the theory that noble dame's children had kept white mice in their nursery befor the ancestral home was converted to more democratic purposes and that one or more of these pampered pets must have escape to indulge in free love.

The after-years were to bring me a friend who remonstratec "You can't sympathise with me for being a drunkard becaus you've never known what it means to kneel down before a bottl of whiskey and say, 'Thank God for you. You're the only pa I've got in the world'." Had I been similarly tempted—he, toc was a war-strain case—I shudder to think of the effect this tin phenomenon might have produced on my nerves.

A larger, and darker, phenomenon presented itself one evenin just before dinner. Answering the bell myself, I faced a man c colour as mighty as that pugilistic champion, Jack Johnson, whos name leaped to the lips of our Contemptibles at their first sight c black-bursting high-explosive shells.

"And what do you want?" I asked.

"Just to see my wife", answered the phenomenon—and gav the name of the entire staff.

By pure evil luck that very Sunday's paper had carried a article in which I quoted my friend Prebendary Gough's prc nouncement on the subject of such mixed marriages, "Christianit must not be made the excuse for miscegenation".

My poor maid quoted my whole paragraph to me before sh left; and I wished that I had never written it. However sure an hard one's general beliefs may be—I learned from this experienc —they are apt to break down when confronted with the individua case.

Another experience at Westbourne Terrace provided comedy i

he shape of an urbane gentleman who called by appointment;
nd came to the point without overmuch ado.

My political articles—said he—were exciting comment in
xalted circles. Had I considered the unwisdom of antagonising
hose who could confer honour? He himself was not actually
mpowered to offer me an honour. But if a knighthood would
nodify some of my opinions . . .

It is presumable that the discovery of my domestic circum-
tances must have modified his opinions. For he never called on
ne in a similar capacity again.

In that same year, 1921, poor Charlie Higham, Coaliton M.P.
or South Islington since 1918, received his knighthood, officially
or good work in raising war loans and encouraging enlistments,
ut according to his own account through sheer high-powered
alesmanship.

"I just went to Lloyd George and asked for it", Charles' story
sed to run. "And when he asked me why I wanted a title, I said,
Because it will be worth £10,000 a year to me in my business'."

Confirmation or denial rests with the higher authority. It seems
fact, however, that the original idea for the cenotaph came from
harles, when he caused a war shrine to be erected in Hyde Park
ome years before the conclusion of hostilities.

Meanwhile another of my friends, Harold Brooke-Alder, whom
had last seen when he rode out to meet our incoming brigade at a
ailway crossing just west of Béthune in 1915, was safely back in
is business—and very upset that I should have lost both mine.

"You ought to have got more for them", he said, over lunch—
ne of the last we were to eat together because, soon afterwards,
e drifted out of my life.

I said, "It's easy to talk like that now. What's the use of
vorrying? I'm earning enough to pay my way".

A final flashback suggests that the statement could not have
peen entirely accurate. For never was a cheque more welcome
han one which tumbled out of an envelope the last post brought
o my maisonette.

Entering under an assumed name, I had won £50—offered by
he Field for the most cogently presented arguments why that
nedium should be used to advertise beer and spirits.

For more than ten years I wondered why my winning answer
vas never printed. Then chance put me next to the husband of
Gertie de S. Wentworth James—a charming woman whose racy
novels entirely belied her own pure character—at a Fleet Street
unch; and I happened to tell him the tale.

"I started that competition in *The Field*", said he. "I'd onl
just got the job of advertising manager. So I didn't know th
real reason why we never carried any liquor advertising."

"And what was the real reason?"

"Our proprietor. He was a staunch teetotaller—and wouldn'
have it in."

§ 2

The Heart of a Child having failed, one of my motives for comin
to London decided me to leave it for a while. An advertisemen
of a cottage to let for the summer months attracted attentio
A letter to the box number produced a kindly man, solicitor b
profession, who had come to know my mother through he
interest in colour prints—his father having been a well-know
collector, Henry Percy Horne.

He produced photographs of the place. Just before we signe
our agreement, he said, "There's one little trouble. My well's th
best for miles. But if there's a really bad drought, it might jus
dry up. Then you'll have to cart your water. If you do, I'll pa
the expense".

Such landlords, I imagine, are rare. So is Harborough Cottag
still standing in the very heart of what hunting men call th
Shires.

Horne had told me its romantic history. Built by "the wicke
Lord Harborough" (a peerage already extinct) in the grounds c
his estate at Stapleford to house a ladylove, it had been trans
ferred, when the ladylove in question proved faithless, beam b
beam and stone by stone, to the adjacent village of Whissendin
Rutland, famous wherever men talk foxhunting for its brook.

Across the road, in a red brick farm, lived "old Stafford" an
"young Stafford" and young Stafford's wife, Dolly, who used t
lend her pony cart, the only available form of transport except on
of those Fords called Tin Lizzies, long past its Detroit prime.

Young Stafford owned a young hunter, which, bolting out of hi
paddock, nearly decapitated me on the laundry wires stretche
across the yard.

I have never been closer to death. But a suave official at th
Ministry of Pensions had already persuaded me—using as on
argument, "You must be making plenty of money by you
writing"—to abandon my modicum of pension; and the inciden
seemed to leave my nerves quite unaffected. I persuaded mysel
accordingly that shellshock and neurasthenia were afflictions o
the past.

Then the big drought set in; and I blessed Horne.

Nowadays there are water mains in Whissendine. That summer we all carted the rare fluid from the few undried wells. Soon the hundred-acre fields of ridge and furrow were brown waves, slippery as ice. Coal was short, too—on account of the big strike. On Sundays, the local baker would cook all our joints.

The Staffords persuaded me to take the cottage on for the winter and try a poor man's luck in the hunting field. I brought a small chestnut mare, whose teeth no longer revealed her age, for the large sum of twenty guineas. For another twelve or so, Gurley and Hassan, the tailors at Oakham, agreed to provide me with a black coat and a striped waistcoat. Saddlery I bought second-hand, and a new whip—I still object to the word "crop", a crop having no lash—for a few shillings.

A pair of old jackboots (relic of Bickley), a pair of ready-made army fieldboots ("misfits from a famous maker", vintage 1915), two pairs of brown breeches (ex the second kit allowance sanctioned by Gowers), and a pre-war tophat which had been languishing on Scotts' shelves since my world tour, eventually completed a costume as natty as it was modest.

Recklessly, I invested in a second quadruped, called Ladybird, brown and almost too high at the shoulder for a stocky man's mounting. This brought my total expenditure on horseflesh up to the tidy sum of forty-five guineas.

Jimmy Finch, secretary of that crack pack the Cottesmore, said he'd "let me off for a pony" (£25) as a subscription.

With the drought over, cub-hunting began.

§ 3

I had never realised, till that afternoon when the rains at last came to Rutland, the truth of the picture in Dorothea Mackellar's lines:

> "Over the thirsty paddocks,
> Watch, after many days,
> The filmy veil of greenness
> That thickens as we gaze".

Neither had I realised, till the first morning I took my chestnut mare out cub-hunting, just what it means to ride a rogue.

As a hack, Polly had always been docility itself. Let her smell hounds, and she went stark staring crazy.

"You try her", I told Stafford after that first experience. He rode at least three stone more than my ten and a half. She stoc fifteen-three. One hour of her—and he took to his sofa t lunchtime.

Polly's next victim was one Wigginton, an ex-jockey—wl used to gallop an old mare he had been given bareback and wit out bridle, her foal thundering after, round the field behind m cottage. He did manage to keep that chestnut nose away from tl ground—one of Polly's more endearing habits was to look f mushrooms at full gallop—by winding the slack of the reins rour his wrists and elbows.

And this same Wigginton could do miracles with any anima I once watched him whistle a hare from its forme.

Nevertheless her owner bestrode Polly at the opening meet the Leicestershire season—the Quorn's at Kirby Gate—open all comers without "capping".

Cardigan outdistancing his Light Brigade to the guns Balaklava must have afforded a poor spectacle compared with tl rider in the pre-war tophat and the brown corduroy breeche whose mount's furious hoofs struck fire from the radiator of 1921 Morris before it cleared the fence at roadside and gallopade still mushroom-gazing, up Gartree Hill.

Whereafter poor Polly was relegated to drawing a hawker cart—last observed halfway through a quickset hedge with hound in full cry two fields off. Those few of you who have read m hunting stories may recognise her as the inspiration for th fictional animal, Mustard Pot. Thus can a little imaginatic "turn the hurt of experience into the pleasure of words".

My string (stabled with Stafford) was thus reduced to Lad bird, who knew considerably more about the game than I di and saved my neck many times. One day I espied from her broa back a red coat topped by a Wellingtonian profile.

Accosted at covert side, O.C. 1st Life Guards nearly topple from his saddle in sheer amaze.

"Good God"! gasped the Vulture, for he it was. "It can't l you." And riding home alone I remembered far-off days when tl slogan of Platt, Schiff, Frankau, and Cooper—revolting befoi their time against those whom modern slang styles "The Hearties —had been "Call me anything but a sportsman".

Also I remembered how the Vulture (otherwise Wyndham) an his âme damnée, the Ghost (otherwise Turnour or Winterton once galloped hired horses with the King's Buckhounds.

Legend runs that the only Eton master out that mornin recognised them—but did not give his two fellow sportsmen away

§ 4

Blood sports, nowadays, are a controversial topic. My own feelings on the subject are that controversy might well be postponed until we have abolished all our slums and provided employment for every soul in our "distressed areas". It will be time enough then, I feel, to consider the fate of the million or so men and women whom the total abolition of huntin', shootin' and fishin'—so gibed at by those who do not enjoy them—would put on the dole.

Some of our puling intellectuals delight to picture foxhunting men and women as brainless idiots who never read a book, and spend all their spare time in the commission of adultery. This does not accord with my own experience.

I find truer pictures in *Reynard the Fox* by our poet laureate, and *The Horn*, a masterpiece by Patrick Chalmers, who has never ridden to hounds in his life.

Forgive this digression from a foxhunter of one season only—two out of whose three days a fortnight in the saddle had to be compensated for by Sundays at his desk.

Some of that work rewrote a novel called *The Love Story of Juliette Brunton*; more went into a tale of ancient Greece, originally suggested to me by Douglas Sladen, the original editor of *Who's Who*.

A vast amount of research eventually produced the first third of our story, some seventy thousand words, to be called, *The Red Boy of Macedon*—its hero Alexander the Great. But the idea of Douglas' name as well as my own appearing on the title page did not please either my new agent, Edmund Cork, who had bought Hughes Massie's business, or Hutchinsons.

Both, I felt, were wrong. But I could not afford to argue; and, by the end of the hunting season, I decided—very reluctantly—that all the good work must go to waste.

I came back to London, unvisited for a whole year, in the spring of 1922. In the February I had been married—at the Oakham registrar's, with only Mr. Lidgett of Furley and Hassan, who cut my one black hunting coat, and a chance met acquaintance for witnesses—to my second wife, Aimée de Burgh.

Aimée, a beautiful woman and fine actress, possessed one of the most perfect voices in the world. Past vicissitudes seemed earnests of our enduring happiness.

My rewritten novel, with its plea for the reformation of the divorce laws (to be renewed ten years later by A. P. Herbert in a book called *Holy Deadlock*), made me another stir in my own country. Even from America, where the cut *Peter Jackson* under the title *Peter Jameson* had fallen almost still born for Knopf's Borzoi press, came a small whisper of success.

The ball seemed at my feet, needing only one kick to send it soaring over the goal bar of ambition.

For some slight record of a fool in his folly, read on.

Part Four

THE BIG NOISE

CHAPTER FORTY-ONE

§ 1

THE original ninety-nine-year lease of "the messuage", 9
Lancaster Gate Terrace, dated 1837, gave permission to construct
a dwelling house on the banks of the West Bourne in the Borough
of Paddington, and forbade any occupant to indulge in the more
noisome professions, among which the Ecclesiastical Commissioners, as ground landlords, specifically excluded the dressing
of tripe.

Undeterred by this prohibition, I took over—from a charming
old gentleman named Hermon—the fag end of his liability at a
rent of £250 a year, plus taxes. Aimée had some furniture, which
Waring and Gillow's hire-purchase system enabled me to supplement at a further liability of some £1,500, payable by instalments
over three years.

Decorators decorated. By midsummer 1922, we were "dans nos
meubles". Once again, a secretary seemed a necessity. Margery
rejoined me and lived out. In, at the beginning, lived a domestic
staff of three, eventually increased to six or seven, eight if you
include a chauffeur.

Considering the 1926 heyday of that megalomaniacal establishment, the mellower mind reaches several peculiar conclusions—
notably, that mere affection may not have been entirely satisfying
to either of the contracting parties. Gundry's still-extant accounts
seem to prove this.

That one of my attempts at psychoanalysis had overreached
itself, is also tolerably plain.

I had discovered—you will remember—that my poverty
phobia was a complex inherited from my father. It appears as
though the subconscious mind, while ridding itself of this thwart,

must have developed an economy phobia, and sought to prove it. courage by the acceptance of more and more financial risk.

There may have been other motives. But attribute th. squandermania to pride chuckling, "Never mind how much yo. spend, you can always earn it", to overaffection, weakness, th. maternal inheritance, or mere vanity and the unworthy desire t. outshine one's fellows—the net result remains unaltered.

Once again work became my god.

The envisaged rewards from this god were twofold, professiona success measured by the gold standard and political influenc. immeasurable even by my own imaginings.

Note a saying by W. A. McWhirter towards the end of th. period we are now considering. On receipt of his usual 1250 word entitled, "If I Were Prime Minister" for the *Sunday Pictorial*, th. Squire, as he is known to his intimates, telephoned:

"That's a good article, Gilbert. Thank heaven you're not".

§ 2

Attach an appropriate speedometer to the spindle outside it. cage, and you will presumably learn the exact pace at which you. pet squirrel chases its tail. But do not ask the squirrel to coun. his own revolutions. He's too busy. Or thinks he is. Whicl amounts—psychologically—to the same thing.

During the four years I spent in my cage at Lancaster Gat. Terrace I resembled that imaginary squirrel to a nicety. Th. abiding wonder is that I found time to make a few friends— among them a novelist whose work is in danger of being forgotten W. L. George.

George, having lost two wives by death, had recently married. dark attractive Yorkshire girl, Kathleen Geipel. Two years olde. than myself, he had been born of British parents in Paris, an. served his time in the French army. Meeting him originally i. 1918, when he was a sections officer at the Ministry of Munition: I had been rather horrified by his pacifist declarations, and hi. admiration for H. G. Wells, then reputed to be "thinking for hal Europe"—with what results we now know.

George still seemed a little too much the socialist for my politica. liking. But I took to him more than I take to most men of th. same occupation as myself.

The Georges lived "just round the corner". He and I used t. talk shop by the hour and politics by the minute. Then we bega. to debate against each other in public, first at literary gathering.

women's clubs—where he was always popular, being known as
the novelist who understands Woman''.

Finally—in the summer of 1924, I imagine—we were invited to
ake opposite sides at the Oxford Union, where George spoke
ven more brilliantly than usual. It struck me, however, that he
vasn't looking quite himself; and I noticed that one of his hands
eemed rather peculiar, as though it had lost some of its strength.

We did not meet again until after our holidays. The hand was
lmost out of action by then. His whole appearance had altered.
Ie might have been ten years older than myself, rather than a
here two, with his scant hair gray at his fine temples and his
ulging eyes.

"The disease is called progressive muscular atrophy", he told
ne, in strict confidence. "And there's no cure for it."

Soon he could only lift a glass by pressing the stem between his
wo dropped wrists.

"But I won't stop working", he said. "I must leave Kathleen
nd my two children enough to be comfortable on." And he
ontinued to dictate books and articles even when he had to take
o a bath chair, even after his throat began to give out. When his
ecretary could no longer understand his mumbles, Kathleen
leputised for her.

She also nursed him, *single-handed*, up to the very end. In all
ny life I have never seen greater devotion in a woman, or more
upreme bravery in a man.

And this was the same man who had pretended to me, at our
irst meeting, "I oughtn't to be in the Ministry of Munitions, you
:now. I ought to be in gaol with the other conscientious objectors
—only I'm too much of a coward to admit my opinions publicly."

It's queer how pride takes us. The one thing W. L. George
vould not admit, you see, was that he'd been spun for physical
lisability each time he tried to enlist.

§ 3

Another good friend of my Lancaster Gate Terrace days was,
.nd still is, Eveleigh Nash, the publisher, and original founder of
Vash's Magazine. As we never did any business together, we could
onfide in each other freely. One day he brought me advance
;alley proofs of a book on Gladstone by an author named Peter
Wright.

A passage caught my eye. I queried it immediately.

"Isn't that a libel, Eveleigh?"

"Don't worry. It's coming out."

But Peter Wright, who thought he knew more about law than his publisher, privily reinserted that passage in the page proofs. The result made a little legal history.

Sir George Hutchinson himself read all my early books, not so much for libels, as for bad language, in which my heroes were all too apt to indulge. His son, now head of the firm, has never—according to his own contention—read a line of my writing.

It is faintly possible that this may have been one cause of those "shallow disagreements" mentioned in the dedication of my first book of short stories. As a sidelight on character—and for sheer orotundity—that dedication is hard to beat.

"To Walter Hutchinson, whose firm's imprint adorns my title pages; in admiration of those commercial gifts I cannot hope to share and in pious memory of all the shallow disagreements we have interred under the deep soil of reconciliation . . ."

The single sentence runs to eighteen lines of italic. (Small wonder if G. B. Stern called me "Mr. Toad" after that famous character in *The Wind in the Willows*, or that a caustic columnist christened me Philbert Swankau.

But I was beginning to make money, I thought I was getting somewhere politically, and my motto—I imagine—must still have been the one which hung over my desk at Gracechurch Street: "Live each day so that you can look every damn man straight in the eye and tell him to go to hell".

I certainly told Greenhough Smith, famous editor of the *Strand Magazine*, that he could seek that warm locality when he rang up to ask me if I would change one sentence in a whole tale. For not yet had life taught me that there could be any pertinence in the suggestion made fifteen years previously by one Edward A. Klin of New York, who is still manufacturing cigars there.

Smiled Ed to my mother, slowly stroking my arm from shoulder to wrist, "If he would only do a little more of this, Mrs. Frankau, and", rudely and rapidly reversing the movement, "a little less of that, he'd get on ever so much better".

By the end of 1922, I had conceived one more ambition, to become a first-class lawn-tennis player. Rubbing people up the wrong way, however, remained my favourite sport.

Proof of this is to be found in my friend Beverley Baxter's book of contemporary reminiscences, *Strange Street*.

§ 4

My private name for Beverley Baxter, here revealed for the first time, is "the inspired gate-crasher". Earliest recollection pictures clock pointing to the sacred hour of eight, and my very self-important self, duly attired for dinner, fuming, "Damn the man! We won't wait for him".

We did, however; and he arrived by twenty past, in tweeds and puffing a half smoked corona, confident that we should appreciate his having brought a friend along with him. The friend, if memory is to be trusted, was in the cinema business and also complete with cigar.

Bax, barely thirty at the time, had already gate-crashed his way—with nothing but a fine war record and one adequate novel for recommendation—via Lord Beaverbrook's *Daily* into the managing editorship of his *Sunday Express*.

Shortly after the above episode Bax gave a stag party at his basement flat in Bickenhall Mansions. Guest of the evening was one of his contributors, "Prince Paul of Oldenbourg", soon to be revealed—by the mischance of police court proceedings—as a Swiss waiter.

On the Prince attended, among others, Edmond Burke, the Covent Garden baritone, Arnold Bennett and my most contumacious self. According to Beverley I spent most of my time contending with my over-dignified colleague that he wrote solely for money. This is still one of my favourite leg-pulls—and never fails to get results.

All I remember of that occasion is how Bennett insisted on smoking his own cigars—and that Burke, ably supported by Bax, subsequently boomed me insensible. This is no reflection on their singing—Bax, among his other accomplishments, possessing an operatic voice. Music, never a pleasure to me, has become sheer torture since the 1914–1918 war.

Years later, by the time he had gate-crashed his triumphant way into the managerial chair of the *Daily Express*, I was to work for Beverley. Later still, we were to have a slight misunderstanding, of which you will hear.

After that, he fell—as I have seen so many fall, myself included, from their high estate in the Street of Misadventure. But Bax fell on his feet, as Public Relations Counsel to the Gaumont British Picture Corporation.

Rumour put his salary at £10,000 a year. Resigning from that

job, he gate-crashed on into the House of Commons, where he
sits for the Wood Green division of Middlesex.

To the modest stipend of the legislator, Bax's talents promptly
added a supplement. He became editorial adviser to Allied
Newspapers; and was soon writing those articles in the *Sunday
Graphic*, which have now been appearing for more than two years.
Even the other man—myself—who was being considered for that
job after Sir John Foster-Fraser's death left it vacant doubts if he
could do it as well.

But between the midsummer of 1922 and the spring of 1926 I never
doubted my powers of competing with any job. Or any situation.

Not even the situation to which I awoke before I had been in
Lancaster Gate Terrace six months.

§ 5

That situation presented itself almost without warning. At one
moment—weary after an even longer morning's work than usual
—I lay somnolent on a big sofa. At the next I heard the door of
the drawing room click open; and my second wife's voice saying
"Your children have come to see you".

Then she closed the door, leaving the three of us alone.

Except once from afar, I had not set eyes on Ursula or Pamela
since 1914. They were unrecognisably older, almost grown up.
It struck me that Ursula, though dark of hair, resembled her
mother—and that Pamela resembled mine.

A prophecy made by Withers, "They'll come back to you long
before they're twenty", flashed through my mind as I asked them
to sit down. I could see that they were at the same time curious
and hostile—the major curiosity Pamela's, the major hostility
Ursula's.

"We'd been hating you like hell for years", they were to confess
later. But for the moment they only required information.

Pamela conducted the main catechism. Ursula, brooding dark
apart, chipped in with supplemental questions. I decided then
and then to treat them as adults, in so far as this was possible
without increasing their hostility, or jeopardising their trans-
parent allegiance.

One could hardly explain to such immature financiers why the
chairs on which they sat still belonged to Waring and Gillow, or
how the manservant who had admitted them owed his regular
wages to the first bank manager ever persuaded that a publisher's
contract and one of those life insurance policies originally taken

out for my world tour (the other I had been forced to surrender ust after the war) were good security for a four-figure overdraft. Neither could one very well produce "This Indenture", whereby 'the settlor covenants" . . . to pay the annuity he is still labouring .o pay as he writes these lines.

.I confined myself, therefore, to the few pertinent facts, and an assurance that both their material welfare and their mother's had been legally protected.

This appeared to surprise them. Their mission accomplished, they rose, and I escorted them to the front door.

We had eschewed sentiment throughout. No hobbledehoy ever kissed more clumsily; no flappers ever submitted cold cheeks with ess grace.

§ 6

A curious sidelight on the fallibility of human recollection is, I eel, provided by Pamela's comment after reading the above.

"I do not wish to argue", she writes. "But the whole object of our visit was to ask whether you thought it was a good thing for is to leave school and get jobs. We thought it very important to begin earning, because we were worried about Dolly's health.

"From 1918 she had been working to supplement the income you gave us, and we were afraid she might have to give her job up.

"As you know, she actually carried on for another two years until the autumn of 1924."

Pamela adds:

"You said, 'Not going back to school for two more years would be like throwing away a gun and trying to shoot with a bow and arrow' ".

It is to be hoped that this, my first counsel to her adolescence—which was certainly followed—will prove some consolation to her maturity should she be forced to save her father from the work-house in his old age.

CHAPTER FORTY-TWO

§ 1

ONE other dramatic entrance into the overlarge drawing room at Lancaster Gate Terrace deserves chronicling, though the date escapes me and I withhold the name on the card presented to me that afternoon.

"Did she say what she wanted to see me about?" I asked.

"She said it was a private matter, sir."

"Well, I don't know the lady. But you can show her up."

That time there appeared in the doorway a woman between thirty and forty, well dressed in a light costume, and not altogether without charm.

She gave a funny little cry when she saw me; and seemed about to collapse.

"But—but you're not you", she stammered.

I supported her as far as the sofa; and offered her tea. She refused. She was shaking like Buldeo's gun by then.

"You're not even like him", she went on. "Let me go. Please. Whatever must you be thinking . . ."

"That he gave you one of my books. He always does that—and autographs them."

"You—you mean I'm not the only one?"

"I'm afraid not. You met him at a country hotel, I expect."

"I shan't tell you anything. I'm going." And, eluding further crossexamination, she went.

Who the man was, I never discovered. He started his game of impersonating me at Tunbridge Wells, sometime in 1917, with an autographed copy of *One of Us* and no small amatory success. The lady in that case pursued him, under my name, via Chatto & Windus, with a letter I left unanswered, presuming it to be a legpull. Her second letter, however, ran to eight pages of Swinburnian rhapsody, with a postscript hinting at blackmail.

I enclosed a photograph of myself with my reply—and heard no more from that victim. The next one wrote provocatively from Bristol; a third from somewhere in the north.

Imagination suggests that there may have been many more—and pictures a phantom army of old ladies, each with her cherished memory, tottering on pious pilgrimage to the family monument in Hampstead Cemetery when I am gone.

Time has mellowed that huge bizarre monument, and the sapling my mother and I planted there is already a stout tree. The old ladies of my imagination will not know its history; which is also queer, and also seems worth chronicling.

Originally Julia commissioned Alfred Gilbert, the sculptor of Eros and many other masterpieces, to design a tomb for my father. Gilbert could only work to inspiration. He took her money, but kept her waiting, until she lost her temper, fulminating an illadvised letter to the press.

Genius, accordingly, abandoned work; and for once my mother's

rtistic sense failed. A serpent-circled ball of gunmetal on a
ripod forms the centre of the monument. Above rises black
marble, relieved only by silver and gold mosaic to represent the
quotation, "Sunset and evening star, and one clear call for
me".

A lesser sculptor enclosed that oriental star in a symbolic
crescent of oriental moon, more reminiscent of Constantinople
than Tennyson.

Said a puzzled cigar merchant—relative of Doris Leslie, whose
good novel *Full Favour* also deals with the fragrant weed—
regarding the newly erected wonder:

"But Arthur wasn't in the *Turkish* tobacco business".

Among those who laughed loudest when Julia first told that
macabre tale was Edward Hulton, with whom my own acquaintance dated from one of my commercial trips to Manchester some
years before the 1914–1918 war, when he took me round his Withy
Grove printing rooms—calling my attention to the "stop-press
box" just swinging into place on what memory pictures as a long
metal arm.

A chance meeting with his wife Millie renewed this acquaintance
shortly after my return to London from the Shires.

§ 2

Sir Edward Hulton had now become a great power in the
Street of Misadventure—and still commanded all his own
ventures, though he rarely visited the huge offices he had built
in Gray's Inn Road, being already a sick man.

He lived like the millionaire he was—in London at Great
Cumberland Place, in the country at Downside, his estate near
Leatherhead—but with a peculiar simplicity all his own. In both
establishments, business conferences went on continually. Yet
business rarely intruded on home life.

Only on a single occasion do I remember broaching a press
affair to him. That was shortly after Mrs. Thompson and her
young lover Bywaters had been sentenced to death for the murder
of her husband—the woman's conviction being almost entirely
due to her own letters.

Those letters, Hulton had acquired.

"But you're not going to publish them", I protested across the
family dinner table at Downside.

"Why not? They'll increase circulation. Somebody else would
have bought 'em if I hadn't. And printed them!"

7*

Nobody could alter Edward's mind once he came to a decisio Even I knew better than to attempt that hopeless task.

His business, as he saw it, was to obtain and sell news. Th political aspect of journalism interested him far less than h racing stud or his greyhounds. Legend has it that he could b difficult. But that side of his character I never saw. Most of m memories show him spending happy hours with Millie and the two children, Betty and Teddy, then in their teens.

Teddy, as I still think of him, has followed in his father's foo steps with all his father's courage. Chamberlain was actually a Munich when he launched that popular weekly illustrated, *Pictu Post*, which topped the million mark within ten weeks.

Betty had all the gifts—looks, brains, money, and a balanc rare among the young women of her class and generation. A she ever wanted was a happy marriage, home life, and a family

"I'm not in a hurry", she told me once. "I don't mean to mak a mistake. It must be the right man, or nobody."

She found her right man some time after her father's deat left her a large fortune, only to die bearing her first child.

§ 3

A different type of man might have tried to use his intimac with Hulton for the furtherance of his finances. But I had alway despised those of my competitors in the cigar trade who currie friendship with their customers for the sake of orders. One boor nevertheless, I did crave.

"Can you get me seats for the Cup Final at Wembley?" I aske him early in 1923.

Characteristically, as in Orpen's picture of him, he inserted on thumb in the armhole of his waistcoat; and asked Millie an Betty if they'd like to go too.

Exiled kings pray for less favours than Cup Final tickets i vain. But four adjacent seats were obtained instanter. W arranged to meet in them. I hired a car; had a hunch, an insisted on walking the last four hundred yards to the turnstile.

Already, as Aimée and I passed through on our way to th stand, handfuls of advance skirmishers were climbing the hig railings. By the time we reached our seats—some forty minute before the kick-off—it seemed as though the public enclosure wouldn't hold another sardine.

"This looks like trouble", I said, as newcomers began to pus oldcomers out of the enclosures on to the oblong of green tur

After another ten minutes, you couldn't see turf at all—only the goal posts and the bandsmen, still playing while the crowd milled all about.

The situation grew ugly, the crowd angrier and angrier. I could see men hostling and women fainting. Millie turned up late, breathless and dishevelled.

"I never thought we'd get through", said blonde Betty, very cool and much amused. "What on earth's going to happen when the King arrives?"

What happened when King George did arrive is history. I never witnessed a greater miracle. As one man—or so at least it seemed—the whole crowd stood to attention for the National Anthem, and sang it through. Then into the thick of the mob on the field outrode some half a dozen mounted policemen—one on a gray.

A foreign mob—furious at the hopeless mismanagement which had oversold some ten thousand tickets—might have pulled those policemen from their horses. This one let them through to the centre of the ground—and presently I perceived a tiny circle of turf again. Round this, the police directing, young men were making a human rope of linked arms.

Soon, there were several of those human ropes, growing longer and longer as the men and girls who composed them—there were quite a number of girls—edged their fellows off the field towards the sidelines and the backlines. Memory suggests that the whole process was accomplished with great good humour, almost as though it were a new game—a kind of gigantic ring-a-ring o' roses with that rider on the gray weaving his way in and out, here, there and everywhere, till the white lines appeared again.

But only some six feet of clear separated those lines from the front line of spectators. Maybe that was why Bolton Wanderers just managed to beat West Ham United in that other game which followed.

Not that I cared which team won. I don't think anybody did. We were all too thrilled at what had gone before—and, speaking for myself again, too proud at this proof that the spirit of self-discipline which won the war had not been killed by five years of political squabbles.

For—throughout all my follies—I clung to one dream.

§ 4

That dream was a fanatic's, a romanticist's, altogether inchoate, and never within the slightest bounds of physical or mental possibility. Call it a poet's Mussolini complex and you will be fairly close to the truth.

The virus of fascism was first introduced into my system by a barman at San Remo about New Year's day 1923. Making holiday at French Menton, I crossed the frontier in a hired car.

Curious to understand the ethics of what was then a new system of government, I asked the barman in question, "But what about the liberty of the subject?"

"There is liberty", he replied, "for all who obey".

The paradox did not strike me. Impressed by his enthusiasm, I returned to England, ready to preach the new creed.

During my absence an ex-captain of infantry, acting butler to the megalomaniacal establishment, had ended one of his letters anent house-cleaning with the trenchant phrase of the war years, "The women are being splendid". Proof that one of them had been splendid was soon visible. I hope that her child inherited its father's sense of humour. But mine was now on the wane.

Further traces of a fascistic outlook must still be observable in a novel of the Lancaster Gate period.

Only eighteen months ago, a Hun company opened negotiations for the film rights. But I made a vow never to do business with that country long before the 1914–1918 war finished. And have kept it ever since.

The novel in question, *Gerald Cranston's Lady*, made me another good friend. One of the big scenes was to take place in an air liner between London and Paris—others in Cranston's coalpit. Theodore Instone, the late Sir Samuel Instone's brother and partner, provided me with both my underground and overground copy— and incidentally brought on a recurrence of what I believe to have been shellshock.

Only private enterprise flew you to Paris in those days. Thanks to Theodore, the Instone Air Line's *City of London* was put at my disposal. Never did that line of the blameless record come so near to losing a passenger's life through sheer fright.

Some half a dozen merry souls went up with me. We hovered over and about London for a bare half-hour. I did just manage to visualise my copy, and not to betray my real feelings. But I drank three double whiskies within ten minutes of our wheels touching terra firma, and how I managed to make the necessary notes when the kindly pilot and I climbed up to the cockpit afterwards I don't know now.

I was not to dare the air again until 1939, when Susan and I flew from Los Angeles to Santa Cantalina—twenty minutes all told.

Another experience I owe Theodore proved almost equally terrifying. Try being let half a mile or so down a new pit-sinking in a bucket if you are anxious to test your nerve. The pit-sinkers themselves were working, almost naked, at the bottom of the shaft, which memory recalls less than ten feet wide at the top.

The coal business interested me enormously. What I saw at Askern, the Instones' Yorkshire pit, and subsequently at Barber Walker & Company's colliery on the famous Barnsley seam, blew away many of those delusions under which an ignorant public still labours.

Any fool can write sob stuff about "the poor coalminers"—and quite a lot of fools have. Factually I found them grand cheery fellows, obstinately British to the core. The "brutal capitalistic owners" I met were model employers of labour—ground between the upper and nether millstones of government interference and politically minded trade unionism.

Time—and good work, some of it by that very Ernest Gowers who was my chief in the propaganda department—have done much to mellow the conditions of 1923.

Nowadays each side realises most of the other's difficulties—though the Englishman's reluctance to leave his home still keeps some pits that should be closed open, and districts that could produce more coal safely short of hands.

But fifteen years ago the fight between capital and labour was a bitter one. And into it, into every fight that offered, pen and tongue wagging with equal fury, went my forty-year-old self.

§ 5

Altruism I had, and sincerity, and a Don Quixote spirit of which I am still unashamed. That I may even have done my mite of good at a time when few worshippers of "The Gods of the Copybook Headings", as Kipling called them, were vocal, is also a possibility.

But I was too intolerant, too intransigeant, too much the diehard. My own point of view, I saw always—the other chap's never. And from a literary point of view, I was on the wrong side.

Your average literary man—why, I have never discovered—leans profitably to the left. I was a convinced rightist. Hence hostility in many quarters—some of which endures.

This I now regret. But at the time, hostility left me cold.

That people should like my books remained a financial necessity. Whether or no they liked my personality seemed completely im-

material. It is a further possibility that I enjoyed makin,
enemies more than I enjoyed making friends.

The only thing that really mattered, when it came to publi
speech or public action, was the certainty fifty-five is so muc)
more chary of voicing than forty used to be, "I know I'm right"

Firm in that conviction, I resigned from the P.E.N. Club whe)
John Galsworthy, its first president, insisted on inviting Gerhar
Hauptmann and a certain Frenchman to one of its early dinners

I had sworn never to break bread with a Boche if I could hel,
it—and have only done so on two subsequent occasions. And tha
pacifist Frenchman seemed to me the last literary figure wh(
should have been invited to represent our ally.

Maybe I was wrong to harbour such prejudices. The years
nevertheless, have proved that I was not so entirely wrong abou
disarmament, protection, and the futility of trusting to th(
League of Nations for our Imperial security.

But the man who says, "I told you so", ought to be in a home

CHAPTER FORTY-THREE

§ I

TOWARDS the middle of 1923 my agent, Cork, always the enthu
siast, rang me up in a considerable state of excitement. The *Dail*
Mail wanted to publish my next book serially. This was some
thing of an innovation—few reputable novels of the perioc
appearing in the dailies before they came out in book form.

I hummed, hawed, and queried the four figure price.

"They'll spend £20,000 on advertising you", said Cork; anc
Sir Andrew Caird, managing director since the death of Lorc
Northcliffe, confirmed this at a personal interview. Memory
suggests that Northcliffe's old editor, Thomas Marlowe, was alsc
present.

The Street of Misadventure is a tough one. But only on one
occasion have I ever known such a word to be worth less than a
bond. That word was given by a lady; and cost me quite enough.

A plot of the *Daily Mail* story evolved itself on my way home

"It sounds a bit sexy", commented Langley Edwards, the
fiction editor, when I told him the idea. "We've got to be careful,
you know."

Higham's advertising slogan for Lucana cigarettes had been

"harmless on account of their absolute purity". I promised that my blonde heroine should live up to it; and departed, not too willingly—I was still considering summer holidays a waste of time—for a furnished house at Speldhurst in Kent.

There, temporarily bereft of Margery, I returned to penwork —9.30 till lunchtime with a late afternoon spell. My teething troubles were nearly over. Now my eyes began to worry me. But I did not realise till the autumn that I should never again write without glasses.

Aimée, always more the gallant than the expert equestrienne, demanded a horse to ride. I warned her never to mount a hireling without first testing the safety bar on its side-saddle. Having disregarded this warning, she was thrown, dragged and nearly crippled for life.

It is possible that husbandly annoyance—to suffer folly gladly has never been among my virtues—outweighed sympathy.

My own recreation was lawn tennis, on a grass court that ran the full length of a garden bounded by a low churchyard wall. Various neighbours called; among them, Admiral Philpotts who commanded the *Warspite* at Jutland, also a keen player.

"I served under a general with the same name as yours", I told him at our first meeting.

"A gunner general?" he asked.

"Yes. He commanded the 24th divisional artillery."

"My brother. It was a toss-up which of us went into the army and which into the navy. He was killed on the Somme. We never knew the details."

I did. For General Philpotts—and no better gunner, no greater gentleman, ever served the Royal Regiment—had been one of those two comrades who walked to their death at the Briqueterie just before I left France. With him, visiting the battery in which they had served as major and subaltern, died his brigade major, Crippen—so fanatically devoted to his profession that he once told me, "No soldier should marry, or have anything to do with a woman".

Coates and I buried those two in adjoining graves. After he had heard my story, the admiral showed me his brother's memorial. It was just on the other side of the churchyard wall.

§ 2

"I gets a little money, and I goes crazy", Edgar Thomas Ware used to say at the poker table; and the quotation is not inapt.

I returned to an enlarged and partially redecorated establishment more confident than ever that I could make twice as much by selling my written words as I had lost by trying to sell cigarettes.

Political journalism meant more to me than my novels and short stories. Only fiction, however, could make me enough money to gratify my supreme ambition—a seat in the House.

Joyously, that November, I sold my first film rights—through the oldest firm of literary agents in England, A. P. Watt & Son—to the company managed by Sir Oswald Stoll. Even my bank manager admitted that this entitled me to run a car.

I ordered my very first—a large blue Armstrong Siddeley limousine, and engaged a chauffeur to drive it, shortly after Christmas. Meanwhile I had acquired a little election experience —and began to wonder whether the conservative party knew its job.

Protection was the issue, and the locale Bow and Bromley, one of Labour's safest citadels. For whom I spoke, I can't remember. But the sitting member was George Lansbury, who personified everything I disliked most. During the war, he had welcomed the bolshevik revolution and spoken of our "Russian comrades". So had his leader, Ramsay MacDonald, of whom I malignly cherished one personal recollection. Travelling on the same boat to India in 1912 he had refused me a subscription to a concert for the benefit of the crew.

I regarded both as traitors, and said so whenever I got the chance.

At one of our meetings, we had to hold the house till the candidate's appearance. The first speaker called on by the chairman had been sent by the party. He began, "I come to you with a message from the chicken farmers of Sussex".

Promptly a heckler shouted, "All my missus ever gives me is a boiled rabbit"; and that speaker sat down to catcalls. It was my turn next; and before I had been on my feet two minutes I was enjoying myself more than I had ever done in my life.

"Sergeant major", they began to yell at me.

"And where the hell would you chaps have been without your sergeant majors?" I yelled back. "Why are the chairs in the Town Hall made of foreign wood? Answer me that, somebody."

"Garn", somebody did answer. "You come and live in Whitechapel."

"My grandfather did. But he had the guts to get out. He didn't stay here to keep the Lansburys."

"Don't you say anything against old George. He's for the people."

"He's a bolshie."

"So am I. So are all of us. Aren't we, boys?"

A chorus approved the sentiment. Somehow I secured a modicum of silence.

"Let's understand one another", I went on. "You chaps don't want an election. You want a revolution."

"Ay. That's what we want."

"Right. Who's going to kill the first baby?"

A complete silence greeted the question.

"Come on", I said. "Let's have an answer. You can't have a proper revolution on Russian lines unless you kill off all the boss class. Now, then, which of you bolshies is game to bayonet one of the bosses' babies?"

Two hundred dumb faces, some of them women's, stared at me in horror. I stared at my loudest heckler.

"What about you?" I asked him.

He hesitated, fidgeting with the muffler round his neck.

"I'd do it", he said at last.

"Would you, you adjectival son of a lady foxhound", said the man standing next to him; but it was the look in the eyes of the women, I fancy, that made him slink away.

Afterwards one very wise in the ways of Bow and Bromley took me by the arm, saying:

"This is the best political nursery in London. It's just a game to them, you know. They like to see how much heckling a speaker will stand. But they'll never let a tory in here. And you can't blame them. Living conditions are too bad."

"That's why we simply must have protection of industry."

But Ramsay MacDonald, pledged to free trade, was forming the first labour cabinet by January 1924, and had "recognised" the Soviet government within a few weeks.

§ 3

An old German quatrain runs roughly:

> "God knows a great deal.
> Yes. But the Herr Professor knows more.
> God knows everything.
> Yes. But the Herr Professor knows it better".

That professorial attitude is common to most young novelists when they sell their first film.

From the moment Jeffery Bernerd, who is still among my friends, brought me the original scenario of *The Love Story of Aliette Brunton*, I convinced myself that I knew far more about the business than he ever could—and, very tactfully, he adopted a few of my suggestions.

Memory of this made me chuckle, only the other day, when I heard that one of my younger colleagues was spending much of his time at a certain British studio, "supervising production".

"We let him think he's the cat's whiskers", said my lady informant. "It gives him a lot of pleasure—and it doesn't do us much harm."

One who is now an even closer friend, Maurice Elvey, was to produce my picture—his wife, Isobel Elsom, in the name part.

Maurice is of middle height, clean-shaven and bespectacled, with a good broad forehead. Strangely for a film man, he comes of Huguenot stock. From beginnings very different from my own, he has made himself a unique position. Responsible for more than a hundred British productions, he can boast that none of them has ever made a loss.

His erudition is as profound as his knowledge of music. He specialises in literature and history. He has marvellous health and a grand sense of humour. For a hobby he collects—or used to collect—model soldiers.

Why Hollywood didn't snatch Maurice up years ago is a mystery. The reasons why he is not among the big noises in his own country are clearer. He cannot pose; he never bluffs; he dislikes extravagance; and rarely smokes a double corona. As a swanker—to put the point briefly—he fails.

I was the poorest judge of a man in those days. But I did recognise that Maurice's enthusiasm equalled my own.

"We're going to shoot the hunting scenes tomorrow", he told me one evening. "Why don't you come along and help?"

For once I gave up a morning's work; donned my old togs; was driven into the country, and helped with the proceedings. A spring sun shone pleasantly; but we managed to find enough trees and hedges without leaves. The shot of myself which duly appeared in the picture did not show me leaping with the first flighters. Nevertheless I returned to town exhilarated by a whole unaccustomed day in the fresh air.

§ 4

This exhilaration must have grown on me while I dressed, donning my three ration medals—familiarly known as Maud, Lily and Kate—for the most important function at which I had yet been invited to speak. The dinner was in aid of a press charity. I owed the invitation to the *Daily Mail*, just about to launch my serial.

Five minutes of tactful modesty, and a couple of those jokes which pass for wit on such occasions, represented the maximum requirement. As usual, I did not prepare my speech.

Stanley Baldwin, leader of the conservative opposition, received the guests of both sexes—who must have numbered between three and five hundred. We shook hands as I came in. For some reason I took the most extraordinary spite to him. This still puzzles me. I knew him for a patriot who had surrendered £100,000 of his personal fortune to the country during the war. But there the spite was, and an element of distrust.

Dinner ran its customary six or seven courses. Near me at the top table sat the Hungarian minister. Looking a little to my right I perceived two faces remembered since Eton days.

Viscount Astor, captain of the boats, very gorgeous in stick-ups and a buttonhole, pop cane slung over his arm, I had only known from afar. Not so the honourable and gallant member for the Horsham and Worthing Division. Twenty years already, he had held that constituency. But to me, he was the same old Ghost, who had ragged m'tutor and written the sporting gossip in the *X*.

We smiled at each other; and I can still remember thinking, "I'll rag him about having been my sub-editor when it's my turn to speak".

Then Baldwin made his speech, and the devil began to whisper in my ear. It must have been the devil. For if there is one thing of which I am utterly certain it is that I was not drunk. Neither can I blame the present Lord Camrose, then Sir William Berry, for what subsequently occurred.

I had never met anyone with a bad word to say for "Bill" Berry or his brother Gomer, now Lord Kemsley, who at the time shared a joint bank account with their eldest brother, Lord Buckland, on which any of the three could draw without consulting the other.

This last fact I learned from Sir William himself. Tall, clean-shaven and reddish of hair, he was so much my ideal businessman of the post-1918 period that I had drawn on his appearance for the hero of my coal novel.

We met outside the banqueting room during a pause between the speeches. Already seething, I said:

"Did you ever hear such a lot of tosh? For two pins I'd get up and say so".

"Why don't you?" he smiled—obviously never dreaming that I would.

Resentment grew on my impetuosity when we resumed our places. Astor made a delightful speech, and referred to me charmingly by name. The devil whispered (this also I recollect with great clarity), "He needn't be so damn partonising". Finally the Ghost rose, in his best ghostly manner, and said among other things, "The conservative party is still here".

That blew the mine. Flashingly I must have recollected two of my gunners talking in the signallers' dugout at Neuve Eglise. "I'll be glad when I'm back in the old factory", one was saying; and the other, "So'll I. But we're not going back to the old conditions." Startlingly, I must have revisualised the men in the dark of the coalpits, that deafening room at a worsted mill, the mufflered figures of the meetings at Bow and Bromley.

Or maybe it was only the exhibitionist in me, the reciter of Horatius, who spoke the truth as he saw it that night.

I orated, if you please, for the best part of half an hour—and that no finer exhibition of bad taste has ever been staged at a London banquet I am utterly sure.

These mellower years can still blush for the figure I cut. But my forty-year-old self didn't care whether some voices shouted "Shut up", or others, "Go on". I just went on, voicing all the accumulated hopes of my war years, all my accumulating disappointment with the years which had followed, all my distrust of Germany, all my hatred of communism, and all my contempt for people who "swilled champagne in London" when they should be looking into and reforming labour conditions in the north.

Why had the leader of the conservative party, "*my* party, *our* party" thrown over protection? Why didn't he "take his coat off" and set about fighting "the traitors within our gates"?

Before I sat down the dinner began to break up. Still out of myself, completely exhausted but in no wise repentant, I went for my hat and coat.

By me, at the cloakroom counter, stood a tall man in what memory suggests to have been a black sarong heavily embroidered with gold.

"What you said", he smiled gravely, "needed saying. I congratulate you. And he told me his name, "Sir Robert Ho Tung", which is writ large in the history of our Empire, and especially of Hong-kong, where his telegraphic address is still the "Longevity" which my maturity wishes him.

But it was a dead friend, the kindest man I ever knew, and one of England's greatest little sportsmen, who carried me off to Prince's Restaurant for supper.

"A glass of wine with you, Gilbert", said Harry Preston, proffering more champagne.

"Some of the old and bold for you, Gilbert", twinkled Harry Preston, proffering more brandy.

But of my speech he said little or nothing. It was too transparently obvious to all at that table—one savagely vociferous lady included—that I had blotted my political copybook for keeps.

§ 5

My butler brought me next morning's newspapers with my early tea.

"Mr. Gilbert Frankau", each reported at the foot of a whole column, "also spoke."

Then, I did not appreciate that my colleagues of the press were being no less kind to me than Harry.

"The Berrys at least", thought the fool in his folly, "might have given me a show."

CHAPTER FORTY-FOUR

§ 1

WHETHER or no my forty-year-old self had enough sense to realise just how blackly it had bespattered its copybook at that press dinner is problematical. In the privacy of my upstairs study, I may have admitted, "You made a complete ass of yourself". But to no other person would the (in his own estimation) famous author of those far-off days ever acknowledge himself wrong.

With the squirrel cage of my misdirected energies whirling always more swiftly, I had no time, and no wish, for contemplation. And since happiness—using the word in its almost universally accepted sense of tranquillity—formed no part of my programme, it never even crossed my mind that my second marriage might go the way of my first.

Of considerably more importance, seemed the success of "my" film, which—Maurice Elvey having departed for America—I was soon assisting to edit, spending all my afternoons at Stoll's studio in Cricklewood.

There, my experiences with Luca Comerio may have proved of some value, the picture eventually grossing £23,000, a big amount for that time. Before it was even trade-shown, Cork sold my novel about the coal business to Fox.

§ 2

The money which Fox Films paid for *Gerald Cranston's Lady* tallied with my own estimate of my commercial value—and went straight to my already swollen head. Almost immediately First National bought one of the few short stories I have ever sold to an American magazine for Doris Kenyon.

Mental record of a conversation which took place shortly afterwards runs like this:

Voice at the other end of the telephone: "What sort of price will you take for the film rights of that story you've got running in the *Mail*?"

My own voice: "Well, I might take ten thousand".

The other voice: "Ten thousand dollars".

My own: "Dollars. Who do you think you're talking to? Guineas!"

Not for nothing had Julia once called me the "half-crown millionaire". Yet that my personal requirements were not on a scale commensurate with my establishment charges the extant figures show. Of the thousands upon thousands paid out during my last three years in Lancaster Gate Terrace they amount only to a trifle.

Nor—though I loved the pose—can I have been altogether the hardboiled businessman, whose motto is the Roman's, "Gold doesn't smell". If I had been I should certainly have jumped at my next film offer, almost as high as Fox's.

The offer came from Berlin via Cork.

"Tell your Hun friend", I said, "that, if he makes it double, he can still go to hell."

That summer of 1924 megalomania began to approach one of its peak periods with the renting of a furnished mansion near

Battle Abbey. The late Lady Mabelle Egerton—to whose shade I owe yet another apology for a series of cantankerous letters—paid her gardeners. But the numbers of my own staff ran into double figures; and Margery's successor lived in.

Still as blind to the domestic as to the financial situation, I continued to worship my old god Work.

Memory recalls many incidents of those six weeks in Sussex, but none of much value to the tale. I re-educated myself as a motorist. I played lawn tennis. I re-met the lady Michael Arlen called Shelmerdine, just affianced with a lieutenant commander in the navy to whom she referred as "my midshipman". I spent a whole afternoon posing countrified for a fashionable photographer.

In September, I returned to town; to my usual double working spells; to first-nighting; to speaking here, there and everywhere; to lunching out and dining out and supping out; to my tennis lessons with Donnisthorpe.

Friends I had; but fortunately no more social aspirations then than I cherish today; and enough resolutions to terminate even my weekends on Sunday night and my own parties—which were many—at the same hour as Cinderella.

Still more fortunately a selfcritical faculty which even the squirrel cage could never quite atrophy warned me that a new story, already as long as the average novel of the period, was not up to standard.

I had been at work on that tale for the best part of six months. In it were to be enshrined all my political theories and all my hopes for the future of the Empire.

The hardboiled businessman I was always aping bewailed the loss of profit; and could only be persuaded by the plea of commercial necessity.

I had to inform him, "This won't sell" . . . before the despised artist and the distressed patriot in me ripped those four hundred pages of typescript to shreds.

§ 3

My good butler, Denham, was a wireless enthusiast, and had made himself a loudspeaker. Borne up from the basement on some mysterious attachment of his own contriving, this heralded the birth of 1925 to some fifty of us.

Within a few weeks the *New York World* was hailing my *Daily Mail* serial, published in volume form by the Century Company, as "one of the dirtiest books in the English language", and the

Boston Post construing it under scare headings as a personal attack on H. G. Wells.

The hardboiled businessman in me—one eye on his American market—duly rejoiced.

Ten years later Wells himself appeared to have read that book, and to be suffering under the same delusion. I cannot divulge the name of my informant. But I can assure my distinguished colleague that, however much I have disagreed with his constantly changing ideologies, and however pernicious I consider his political influence to have been during the post-1918 period, his blameless private life never was and never will be any concern of mine.

Coincident with the arrival of these reviews—and what further rejoicing there would be every time the daily envelope of press cuttings was a really fat one!—came an S O S from Colonel Roberts, once of the *Wipers Times*.

"I'm in a hell of a mess, Gilbert, old lad," he told me. "And unless you can see me out, I'm sunk."

The affair was simple, but presently of world interest. At Roberts' instigation the *Daily News* and its stable companion the *Star* had sponsored a crossword puzzle marathon—the mania then being in its infancy—for a first prize of £5,000.

"It's to be an eliminating contest, old son", continued Roberts. "Here's the first puzzle. My own. Child's play, of course. Just to get 'em in. We've had more than a hundred thousand entries, at a bob a nob, already. What I want you to do is to knock the lot out in four more rounds."

"So that you won't have to part with the £5,000?"

"No, you suspicious ass. The cash is in the till. Otherwise the papers wouldn't have touched the scheme with a barge pole. But it's no good if a hundred thousand people have to share it."

I had no experience of solving, far less of constructing, crossword puzzles. But a comrade of the 24th Division could not be left in the lurch.

"You're on", said I. "What are the orders?"

My orders for round two were to spare my punches, but floor at least half my opponents. "Jumping mice" figured among the clues; but memory suggests that you had either to reverse, curtail or decapitate them.

For round three I dredged *Webster*, Lemprière's *Classical Dictionary*, and most of the miscellaneous knowledge I possessed. Decapitations (removal of the first letter) and curtailments (removal of the last) were double and triple by then—and studious moneygrubbers cursing me as far away as San Francisco.

Round four demanded a knowledge of French, Spanish, German, Italian and the higher mathematics. But punch-drunk stalwarts still refused to take the count.

"There are three hundred odd left. Finish 'em off before the bell goes", telephoned Roberts; and, sealing the last solution, I did.

A London syndicate—which included F. M. Atkinson, secretary of the Poets' Club, Edmund Dulac, the artist, and "Da" Marks, the barrister—eventually trousered Roberts' boodle. But even they failed to solve all the clues.

My own remuneration was a modest £100. I have never written harder for less money, or earned more opprobrium by my unpaid speeches, in my whole life. Even to this day chance acquaintances are apt to give me the salute of the clenched fist, not as a profession of communistic comradeship, but as one-time battlers in that mammoth no-alternative scrap.

CHAPTER FORTY-FIVE

§ 1

I could not use the word "zip", as generally understood nowadays, in any of my crossword puzzles; because there was no authority for it.

"*Attrib.*", reads the present authority of the *Oxford Dictionary*, "in the trade name of a 'lightning fastener', a device by which an opening is closed by the interlocking of metal strips placed on adjacent edges. 1925."

Not rash enough to believe, like one of my bygone confrères, who wanted to leave a perpetual trust fund for the printing of his novels, that my own will have the ear of posterity, I hereby claim —for all time—my fourth share in the coining of that trade name.

Give the remaining credits to Charlie Higham, Commander Ellis of Imperial Chemical Industries, and Miss Peggy O'Neil.

The lightning fastener had been invented, to my knowledge, for the best part of twenty years. Commercially, however, its success tarried till the day Charles telephoned:

"If you feel like making a short speech and undressing one of our loveliest actresses, come along to a little lunch I'm giving at a private room in the Savoy".

He explained the stunt. Miss O'Neil's dress would have no hooks or buttons—only lightning fasteners. Accordingly I need not fumble when she rose beside me and the magnesium—then, publicity had no Sasha bulbs—flashed in the pan.

"Nothing could be easier", I told my audience, with the camera-man just ready to press his trigger. "Zip—it's on. Zip—it's off." And I went back to my work, never dreaming myself among the immortals.

For it was not until ten years later that I was to sit breakfasting, on my way to see coal turned into petrol at Billingham, with the present Lord Melchett and A. P. Herbert.

"I've got a vague idea of running for the House of Commons", said Herbert on that occasion. "How does one put up for a university constituency?"

Melchett, who happened to know, told him; turned the talk on his latest book, *What a Word*, in which he poked good Herbertian fun at governmental and business English, and finally produced the axiom:

"Nothing exists until somebody has given it a name".

Whereupon Ellis poked his head over the low partition; and announced:

"Well, you're sitting with someone who gave something a name that is now universal. Frankau's responsible for zip".

And he went on to tell us how he had rushed straight back from that long-ago lunch party to rewrite half his leaflets.

But when he attempted to register my onomatopoeic word, the competent authority would have none of it—and if you order zips from the Nobel branch of Imperial Chemical Industries you must still ask for their Lightning Fasteners.

America uses "zipper" instead of zip. I claim a fourth share in that word too.

§ 2

Similar stunts were legion. With others, including G. K. Chesterton, whose method struck me as too academic, I debated the merits of plays immediately after their performance. Alone, on the stage of a different theatre, I opened a dress show for Poiret. Constantly you could hear my voice uplifted either at the Poets' Club, still presided over by my old friend, Harry Simpson, or some Glasgow High School dinner, in Harrods' book depart-ment, or Whiteley's, or Selfridge's, or the little bookshop founded by Sidney and Ethel Gutman in Bermondsey. I wrote a prologue for the film of *Anna Christie*, and held an audition to discover which of the hundred odd applicants recited it best.

So assiduously did I seek the limelight that Hall Caine himself felt moved to admiration.

One day I was taken to tea with him in his Hampstead home; and, looking on that worn kindly bearded face, I remembered how, in his own youth, men had paraphrased the title of one of his novels, *The Deemster*, to make him a nickname.

"The Boomster", he had been called in those far-off days, when—according to Pawling—he would sneak into Heinemann's office by the trade entrance to spend many a clandestine hour drafting their advertisements for his bestsellers.

I knew, too, that it was he who had revolutionised the book trade by insisting that his novels should be published in one volume at 6s. (4s. 6d., as long as you didn't buy them on a railway bookstall!) instead of in three volumes at half a guinea apiece.

How, accordingly, could I—already profiting through that revolution—be angry when he said, maybe with just a touch of envy:

"You are lucky, young man, to be writing novels at a time when a novelist is no longer expected to be a gentleman"?

The implied criticism did not even sting.

Only one thing stung as the spring of 1925 warmed to the summer. Fox showed his superfilm—still entitled *Gerald Cranston's Lady*, for mad cables threatening to spend every penny paid me for it in the American law courts had erupted from Lancaster Gate Terrace at the mere suggestion of a change—at the Empire.

Eddie Goulding, subsequently to produce *Grand Hotel*, appeared to be responsible for the scenario. Alma Rubens, later to die tragically, starred with James Kirkwood. After their final close-up, the author was led away almost in tears.

I believe I did actually drop one tear when my great coal-strike scene—they never even mentioned that Cranston was in the coal business—metamorphosed itself into a proletarian riot outside the hero's mansion, with New York mounted policemen—staves lifted like sabres—charging madly down a pseudo Park Lane.

Or maybe that tear was wrung from the eyes of the hard-boiled businessman I still imagined myself, when the earl I had taken such care to picture shabbily clad, utterly decent, and altogether the very old Etonian, first appeared in his Balfour monocle, his gleaming topper and his white spats.

"That's how Americans always imagine an earl", Eddie Goulding was to tell me later.

But, "The screen", said the fool in his folly, "must go my way. Not I the screen's".

Enthusiastically, quixotically, I embarked on yet another campaign, pouring out letters to the press, pouring out speeches at trade gatherings—to one of which, with his dark orchidaceous bride, came Jack Dempsey.

I took the chair at that lunch; and added yet one more blot to the copybook when I suggested there were too many crooks in the British cinema business. Publicly, too, I opposed the new idea of a quota. Did Great Britain need the protection of a quota while *I* was game to produce and direct a picture, just to show how the thing should be done?

But that thought I did not broach in my private letter to Lord Rothermere, merely asking whether he would grant me an interview "on a matter of national importance".

Very promptly he did.

§ 3

The main impression of my one and only talk with the personality I have heard more abused than most—though nobody did more to stimulate our rearmament—is of a biggish man, very quiet, slightly diffident, and poorly housed in a top flat at Savoy Chambers.

Lord Rothermere "received me most politely". Nobody could have been a more attentive listener to a more crazy scheme—which boiled down to the request that the *Daily Mail* should find the capital to make a film of *Peter Jackson, Cigar Merchant*, with its author in sole command.

"Put your ideas in writing, and I'll consider them", said his lordship.

I spent a whole day composing that letter. After about a week, he replied that he had considered the matter with his associates and regretted that they could not see eye to eye with me. Wise men all!

In the meantime, having finished my magnum opus, which my old friend David Whitelaw, no mean crime novelist himself and the inventor of the game called Lexicon, was running serially in the *London Magazine*, I at last felt the necessity of a summer holiday, and decided to spend it motoring on the continent—a practice to which I have been addicted ever since.

Just before I left England, that great social reformer, Mrs. Cecil Chesterton, who has done so much good with her hostels, invited me to speak at one of her meetings.

One phrase meant only to rouse a laugh—"You women are just a lot of sleek jungle cats, always on the prowl for men and money"—ran like fire over stubble clean round the stunt press of the English-speaking world.

Even Scottish New Zealand took my jesting words as a serious pronouncement on feminism. It is just conceivable—though I still had no more idea than the man in the moon of jeopardised domestic tranquillity—that they came from the heart.

CHAPTER FORTY-SIX

§ 1

EVENTUALLY, that continental motor trip—on which, of course, my self-importance must be accompanied by a chauffeur—was to change the whole course of my life. But nothing warned me of this as I stood talking, on an August morning in Venice, to the manager of the Grand Hotel, who had been chief reception clerk at the Ritz in London when Julia moved there from Clarges Street.

"A lady I met just before I came away", said I, "told me I must stay at a place called Beauvallon in the South of France. And now the only hotel there wires they can't give us a room."

Signore Mella sent another wire, indicating that I was a "beautiful client". The Golf Hotel, Beauvallon, relented. Arriving there—fascinated alike by the beauties of the bay of St. Tropez, a lady's pleas, and his half-crown millionairedom—the fool in his folly decided a mere London establishment incommensurate with grandeur. In addition he must have his own villa on the Côte des Maures.

Further auto-persuaded that this would mean cheaper holidays for the future—not yet forty-two I could always convince myself that an expense was really an economy—I returned to London the proud possessor of my own acre, and a few odd metres over, in France.

To build that villa should only cost "a thousand or so". And here came Mr. Wells of Harper & Brothers, the American publishers, offering to take me over from the Century Company on a four-book contract.

Would I—asked Mr. Wells—undertake a publicity tour in the States?

Would I not? Before I went, however, my *Masterson*, its English publication fixed for January, must trump all the home tricks.

More royalties were not the main urge. The one white flame had flared again, the one altruistic dream—stimulated maybe by a night in Ypres, where men still disinterred the bodies from the blood-soaked soil—had returned to me while I corrected and re-corrected those proofs.

Good or bad—secretly I thought it rather good—this book, which had cost me so much labour, contained something more than its *Story of an English Gentleman*. It preached all the truths and all the warnings I had shouted from platforms or striven to make clear in my articles.

Let the quietists call me a stunt merchant. Let Leftists think me the mere moneygrubber. I would push the British sales of *Masterson* to fifty thousand copies before I sailed from Southampton.

As an advertising medium, what price the B.B.C.?

§ 2

Then, as now, the British Broadcasting Corporation, already moved to Savoy Hill from its two original floors at Marconi House, had no price. Yet surely they would accept, from the first scribe who ever read one of his stories, perched precarious on packing cases before the tin megaphone of Eckersley's devising, a little talk entitled, "An author's feelings on publication day"?

Surely if, by the merest coincidence, that talk synchronised with the publication day of one of the talker's own novels, his announcer could be induced to mention the title of said novel?

My script, duly submitted, met with approval. For once Sir John Reith must have been caught napping. The announcement was duly broadcast. What followed—Walter Hutchinson, his sales staff, headed by one Rex Flatau, my friends on the press, and my friends the booksellers backing me like Trojans—was money for jam.

Even the left wing of the press slaughtered me in columns; and attacked the B.B.C. for permitting propaganda. Not even a strike of the packers in the book trade—which prevented my poor friend W. L. George seeing his last novel published before death took him—was allowed to interfere.

On one day alone I delivered a thousand copies to our London booksellers in my own car; and they filled their windows with them. Only in Liverpool, during a whirlwind tour of the provinces, did I find a doubting Thomas, who swore:

"I won't show a copy. You've made them start the Grand National with a gate".

And when I protested, "But I came up last year on purpose to see the race. And it was started with a gate", that bookseller still doubted, saying that he'd been there himself, and moreover that he had never missed a National since the 'eighties.

Nor would any word of mine persuade him that my eyesight had not failed me when I watched the faraway tapes go up from my seat on the Canal Turn stand. Only the word of the clerk of the Aintree course—telephoned to in a frenzy—carried conviction.

Whereupon, the doubter promised generous amends; and had actually re-dressed his window before I lunched with the proprietors of Lewis' Bon Marché; and one rushed in on us chuckling, "Have you seen the *Echo*?"

We also chuckled.

But since such mistakes will happen, even in metropolitan composing rooms, and since the fault for that one unfortunate phrase was more my own than the young reporter's who took down my "Striking Defence of Modern Woman" a shade too literally, it shall not be repeated here.

Nor—here—would I venture to suggest that the B.B.C.'s memory resembles the elephant's.

It was, of course, purely an accident when, some thirteen years later, the Columbia Broadcasting Company of New York arranged a talk—also to advertise one of my novels—between myself, Mary Astor and Orson Welles, that the engineers at Portland Place, London, misunderstood their instructions, with the result that I faced a microphone which would carry no word across the Atlantic.

This at 3.15 a.m.

§ 3

Then, as always, the press of Great Britain was more interested in a novelist's views on women than in his political opinions. Nevertheless, during those last weeks before I boarded the *Berengaria* I managed to wave my political torch frequently—and some record of those wavings, sheer chance has preserved.

The mellowing mind, reading those old cuttings, marvels alike at the selfconfidence and at the intransigeance of two and forty. But at least I was sincere.

The stunt merchant, for all his stunting, had a creed.

He believed in his country. He believed in individual liberty.

That he held his country to have been misgoverned for eight long years, that he admired a different system of government, which time has proved the very antithesis of individual liberty, that he could neither moderate his language nor realise an equal sincerity in some of his opponents—these facts, also, are clear from the records.

Unclear remains the complexity of the motives which were taking me to the United States.

I certainly welcomed the opportunity to preach my creed, to warn America against what I held to be the tyrannies of trade unionism, the fallacies of socialism and the abortive experiment of communism. I certainly believed—of this the cuttings leave no doubt—that the average English lecturer misrepresented England to the Americans.

"I'm going to tell them the Old Country's not done yet", says forty-two.

Add one more good motive—that old dream of an Anglo-American alliance to preserve world peace, originally inspired by Mary Elizabeth Bradley, before you condemn the altruist.

Yet that the egoist expected the resultant publicity to sell tens of thousands of copies of his novel can no more be denied than that he hoped to sell film rights in Hollywood.

This, I admitted—privately—at the time.

What I would not admit—when I let my house furnished, and stored my car, and sent my wife away to the South of France— was that only the tattered banners of chivalry were still fluttering over affection's citadel.

Once before—remember—my secret urge had been escape.

CHAPTER FORTY-SEVEN

§ 1

A TRAVEL book entitled *My Unsentimental Journey*, which may have its slight historical value in the distant future, relates how England's most voluble and most self-opinionated author—having stood drinks to those deck reporters whom Theodore Roosevelt once called "the outposts of American journalism"—arrived at the Plaza Hotel, New York, on Saturday, March 27th, 1926.

There, in the gloomiest of suites—which I changed immediately—I found Miss Ruth Raphael, "a smiling, large-eyed, dark-haired lady", Harpers' publicity woman, who said:

"I've made a few appointments for you".

The book, which is in diary form, further states: "My enemies say that I like publicity; and in a way I suppose I do". The mellowing mind finds this phrase a trifle disingenuous when applied to the self of that time.

"God's own gift to a sob sister", as an admiring American colleague phrased it, I must have spoken fifty thousand words of goodish sex copy that first afternoon. Memory suggests that I rehashed nearly every "woman" article I had written for British magazines and newspapers since 1921.

But the *New York Times* was "not interested in sugar daddies, and butter-and-egg men and cake eaters", which last I had discovered to be Americanese for "a lounge lizard or a gigolo"; and published my political views verbatim next day.

It is a queer reflection on time's crazy whirligig to discover that, among those mentioned as socialist-bolsheviks, I find "Comrade Cynthia Mosley". The main attack, however—duly headlined—was on Bernard Shaw, whose war record my intransigeance felt to be unpardonable, and H. G. Wells.

With this, my speechifying and my broadcasting, mostly on the same subjects, I managed to kick up as much dust as any other fanatic who believes himself to have a mission.

Take such activities, the visiting of booksellers, theatre-goings, prizefight-goings, public lunches and public dinners, personal contacts, sight-seeing, the inspection of many factories, much tennis-playing, a little horseback-riding and many a night of sleeplessness brought on by over-exertion and over-excitement, as the general background of the next three months.

Towards the payment of my expenses—remember that I never took a dollar for any of these activities—I had further undertaken, if you please, to supply the *Sunday Pictorial* with my regular monthly articles while still en route; and to write a minimum of fifty thousand words dealing with my American experiences for our leading right-wing newspaper, the *Morning Post*.

The opportunity of one really new experience presented itself within nine days of my arrival in dry New York.

At seven o'clock on Monday morning, the 5th of April—just as was recovering from an attack of influenza—the telephone woke me.

8

Would I "cover" the hanging of a man called Gerald Chapman for the *New York Evening Journal*? Could I leave for Hartford, Connecticut, on the two o'clock train?

The *Sunday Pictorial* of those happy days paid me at the same rate as Arnold Bennett, 2s. a word. Heast's paper offered me £20 and my expenses for eight hundred words to be syndicated in eighty other newspapers.

I demanded more vainly; promised to decide within half an hour; wondered if shellshocked nerves would stand up to the strain; wondered whether the offer could be a "dare" (factually, I discovered later, it was, one man in that office having said to another, "Captain or no captain, I'll bet you five bucks he won't have enough sand"); and rang back to say I'd go.

§ 2

Among my few intelligent decisions since reaching New York had been that I should never accomplish the whirlwind coast to coast publicity trip of Miss Raphael's planning without a good valet-courier.

By sheer marvellous luck a treasure was already found. His name is Robert Alfonso Smith; and he is now living, very happily married, at Minehead in Somerset. What I owe to his fidelity, to his intelligence, and to his unremitting care for a mere temporary employer, mere words cannot hope to repay.

"A hanging, sir", said Robert Alfonso when I broke the news. "I hope you're up to it."

Memory suggests—for he is a very meticulous man—that he may have asked me whether I should need his company, and a dinner jacket.

But only a great chap named Spiro, reporter on the *Evening Journal*, travelled with me to Hartford; telling me Chapman's history the while.

The man was a killer of the most desperate. But whether he killed the one policeman for whose murder they were about to hang him is still disputed by American criminologists. He and his band certainly got away with the biggest bank-van robbery ever committed—two and a half million dollars' worth of bearer securities—without taking a life.

At the Bond Hotel we found one of Spiro's colleagues named Henry. He told us the story of Chapman's last appeal for clemency, heard that afternoon.

"Some fighter. Believe me, he gave them hell."

The weather was icy, the hanging to take place at midnight. Spiro had work to do. I walked the town. "Broad tram-clanging streets, at least one fine set-back skyscraper, a domed State Capitol impressively illuminated, Georgian-looking churches, a good park, rows upon rows of frame houses", reads the book.

"Shaky and seeking companionship", it continues, "I introduced myself to a friendly bookseller, just about to close up store for the night; received some counsel, and a mild cigar.

The mellowing mind feels that "shaky" is another piece of disingenuity. "Sanguinary funk" would be a better description of my mood while I ate a lonely dinner. But any humanitarianism experienced must have been purely personal.

I had no more conscientious objection to capital punishment then than I have now. America, for all I cared, could hang, draw, quarter, electrocute or asphyxiate all its bandits.

My one conscientious objection was to disgracing myself in a foreign country before at least twenty fellow-journalists. If they could stick this sight—and turn out their copy immediately afterwards—so could I.

Whiskey might have helped some people. But I had not yet taken to toting a hip flask—and am still unable to write a decent line except cold sober.

Ten-thirty saw me in a taxi with Spiro and various others. Two women were on their knees just outside the huge gloomy bulk of Wetherfield Prison—or so my companions told me.

Subconsciously—I carried neither paper nor pencil—I must have made my first note.

§ 3

In a large businesslike office, a courteous man, about ten years my junior—Bradley by name and parole agent, whatever that might mean, of the prison—was regaling some sixty other pressmen with coffee and sandwiches, cakes and cigars. The battery of typewriters in this room had momentarily ceased fire; but the telegraph instruments hidden by a partition still tapped furious Morse.

"What do you imagine he's thinking about?" asked Spiro, as we watched a large clock.

At eight minutes to twelve exactly Bradley signalled to some fourteen of us; and we followed him downstairs to the outer hall of the gaol. Except in the air, I had hitherto found actual ordeals less terrifying than my apprehension of them. The knowledge must have been heartening. From the moment we gathered round Bradley and he asked us to make as little noise as possible because we should be passing the cells where they kept the criminal lunatics, my mind began to register every sight, every sound, and every personal sensation.

Pride, the realisation that I must have seen many worse sight in the war than the one we were about to witness, and a curiosity I recognised slightly ghoulish, were all present to the registering mind.

The prison officer in the blue cap who had originally queried my right of entry was chewing another cigar. He unlocked a gate in the high white bars. Beyond these rose the latticed staircase I had seen on the films. The film of my own mind snapshotted the incurious eyes of a coloured boy at a telephone switchboard.

We veered right and away from the staircases. Another iron gate was unlocked. Another clock indicated that the hanging would take place in less than five minutes.

Two by two we walked through a dim chapel. A single bulb showed thin steel pillars and plain white walls. The next room was the library. Almost at once, we were filing past the cage-like cells which housed the criminally insane.

A twelve-inch grille in one cage door was open. Through it stared a blank hopeless face, more bestial than human. By it stood another prison officer. Neither of the faces twitched so much as an eyelid while I went by.

The microphone of the mind recorded no sound either—except the noise our feet made on the metal floor.

Up a short staircase and down again, we entered a bright corridor which memory suggests to have been carpeted. I did not realise, until later, that the closed door we passed was that of the condemned cell.

An open door opposite admitted us into a room with green walls, twenty or more feet high. Metal water pipes, their protecting felt banded on with nickel, upran those walls. On a floor of reddish concrete, I perceived a rough circle of green chalk.

The man next to me whispered, "That's where they'll stand him". I took a back seat in one of six church-like pews at the far end of the room.

A new system of mechanical hanging was to be used for the first time. A yellow rope, ending in a noose, drooped from the centre of the ceiling to a black hook near the still-open door. Two more officers in blue stood by the noose. One of these focused my attention. He seemed so out of the picture, with his white moustache, his slight tendency to paunchiness, and his kindly face.

We were hardly seated when Chapman, attended by a florid Roman Catholic priest, entered the hanging room; and the door closed.

§ 4

At this point, I must have keyed my mind to its highest pitch of sensitivity. How many pictures the mental camera took in the next few seconds is beyond computation.

Developed, those pictures were to show a tall figure with manacled wrists, in a white shirt open at the neck and loose black clothing. The shoes may have been felt. I cannot remember them making any sound. At a touch on its shoulder, the feet of the figure were inside the circle of green chalk.

The face of the figure was completely colourless and as completely immobile. Chapman may have been doped. But the immediate impression he made on me was that of a martyr, newly shriven. I can still see those thin lips; and the pale blue eyes looking either to heaven—or only to where that yellow rope drooped through the hole in the green ceiling.

Swiftly one of the men by the door knelt to strap Chapman's knees and ankles. The other—he of the kindly countenance and the white moustache—lifted the noose, and tightened the slip knot round the bare neck.

Who slipped the high black cowl on, I am not sure.

Chapman's figure, now, was that of some hideous black and white buffoon. Immediately, weights clanged as someone pressed an invisible pedal; the yellow rope whipped through the hole, and the buffoon leaped in a long curve to the ceiling.

The drop was vertical. With a wrench and a jerk, the straight rope tautened. Less than six yards from me swayed the black shrouded shape—its feet well clear of the concrete floor.

Two men steadied the swaying shape. For long seconds, it hung rigid, "almost as a carcass, sacking-sheathed in a butcher's shop". Then, horribly, the knees of the carcass bent, the legs opened, and the feet were lifted high.

For the fraction of a second, heavy breathing distracted my attention. I turned. The young reporter at my side gave me one awful glance through his horn-rimmed spectacles. His eyes might have been a drunkard's. His shaking fingers tried to make another note. But the pencil skidded clean off the yellow paper.

When I next looked at the thing which had been Gerald Chapman its elbows were bending and its hands clenching. "He's quite dead", I whispered without taking my eyes away.

But the travesty of life continued for the best part of five minutes; and all that time—though the breathing at my side continued also—my forty-two-year-old self must have watched every movement, coolly, scientifically, objectively, standing to obtain a better view.

The record in the book proves that the mental camera missed nothing—except whether the instrument used by one of the two doctors who finally opened the black jacket and the white shirt was a stethoscope. Even that last touch of tragicomedy—the man who so nearly forgot to pluck off his derby hat as he carried in the wicker coffin—is not missed.

Only when the mechanism lowered the thing which had been Gerald Chapman, when a man uncowled the white face, recovering it with clean linen before others strapped the wicker lid on the coffin, can the personal reaction have begun.

§ 5

Spiro, if he is still alive, may remember the full intensity of that personal reaction. According to plan, he was sitting at one of the fourteen typewriters when we returned to Bradley's room.

I dictated my stuff to him. The others clacked theirs off themselves. Every time I stopped, Spiro damned my eyes—and I damned his. We finished last, with not more than five minutes to spare.

The others reported—subject to the limits of decency—what they had seen. I took a different line.

The death meted out to Chapman, I felt, had been quicker and more merciful than most deaths in battle. I said so—and suggested a little sympathy for his victim and his victim's widow.

Next day every Hearst paper carried the banner headline:

" 'Couldn't Even Pray For Him', Says Gilbert Frankau British Novelist".

Eleven years were to go by before the same press offered me another experience, in a telegram which must have cost their London office the best part of ten shillings and concluded with the promise of a hundred pounds.

But I wouldn't have "covered" the Duke of Windsor's wedding to Wallis Simpson for double.

The psychological conclusions are for you to draw.

CHAPTER FORTY-EIGHT

§ 1

SLEPT four hours in Hartford; and was back in New York by lunchtime next day. My multifarious personal occupations gave me little time for reflection. But the enormous changes wrought since my first visit in 1905 made a profound impression, which I summed up thus.

"Time has utterly destroyed the Fifth Avenue of the few daintily clad women strolling for their pleasure of a morning, and the fine harness horses. Almost the last of its residences, the Vanderbilt, is being razed.

"And the rest of New York is no longer the old Manhattan. I doubt even whether it is any longer American. It is Cosmopolis; a monstrous mechanical Frankenstein of a city, full of hectic rather than of active people, all crazy with the zest for life."

It is to be doubted, nevertheless, whether any single inhabitant of Cosmopolis can have been as hectic or as crazy with the zest for life as myself.

Reports of my anti-communist speeches alone would fill an entire volume. The headline, "Frankau Heckled By Jeering Reds", which followed a meeting at the down-town Civic Club is typical.

"He'd be better with his mother", said a Brooklyn newstand man to a lady friend of mine as he scanned that headline.

"But his mother's dead", protested the lady.

"Sure. And so'll he be if he don't get out of town."

Anonymous letters, about this time, were many; but taken no more seriously than the single threat.

Meanwhile, as happens with all fanatics, my sense of humour was again deserting me: and only revived on one occasion when the Dutch Treat Club invited me to speak on the strict understanding that I should eschew politics.

Nobody could have summed up the value of his work to the American public better than Britain's most voluble author when he said:

"So popular are my short stories in this market that when I offered to pay the *Saturday Evening Post* its maximum advertising rates, which I believe to be in the neighbourhood of seven thousand dollars a page, to publish one that would have run to at

least ten pages, the editor refused on the ground that he could no
afford to jeopardise his circulation for the sake of a little mor
revenue".

Much truth was symbolised by the fable; but a fool in his foll
imagined himself to be at last conquering that country which ha
always been—financially speaking—his promised land.

There were hints, in a new York office, of contracts waitin;
when I reached Hollywood. So far Harpers seemed to approve m
efforts. My expenses, in the neighbourhood of six hundred dollar
weekly, included six dollars ("approximately twenty-seve
shillings") for two portions of baby lamb at the Old Colon
Restaurant.

This item is on the record. Not on the record is a certain con
versation which took place over a half-bottle of vintage cham
pagne in the privacy of my suite at the Plaza.

Charles Higham, who enjoyed the "freedom of the port", ha
several such bottles when he arrived at the Ritz. Generously—
how generously only those who experienced prohibition wil
realise—he presented me with some of his stock.

"You were always a great hand at kidding yourself, Gilbert"
declared the bright-eyed young woman who shared that Clicquot
"But it's no use trying to kid me that your marriage is happy
I know you too well."

The tattered banners of chivalry, however, still flew.

§ 2

Time has modified a few of the political beliefs I voiced in th
United States of 1926.

But one of them—my certainty that there will never b
permanent peace on this planet unless the English-speakin
races join hands to enforce it—still holds. Whether this piou
hope will ever fructuate seems a different kettle of fish. No
least of present-day hindrances is our still-outstanding wa
debt.

Other difficulties were pointed out to me, at a time when w
were still making regular payments, by that well-known banke
and philanthropist, Otto Kahn.

He gave me lunch, "after we had walked the deep canyon c
Wall Street, with red brick Trinity Church tiny at the end of it'
in a private room at the Bankers' Club; and made me promise hir
anonymity before he would state his views.

His shade, something tells me, would wish the seal of secrec broken. Living, he shared my fervent belief in Anglo-American co-operation; and, very curiously in the light of recent tendencies in Italy, my delusions about fascism.

His interpretation of boom-time prohibition-time America still contains much truth.

"Never forget", he told me, "that the men of this continent have had to make a civilisation within a hundred and fifty years. They've had no time to spare for politics, for culture, for contemplative thought. They've been too busy—they're still too busy—pioneering."

It was among the women—he maintained—that one must mainly seek the lovers of good books and good pictures and good music.

"They're always grasping after knowledge", he said. "And after happiness. That's why it's so easy for anybody to preach a new religion or inculcate some new theory of life."

And he concluded, "Generally speaking, we have no traditions. In one way that's a loss. But in more ways it's a gain, because we don't sit on the man with new ideas. The British Empire has succeeded in spite of geography. The United States are succeeding because of it. Big men made your country. Our country makes men and women big".

Otto Kahn loved both countries. To pretend that the man who lunched with him on that blue day of a long-ago springtime learned to love America during the weeks which followed would be as hypocritical as the description of himself which ends the New York section of my travel book.

The "truth to tell, very homesick Londoner" was certainly not homesick for London. In the only words of French understood wherever English is spoken: Cherchez la femme!

§ 3

Looking back on a six-thousand-mile itinerary which covered Boston, Washington, Philadelphia, Chicago, Detroit, Kansas City, Denver, Salt Lake City, San Francisco, Los Angeles, the Grand Canyon, Cleveland, Cincinnati and Pittsburg between the 16th of that April and the 23rd of June, I am not in the least surprised that I did not learn to love America.

The only thing which surprises me is that I survived.

It is impossible to exaggerate the kindness and the courtesy I encountered everywhere. But American kindness, and American anxiety that the stranger shall see all the sights within her wide

8*

gates, can kill any man who has not yet learned the limitations of his own physique.

Had I contented myself merely with giving interviews, broadcasting, speechifying and visiting every bookseller of importance in every town at which I "stopped over", my task would have been sufficiently burdensome. Add the perpetual gathering of copy for my articles, a passion for physical exercise, a constant round of not-always-too-decorous evening entertainment—and you will begin to realise just how much I really do owe to the assiduity of Robert Alfonso Smith.

He and I spent a whole weekend in Boston, where I appear to have enjoyed a "few moments' peace at the Somerset Club, which is sheer Piccadilly, even down to the bow windows"; and where one George Lewis junior mounted me on the sort of hunter I would have given my eyes for at Whissendine.

The Norfolk Hunt ends its season with the Christmas snowfalls. So we could only hack . . . over stone walls.

That night I rang up Ellery Sedgwick, whose *Atlantic Monthly* had published one or two of my war poems; and he at once asked me to dinner. I have often wondered how many English editors would have behaved in the same way to an American contributor.

Anglophile Sedgwick's prognostications about the future of the Empire are summed up in the phrases, "So much class hatred. So much laziness. The lack of intellect in your parliamentary debates".

But if he was a little gloomy the two young men—one, I fancy, his nephew—to whom he introduced me were the reverse. Thanks to them, I saw Harvard *and* the Porcellian, which is the most exclusive club in the world.

Maturity hopes that the clock there, familiarly known as the Old Bitch, still ticks; and that a second hero has successfully swallowed his way through the "Day's Drink", which begins at dawn with gin and Hunyadi Janos to conclude with port at dusk. Only one had accomplished this feat between 1790, when "The Pork" was founded, and 1926.

Yale's Skull and Bones Club, says the book, is a "similar institution"; but "Yale"—according to my two informants—"is only out for success".

In the Yale spirit rather than the Harvard ("*We* only try to educate a man to be a gentleman", quotes the book) England's most voluble author fared on.

§ 4

My Unsentimental Journey notes, with considerable surprise, that Philadelphia's Broad Street is fourteen miles long, and records a happy twenty-four hours under the hospitable roof of Mr. Charlton Yarnall at Crum Creek farm in the Radnor Hunt country. The Sesqui-Centennial Exhibition was still a-building, but the *Philadelphia Inquirer* already had its new plant. Mr. Sydney Williams, literary editor of that fine newspaper, acquires one of many honourable mentions.

Fifty-five hopes that the Franklin Inn is still the same cheery tavern in which he lunched when he was forty-two.

In Washington, I experienced a return of my old shellshock tempers; cursing the receptionist of the Mayflower Hotel, who made prompt amends for a forgotten reservation by giving me the presidential suite. Already a little jaded, I had my first experience of insomnia. A wiser man would have put the brakes on. I accelerated. I would.

One of the best friends I ever had, F. A. D. Hancock, originally met in Venice on that very morning which was to change the whole course of my life, shepherded me round Washington. The name of Natalie, his widow, was still a household word for children's clothes when I visited America in 1939.

The history of that undertaking is dramatic. Natalie began plying her own needle for bare necessities; and became "head of a great and growing business, all in children's garments of her own designing, in stuffs of her own choosing, sewn for her by hundreds and hundreds of similar gentlewomen up and down this enormous land".

Hancock, who managed that concern until death took him, was an Englishman, too stubborn to take out his naturalisation papers, but with a grand sense of humour. He it was who told me the tale of General Scott's equestrian statue.

Never did sculptor sculpt a more obvious mare than the docile creature bestridden by the effigy of that general, victor of Vera Cruz and commander of the Capital City at the outbreak of the Civil War. Yet never did a Spartan mother demand a dourer promise than Scott's.

"Swear to me, Winfield, my son", she said, with the eighteenth century just passing into the nineteenth, "that never, so long as you live, will you mount any horse but a stallion."

This oath, Winfield Scott took and kept. Not even a gelding ever felt the pressure of his legs.

But the poor sculptor heard this true tale too late—and must needs sacrifice art to accuracy by the addition of pendulous bronze. I make believe-it-or-not Ripley a present of the curiosity, reserving only my paraphrase of Horatius which begins:

"They hang nearby the Capitol,
  Plain for all folk to see".

Needless to say, that parody does not appear in the book.

CHAPTER FORTY-NINE

§ 1

THE contrast between my pigeon-haunted bedroom in the Old Chicago Club and the presidential suite at the Mayflower, Washington, is still vivid. So is the leopard skin coat worn by blonde Fanny Brewer, literary critic of the *Chicago Tribune*, when she showed me the whole of her great city from the roof of that newspaper's building. Memory suggests that I may have conceived a platonic tendresse for the lady in question—and for various others on my hectic way.

But the way was too hectic for much dalliance; and the General Strike turned my thoughts home.

Here, the book loses all disingenuity. It tells how I wired to the embassy in Washington to know if officers on the reserve had been recalled, and of my cable to John Withers, who answered, "Position serious but not desperate. No necessity for immediate return".

That was at Detroit on the 5th of May. By Sunday the 9th I was through with Cleveland, where I prophesied the exact day on which the strike ended, and making my way to the booksellers' convention at St. Louis. There I committed one blazing indiscretion—it was no worse!—for which these mellower years still blush and crave indulgence.

There, too, a scribble in the private diary from which I afterwards wrote the book, notes: "Commercially speaking, I feel the trip's going to be a wash-out. I can only hope I'm doing my bit to improve Anglo-American relationships. The way Baldwin settled the strike has shown them we're not quite down and out yet".

Noted also are the facts: "Who told me American reporters garbled interviews? He's a liar. I've never been reported so accurately"; and that I reached the Hotel Muehlback in Kansas City by Sunday, May 15th.

§ 2

Sinclair Lewis was in Kansas City, "collecting parsons", to use his quoted phraseology, for a new book, *Elmer Gantry*. We had disliked the idea of each other for years—and as good as fell into each other's arms within two minutes of our meeting at the Doubleday Page bookshop.

"Damn it, Gilbert", says the "Red" Lewis of the book, who "seems even taller than he is, derives his nickname from his hair rather than from his politics, and possesses a pair of gray eyes that miss very little"; "damn it, you're a regular fellow after all, even if you are a hardshell tory." And I concluded our subsequent proceedings on neat absinthe towards two o'clock in the morning.

Our host was giving demonstrations of Wild West gunplay by then; and I had to assist a certain cavalry lieutenant downstairs. He insisted on driving me back to the hotel, however; and accomplished the drive successfully at a little over walking pace. Never in my life have I clung so hard to a handbrake. He thought the plugs were not sparking—bless his innocent heart.

Red appeared in my bedroom just as I was falling asleep to tell me why he had left the party. Balzac himself couldn't have ended one of his "droll tales" better. I reminded him of the story he told when we met recently—but, like the parody of Horatius, it can never see print.

Thanks to Sinclair Lewis I met many interesting people, among them a man whose name—if I can judge by the newspapers—is more familiar throughout the States in 1939 than it was in 1926. He is described in my record as a "thin, pale, over-manicured youth, W. E. Browder, head of the Kansas Communist Party", and professes, inter alia:

"I'm an out and out Leninite. We must organise the proletariat and teach them how to shoot all the capitalists, all the bluffers and all the bunk merchants".

My book gives him four pages; Clarence Darrow—whom Red called "the last representative of the Jeffersonian tradition"— rather less.

Thinking over the whole crazy trip in these calmer after-years, I fancy Darrow to have been the most impressive personality I encountered between coast and coast.

Carson himself could not have improved on that question he put to William Jennings Bryan, briefed by the State of Tennessee to prosecute a high-school science teacher because he had taught the Darwinian theory, in the Dayton "Monkey Trial" of 1925.

"Then you believe, Mr. Bryan", suggested Darrow, "that God made Himself in your image?"

Yet Bryan, who died within a few days of the victory, won his case—and as late as 1932 the State of Tennessee was contemplating the erection of a fundamentalist university to celebrate his victory—and globe-trotting Britishers still delude themselves that they understand America, just as globe-trotting Americans still delude themselves that they understand Great Britain.

Thanks also to Sinclair—and to many others—and to a trained sense for cosmopolitan values—I was at least saved from that egregious error, and from the more dangerous generalisations, of which last this is almost the sole example to be found in the book.

Sinclair Lewis: "It's the real honest-to-God simplicity of the average American that defeats you Britishers".

Myself: "You mean your children".

Sinclair: "That's about it. And because we're like that, you never feel really comfortable with us. Even Hughie Walpole doesn't. Though he pretends to—and does it damn well".

Myself: "But if you're children, what are we?"

Sinclair: "The devil! I married an Englishwoman and I lived in London for years. But you're beyond me. I wouldn't risk putting an English character into one of my books for anything. Don't you risk putting an American character into one of yours".

Myself: "We'll see about that".

And I did—sketching him, I still flatter myself—rather well.

§ 3

"There are more sheep in Denver", the book quotes from a notice on one of the trolleys there, "and it's a great place to live".

But for those unacclimatised to mountain air, who travel "sans suite et sans sweetie"—as my forty-two-year-old-self described it to one Peter Hagner Holme of the Cactus Club which I had been asked to address—it's a "hell of a place to sleep in", especially if, being unmusical, you happen to strike a "music convention".

"Thank Gawd 'e can sing", a tinker's wife had roared back,

when I roared from my study window in Berkshire that she should stop her "miserable urchin" from serenading me.

In daytime Denver, brass bands serenaded my forty-two-year-old-self hourly—and string bands by night. A tribute, therefore, is paid to Mr. Bellamy, one of my many friendly booksellers, who took me into the silence of the mountains, and showed me a silver-fox farm, of which there were none in England then.

Harry Kendal, one of the few actors with whom I ever feel at home, was in that town, playing a trifle called *Naughty Cinderella* with Irene Bordoni; and the record tells how we chaffed each other about the commercial fate of a song of mine, for which he wrote the music, in *The Heart of a Child*. The publishers of that song had gone broke.

"*I* never got my royalties from them", grumbles Harry.

"You didn't ask hard enough", say I. "Otherwise you'd have had your fiver too." And I depart for Salt Lake City, otherwise Zion, otherwise Deseret (which means "Busy Bee") beyond the Wasatch Hills.

I was happier in the city of the Mormons than in any other I glimpsed on that crazy journey. And I am still amazed—though no world delusion dies harder—when I find people who believe that modern Mormons practise polygamy. Factually, there is no dourer and no cleanlier creed. Your true Mormon neither smokes, drinks, swears nor prevaricates. Even tea and coffee are taken in the strictest moderation. And ten per cent. of a man's income is given to the Church.

Polygamy was legally abolished in 1896. The penalty for it is excommunication. And if anybody who has seen the lovely maidens there, still imagines that the male citizens of Zion cross half America and the whole Atlantic for the purpose of luring peroxided British barmaids into their harems, he should be locked up in a lunatic asylum without more ado.

That grand woman, Susa Y. Gates, one of Brigham Young's half a hundred children, since dead, was among those who taught me to appreciate the greatest pioneering achievement in American history.

You could put five Englands into the State of Utah—and there is no square yard of that territory which does not owe something to the man who was a mere jest to music-hall comedians in the days of my own youth.

Meanwhile the streets he traced from his covered wagon in 1847 are still the only town thoroughfares in the world broad enough to handle modern motor traffic—and on the main one he allotted land in perpetuity for the churches of every other denomination, including a synagogue.

Such facts, and many more, are to be found both in *My Unsentimental Journey* and in various articles I wrote thirteen years ago.

Recent experience confirms every one.

§ 4

I stayed four days in Salt Lake City.

Clarence C. Neslen, then Mayor, and Doctor Levi Edgar Young, and Clarence Snow (whose father and Orson Pratt were with Brigham Young when he first pointed down to Zion, saying, "This is the place") and Counsellor Anthony W. Ivins, and President Heber Grant wanted me to return and write another book, a dispassionate survey of Mormon history. They promised to put all their archives, which contain shorthand notes of speeches extending back for more than sixty years, at my disposal.

How much that promise, worth more than any bond, tempted me, I can still recall.

I needed rest by then; and even my selfconfidence began to evaporate. Commercially speaking, all my efforts *had* been a wash-out. *Masterson* wasn't selling as a novel should sell in boom-time America. I might kid myself about a lot of things—but not about that.

Twenty-six hours more took me to San Francisco—the book narrates—its bay still bridgeless and no roof cocktail bar to pack the elevators of the Mark Hopkins Hotel.

A boy who had already passed on played a strange part in my visit. Asked to say a few words at the auditorium of Smith Elder's bookshop, I abandon my usual rhetoric and re-tell the published story of *My Friend Batstone*, a heroic American who joined the British army and served in my own brigade.

"The story happens to be true", I conclude. "The chap's real name was Butters. I know he came from California."

More than half my audience had been personally acquainted with Harry Butters, one of whose letters "did more than any other single piece of propaganda to bring America into the 1914–1918 war".

George Douglas, who had taken me up to the platform, reported —in the *San Francisco Bulletin* of June 5th, 1926—that I "sat with staring eyes and a look of utter bewilderment" when I heard this; and his report states the cold truth.

The whole incident still seems spooky. For I had loved Harry Butters better than most men, and helped him more than a little; and there are only two books in the world, so far as I know, which tell the story of the 24th divisional artillery between its firing practice on Salisbury Plain in July 1915 and the fighting on the Somme thirteen months later.

One of these is my own *Peter Jackson*. The other, called *Harry Butters, R.F.A. An American Citizen*, consists mainly of his letters home during that period, edited by Mrs. Denis O'Sullivan, who gave me a copy, which I still cherish, before I left for Hollywood.

§ 5

My forty-two-year-old self was to spend a whole fortnight in Hollywood—and to hate it like hell.

CHAPTER FIFTY

§ 1

THE Hollywood section of *My Unsentimental Journey* still strikes me as a nice piece of journalism. Localities are neatly described. It contains competent thumbnail sketches of various celebrities— including Charlie Chaplin, Elinor Glyn, William Randolph Hearst, Irving Thalberg, Colleen Moore, Virginia Valli and many others.

But you can search those thirty-six pages vainly for one plain word of the autobiographical truth.

A very short-lived love affair is still carefully concealed. I do not even hint at my reactions to the letters I received from Beauvallon, where Aimée had been staying ever since she left England.

Three further truths seem plain—and pertinent—to the mellowed mind.

First: as the supreme Frankau fan, I had never stooped to being a movie fan. Secondly: I still hugged my pet delusion about knowing everybody else's business—the movie business included —better than anybody else ever could. And thirdly: the only thing I wanted from Hollywood was the largest possible emolument for the shortest possible stay.

Memory suggests a hundred-thousand-dollar contract for three subjects (four, if it came to bargaining) as the minimum aspiration of an obstinate man, only a few years this side of shellshock, already pretty well at the end of his nervous tether, not a single line of his *Morning Post* stuff yet fit for publication, and down to the last thousand or so of his savings.

Credit the psychological balance sheet, however, with three items. A chivalry which demanded the making good of a promise: that I would return with enough money to build a lady her villa in the South of France. An independence which could—and did— tell any man to go to the devil rather than fawn on him for praise or money. And a lack of selfpity which never sought to lay my own lack of fortune at anybody else's door.

Meanwhile imagine the debits on the financial side of the balance sheet mounting at the rate of some £20 a day.

§ 2

The old record seems to betray my old self soon realising that the silent galaxy (not yet had the screen spoken) might deem their starhoods more brilliant than my own.

One of the few genuine compliments the book pays is to Colleen Moore.

She and her husband, John McCormick, had dined with me when on a visit to London. Memory suggests that I conceived great expectations from McCormick's connection with First National.

Dining with them at the Cocoanut Grove (the dance-supper room at the Hotel Ambassador) I report that Colleen and "the opulent Pola Negri, glittering with barbaric jewels like the Queen of Sheba", are the only heroines of the silver screen not "mass-produced by the same beauty parlour and the same dressmaker", and I let the overbold pen continue:

"As for the heroes of the silver screen, once they have donned their tuxedos, they are very like other gentlemen in tuxedos . . . only rather less so than more".

Their dinner jackets may or may not have been the reason why I decided to wear tails and a topper on every possible opportunity.

That Robert Alfonso never let me leave the hall of the hotel at any hour or in any attire unless he were personally present to hand me the requisite hat, stick, coat or gloves, was a service as much appreciated as all his others, including the private whisper, "Got your little tin, sir?" to remind me of a certain powder, which a recent discovery called "Dentesive" has now supplanted in my favour. Note carefully, however, that the touch of public showmanship was not a touch of genius—both of us having been brought up to such ways.

Otherwise you will not fully relish the dénouement of my Hollywood adventure (over which the book skates very tactfully) headed in my unpublished notes: "Words of wisdom from a goddess in a machine".

My extravagances stopped at hiring my own machine, as the America of 1926 called a car. But plenty of free transport seems to have been available—and the copyhunter did not miss much. Down town and up, I went everywhere a reporter should.

The Hollywood Athletic Club forgot to send me a membership card; but the Los Angeles University Club and the Californian were less remiss.

The book further records—with all the gusto of the disgruntled —how both institutions warn me not to introduce anyone even remotely connected with pictures; and how every down-town reporter begins his interview with the admonishment, "No movie stuff, Captain. They're not news any more with us", and how a long-eclipsed star named Clara Bow manages to crash her way into those carefully guarded news columns because her suitor, not content with having tried to "rush her off her feet" before they were "properly acquainted", attempts suicide into the bargain.

Meanwhile the more studios I visited, the angrier I grew. My idea of an author's importance to a picture, you see, paralleled that of my young colleague, referred to in a previous chapter. If I couldn't be the cat's whiskers, I just wouldn't play.

One magnate, I appear to have told, "You people can't see you're killing your own business by putting the cart before the horse" (the horse, needless to say, being such celebrated authors as myself); and to another, Cecil B. de Mille, I read a long homily about his recent production, *The Volga Boatman*.

The book pictures him receiving my statement that I considered the masterpiece "an even worse piece of historical perversion and a better piece of pro-revolutionary propaganda, than most", in the right spirit. His manners were certainly better than mine.

Poor Irving Thalberg's manners were always exquisite; but his kindly suggestion that I should submit a few ideas aroused the very worst.

No hint of our business discussion is to be found in the public record. I believe I cut it short with the terse statement that I had not come to Hollywood to chase shadows, and that he knew where to find me if he wanted me.

Whereafter, commercially speaking, I sulked.

§ 3

The public record shows that I did not sulk in my tent, except of a morning, when—reverting to my old habits—I worked away at my stuff for the *Post*. It contains the usual report of speeches made, of places observed, of a prize fight attended, of violent tennis lessons from one Golderer, the hotel professional, and a meeting with Elinor Glyn.

Years later a few incautious words at a London dinner were to give the lady in question much offence. The last time we met, however, she told me that I was forgiven "because I was the father of Pamela".

Nobody—Pamela or no Pamela—could have been kinder or more informative than the lady in question when I claimed her acquaintance in the Cocoanut Grove.

"Do join us", she is reported as saying. "This is my dancing partner. He takes pity on me once a week. Not so bad for a grandmother, am I?"

And the record continues:

"She has outlived time—this queer Ninon de l'Enclos of a woman with the slim hands and the almost youthful body and the magnetic eyes (violet, I think they are) that stare at you from under her still-red hair".

Thanks to her I attended one of Marion Davies' parties, where "our hostess, blonde, blue-eyed and a trifle affairée, with one of those tiny stutters which are so fascinating in a woman, received me as a hostess should".

I seemed so dead beat by then that Robert Alfonso scorned the blandishments of a particularly grim institution known as the "Breakfast Club" on his own initiative, telling me subsequently, "You're not up to making any more speeches, sir. Especially at half-past eight in the morning". This was the only invitation to oratory refused between coast and coast.

Meanwhile he had booked our reservations, and we were due to leave by the Santa Fé within forty-eight hours.

§ 4

Re-reading my account of Marion Davies' long-ago party, the more experienced writer finds little to condemn. My slightly self-conscious journalese is beautifully convincing—and quite sufficiently accurate.

Here I meet Tom Mix, "rugged and a trifle shy with a most

attractive Mrs. Tom". There I observe Rudolph Valentino, and think—rightly, since death's seal was already on him—that he is 'looking ill".

"The most expressive eyes ever set in a human countenance" proclaim "a smallish youthful man, slightly negligé of smoking jacket, slightly sallow of cheek, slightly curly of Oriental hair and slightly thick of clean-shaven lip" to be "none other than Charlie Chaplin".

Mindful of my duty to my newspaper, I manage a lightning interview with Chaplin before we "file more than a hundred and fifty strong down the stairs and across the packed Cocoanut Grove to where, screened from the public eye, we found some two dozen tables and a special orchestra".

I sit between Louise Fazenda and Agnes Ayres. I observe William Randolph Hearst, and relate the old chestnut which makes him say, "No money in the moving picture business? You're wrong about that, sir. There are at least two million dollars of mine".

Then I chronicle the entrance of Gertrude Lawrence, and of a Beatrice Lillie not yet celebrated for her rebuke to the spouse of a Chicago meat-packing king.

This lady, chafing for her favourite hairdresser, remarked in a loud voice on being told that he was busy with Miss Lillie, "How much longer have I got to be kept waiting for that adjectival actress?"

"Please give Lady Peel's compliments to the pork butcher's wife", called out Beatrice through the screening curtains, "and say that she won't be very long."

But that good story still slumbered in the womb of time. My own now records the arrival of Irene Bordoni "looking her very Frenchiest", and "a tiny little woman with eyes almost as expressive as Chaplin's own".

The little woman's name is Raquel Meller. Losing no opportunity to flaunt my own erudition, I duly report that our conversation was in Spanish, and that she told me she was "bored to death".

Shortly after which the less erudite Charlie Chaplin "seized a fiddle from one of the musicians, pretended to be a fiddler, pretended to be Charlot", and finally—Raquel Meller's boredom still unrelieved—"began to dance for us, and suddenly flung up two hands, and began to quiver with his hands, and to quiver with all his body, and so sank, all in a heap of quivering Pavlova feathers, to the floor".

"Only then it was", reads on the journalese, "that miming genius recognised miming genius, and Raquel Meller's boredom fell from her as a shawl from white shoulders, and she applauded with the rest of us, crying, 'The death of the swan. See you? The veritable Death of the Swan' ".

And the selfconscious writer adds, "But I, once I had seen this thing, said good night and went my way rejoicing; because it seemed to make all my days in Hollywood worth while".

§ 5

No blacker lie, no more deliberate perversion of the auto-biographical verities than the above sentence ever deflowered a virgin page with ink. Every houri in Hollywood could have sunk quivering at my feet on that evening—and I should still have loathed the place.

It had kept its dollars. All I had kept was my panache. That this had been observed from high Olympus, I did not know till the following afternoon.

CHAPTER FIFTY-ONE

§ 1

OLYMPUS, on that long-ago occasion, must be imagined as a suite at the Hotel Ambassador not unadjacent to my own. The goddess who dwelt there—memory insists—was English. We had met once, maybe twice, altogether casually. She summoned me from making my notes about the Marion Davies party to the phone.

"I want to see you privately", she said. "Will you be in at teatime?"

Mortal man could but obey the command of heaven—and tell mortal valet to make himself scarce from four o'clock onwards. Mortal man—it must be admitted—was a little puzzled, and still more so when, at the time appointed, the phone rang again.

"I think I'd better not have tea with you", said the goddess that time; and she indicated the whereabouts of her machine, which she had parked out of sight of the main entrance.

"Give me five minutes", she further commanded. "Don't say anything. Just get in."

The engine of the saloon was already running when I joined her. I noticed that she was occupying the passenger seat.

"Can you drive?" she asked.

"Yes."

"Then drive anywhere you like. And listen. I've got a lot to say to you. Someone told me you intended leaving to-morrow. You'll be mad if you do."

An American goddess—I knew by then—would have used the word "crazy" to express her meaning. I answered in our own language as I let in gear:

"I'd be madder if I stayed. My bill this week is over eight hundred dollars. Thalberg doesn't want my film rights. McCormick doesn't. De Mille won't look at 'em. I've talked to the Fox people——"

"Not too pleasantly, I gather", smiled my heavenly companion. "And not for very long. You've played your cards beautifully so far."

"I beg your pardon."

She repeated her last sentence. Some street or other slid by.

"All you have to do now", she went on, "is to move out of your suite and take one of the hotel cottages. You see, you've got 'em all guessing."

"Got who guessing?"

"The women, of course. They can't imagine what you're up to. They've never seen anyone like you. They still can't believe you're quite real—with your valet waiting in the hall to hand you your hat and coat, and open the door every time you take a taxi."

She smiled again; and memory suggests that she may have laid a largeish hand—she was a largeish size in goddesses—on my knee. Then she revealed the name under which she had once glittered in the Hollywood firmament; and my surprised foot trod on the two-wheel brakes. She said gently, "Don't stop".

"I don't call myself that any more", she went on. "There are—reasons. But I wasn't a leading woman all those years without getting to know this place. So please do as I tell you. Cancel your reservations, take that cottage, and stay."

I remember objecting that I disliked the place and that I couldn't afford to stay. She brushed both objections aside.

"You can't afford to go", she said. "There's a fortune waiting for you."

"A fortune?"

"Twenty thousand pounds, anyway. And you can earn it in less than six months."

"How?"

"Eventually, by selling stories."

"But the men here don't want my stories."

"The men don't buy stories for themselves. They buy them mainly, for their leading women. And if one of those women happens to take a fancy to you——"

She broke off. I slowed the machine, and stared at her.

"There should be more than one", she continued. "Go on playing your cards properly. Or improperly. And the contracts will follow."

"You can't mean——"

"But that's exactly what I do mean." For the first time, she laughed aloud. "Don't pretend you're a simpleton."

Maybe I was. Maybe I still am. The goddess, however, continued to plead with me, and to insist that she knew herself right.

"Stay six months", she pleaded. "You can clean up in that time."

I believe I mentioned that I had a wife, and that she might wish to join me. I believe this objection also was brushed aside with a quiet, "She mustn't. It would spoil everything". I believe I promised to consider the advice of the goddess.

I know I reparked her machine near the hotel; and that her heavenly hand rested, just for a moment, in my own before she returned unseen to Olympus. I know also—being no simpleton when confronted with tangible evidence—that her own motives were purely altruistic; and that I have never set eyes on her from that day to this.

But you must decide for yourself whether she spoke the truth; and whether a mysterious phone call about six o'clock that night (from a producer who must remain nameless, asking me how much longer I intended to stay) represented the earthly confirmation of the divine foresight.

For my forty-two-year-old self never interviewed that producer. By sunset Robert Alfonso and I were beyond the orange groves of San Bernadino.

§ 2

It appears from my book that the night of June 14th, 1926, was warm and starry; that "the orange groves give way to primeval desert, where only the yucca flowers—white spikes of bell-blossom, pricking high above dark clumps of leaves".

The published record quotes Kipling's "Asleep beneath the
uccas, the city takes its ease"; the private diary Byron's:

> "The prisoned eagle will not pair, nor I
> Serve a Sultana's sensual phantasy".

But the truth lies even deeper—and even the diary keeps it hid.
Next day I breakfasted with "Manager Patrosso", from whom
heard less than two years ago, at his El Tovar Hotel on the
Grand Canyon of the Arizona, and peered out across the Painted
Desert. Then I railroaded on, all Tuesday night and all Wednes-
day, by the old trail to Las Vegas, and away from Las Vegas,
back through Kansas City and St. Louis of the unfortunate
memory, to Cincinnati.

I stopped over in Cincinnati, where the hotel bootlegger was
clept "Muck" (another present for Ripley); and again in
Pittsburgh.

There I gave my last newspaper interviews, and broadcast my
final message, from station KDKA, and visited my ultimate
works, the Edgar Thompson steel mill.

Thence—no single item of the whole crazy coast-to-coast
programme omitted—I arrived in New York, whacked to the
wide and wholly conscious of failure. A hundred speeches,
innumerable visits, a thousand columns of publicity, and un-
limited personal expenses had sold exactly eighteen thousand
copies of the two-dollar novel I had set out to boom.

Harpers proved as kind as the circumstances allowed. That
they could only sell three thousand copies of my next novel, and
that they were presently to crave release from their contract,
on the grounds that their enthusiasm had become less fiery than
of yore, may or may not have been attributable to the powerful
impact of my forty-two-year-old personality on those audiences I
so scrupulously informed:

"You behold before you a rare phenomenon. The only British
author who has ever bought his own ticket to the United States".

Certain is that *My Unsentimental Journey* has never yet found
an American publisher, although no word in it is unkind, and
few are even critical. It further contains a positive mine of
information, set down, as the preface states, "half in fun and half
in seriousness"—and is utterly reticent about the true happenings
of that last week in summertime New York.

§ 3

I don't think I kidded myself much—my last night in summer time New York. Or next day, when Robert Alfonso and I shook hands as friends should—and a situation already thirteen years gone in time duplicated itself on the old *Mauretania*.

The commercial fiasco didn't matter a damn to me. Nothing seemed to matter—because the second situation was even more hopeless than the first had been—except that unpalatable knowledge of re-arisen love.

But because the knowledge was so unpalatable chivalry refused to admit its truth.

I had ordered and drunk a whole bottle of champagne in my tiny cabin on E deck—the only occasion I have ever done such a thing—before the Statue of Liberty sank behind us. And I paid for three cases of the same vintage ere we docked.

Prohibition, forcing a wine drinker to content himself with ginger ale and whiskey, may have had a little to do with this unusual insobriety. So may the 4th of July celebrations. So may Captain Sir Harry Rostron's well-deserved knighthood, of which we received wireless news on the 5th, and which we also celebrated. Nor can my hatred of failure be held altogether blameless. The real blame for that last puppy riot across the Atlantic, however, lay deeper.

"It's no good, Gilbert dear", memory kept on repeating. "We've been through all this before. It wouldn't work, and we both know it. You've just got to go back and do your best".

§ 4

I was to do my best for nearly four more years.

Part Five

APPROACH TO SANITY

CHAPTER FIFTY-TWO

§ 1

BACK in London after that last puppy riot, I begged Pollock of the *Morning Post* for a few weeks' grace, and took train to Beauvallon. There, working myself and my unfortunate secretary, Nancy James, nearly to death through a South of France heat wave, I finished off my travel articles. Almost simultaneously I came to a mad decision of which I still fail to understand the predominant urge.

Conceivable influences were sheer physical and mental fatigue, mere disgruntlement, the prospect of reducing my inordinate expenses, the hope of saving a matrimonial position already felt to be in jeopardy, the peculiar fascination of a locality far from the fashionable Riviera, and the Hancocks who, arriving towards the end of August, volunteered to lend me several thousand dollars on mortgage if I made up my mind to build a villa.

Stark fact is that, having decided to accept this kindly offer, I further decided to spend "the evening of my days" in exile at the ripe age of forty-two.

The quoted phrase, which I distinctly remember myself using, was spoken in all seriousness. Before the Hancocks left I had called in an optimistic architect, whom we will call Monsieur Chose.

Monsieur Chose soon produced a set of plans, an estimate, and a local builder. Guilelessly signing the contract, I imagined that my new house would be ready for occupation before the mimosa bloomed.

§ 2

The indefatigable Cork, who paid me a visit while these negotiations were in progress—and nearly lost his life, to say nothing of Nancy James's, when the hotel car skidded on the coast road—had initiated another good serial deal with Percy (now Sir Percy) Everett of the Newnes-Pearson group.

Dashing home, I clinched this; and returned, sans Nancy, who disapproved of exile, to a small local villa I had rented for the winter from one of the Perrins, famous for their gloves. "The Yellow Peril", as a new 9 h.p. Renault camionette came to be known from Marseilles to Mentone, was already standing in the Perrin garage. Some eight square metres of masonry erected by the local builder before he realised that payments in advance were foreign to one foreigner's nature, were still standing on my acre of estate.

The house in Lancaster Gate Terrace, though on the market, had not yet found a tenant. Accordingly, I might still have altered my decision. That I would have done so in certain circumstances seems proved by the recollection of a talk I had with the first Lord Melchett, who came to spend Christmas at the Golf Hotel with his wife.

He was a man whom I admired greatly, alike for his quick intellect, his personal kindnesses, and a certain quality which I can only describe as elephantine—a combination of strength and wisdom I have never since encountered. Proof of this had been given some year previously over an article of mine, containing a more than usually virulent attack on our trade unions and their leaders.

As Melchett was trying to bring about better relations between the unions and the employers' federations, my editor thought it would be only fair to let him see a proof of the article before it appeared.

One of his coadjutors, present when I interviewed him, was completely horrified.

"This is bound to do a great deal of harm", he protested.

"On the contrary", Melchett had said on that occasion. "The views which Gilbert has voiced here are held by a great many people. It is just as well that the trade union leaders should read them."

On this occasion at Beauvallon, he asked me point blank why I had decided to exile myself—and I opened my whole heart to him.

"No paper in England", I said, "will let me write what I really feel."

He then discussed, with another of his coadjutors, the question of buying me a paper.

"How about *The Spectator*?" I can hear him saying. "We might get hold of that fairly cheaply."

But nothing further transpired except a very pleasant visit to Cannes—returning from which I found no more metres of masonry.

My local builder had gone placidly broke.

§ 3

Somewhere about this time, my old friend Lady Drogheda came cruising over the Esterels with the lady I had met thirteen years before at King's House in Jamaica, "Mouse" Dennistoun, now interested in architecture.

We had the cheeriest of lunches at a little restaurant in Sainte Maxime called the Hermitage. I told Mrs. Dennistoun that I was fed up with Monsieur Chose who had not yet found me another builder. But she decided that to send workmen from Cannes into the fastnesses of Beauvallon would be beyond her powers.

My next architect, whom we will call Monsieur Autrechose, was not so diffident. He also produced plans, and an estimate, but still no builder. By then 1926 was well into 1927; and my new novel under way. Memory recalls the peculiar horror of a tartan-esque wallpaper in the bedroom I used for my study at the Villa Perrin, and frightful storms, and oil lamps of an evening, and Walter Creighton, the originator of the Tattoos at Aldershot, who came to stay.

Walter may recall an accident with his Amilcar, and how—forgetting to appear before the magistrate—he was only just saved from incarceration at my especial pleading. Meanwhile—more determined than ever not to be defeated by mere archi-tects—I had encountered, chancely at the local post office, a young French "engineer", named Robert Plumier, to whom I took an instant fancy. This was one of the best hunches I ever had in my life.

Plumier lived in Sainte Maxime, but was employed in the inland bauxite mines near Brignolles. I told him my difficulties.

"Could you supervise the building of a house in your spare time?" I asked.

"If I had the plans, mon capitaine."

"We'll use Chose's plans", said I. "Autrechose can go to hell."

Within ten days we had engaged our équipe, under a grand foreman named Castelvetri; bought our first lot of material, and were tearing down the old masonry to start afresh.

Never shall I forget Plumier's face and Castelvetri's when I issued my original instructions:

"Understand one thing, both of you. I don't want any economies."

"No economies?"

"Not one. Labour or materials, everything in this house we're going to build has got to be the very best that money can buy.'

You have to know France, and Frenchmen—you should have known what the Midi was like in the building boom, then beginning—to realise that this instruction was not nearly so foolish as it looks on paper.

For proof of wisdom, I adduce the subsequent happening at the Villa Perrin, from which I moved to another before my own walls were manhigh from the ground.

This move, enforced by the collapse of the main drain piping entailed the breaking of an agreement, but no damages—that invaluable official of the French law courts a "huissier" (usher' providing me with a signed paper "constatant" (witnessing) that a most nauseous odour proceeded from my "septic tank".

False economy number one having been duly rectified, another tenant occupied the Villa Perrin, and proceeded to smoke an after-dinner cigar on the very same balcony where I had been wont to smoke mine.

False economy number two then became apparent with a crash The cement pillars supporting the balcony buckled, plunging the smoker to his death.

It was rumoured in Sainte Maxime that the resultant action cost the unfortunate Perrin more than the villa and the land put together.

My own job cost more than a million francs. (Monsieur Chose had originally budgeted for two hundred thousand.)

But it should be standing long after I am dust.

CHAPTER FIFTY-THREE

§ I

THE French phrase "folie de pierre" is untranslatable; and the full tale of the building of "Mas Natalie", as my gratitude for the original loan decided to call it, too long to tell here.

Suffices that my mornings were devoted, as usual, to earning money; and my afternoons to supervising Plumier's spending of it. Within three months we celebrated the placing of the first roof beam with the customary midday feast to our workpeople.

They were a polyglot crowd. I made my little speech in three languages. Castelvetri, a great ox of a man with red hair, drank three litres of the local white wine, an identical quantity of the local red wine, and at least six glasses of the local brandy, which burns like methylated spirit and tastes rather like sulphuric acid, before he replied.

To realise him still completely sober was rather shattering—but not so shattering as the telegram received a while later from Cork.

"First half of serial for *Home Notes* received", wired Cork. 'Everett desperately worried. Stop. Fears must cancel agreement unless you can assure him of Margery's moral behaviour during rest of book."

Margery being my heroine, and ruin staring me in the face without Everett's money, I wired back the requisite guarantee. Whereafter both creations waxed apace—the creation in stone only slightly handicapped by the discovery that Monsieur Chose had forgotten that the kitchen would need a chimney and that the front door—owing to the slope of the ground—would only be approachable by a motorcar which could climb up and down steps.

But Castelvetri, whose craftsmanship also copied a sixteenth-century stone staircase in masonry by eye alone, solved our first difficulty; and the acquirement of more land did away with the second.

By August 1927, the furniture from Lancaster Gate Terrace—let at last, though without a penny of premium—had left England. The size of the new mansion made further purchases necessary. In Cannes were the best furniture shops—and my friend, W. J. Locke.

§ 2

Posterity can put its own value on the literary achievements of the late W. J. Locke. But to those of us whom he honoured with his friendship, there will remain—so long as we live—the memory of a great gentleman, honourable in all he did, thought or said.

Rising sixty-five that summer, Will Locke was at the very apex of his vogue as a storyteller. Tall, clean-shaven, slightly emaciated, he looked at once the scholar and the dandy. A weak chest—and not, as the very few who did not appreciate him would have it, the wish to escape income tax—having forced him to leave England, he kept open house at the Villa des Arcades.

One had only to telephone to his wife, also called Aimée; to Sheila, his beautiful adopted daughter, something of whose history you will find in his book *Stella Maris*, and who has since died untimely, or to his secretary, Mary Chaldecott, who copied all my manuscripts for me during this period—and one's room would be ready next day.

Will's working hours were as peculiar, and as particularised, as my own. He used the pen exclusively—retiring to his study at 10.30 p.m. precisely, and going up to bed some four hours later. This habit—he once told me—had become ingrained during the ten years (1897–1907) he was secretary to the Royal Institute of British Architects, and only wrote as a side line.

Not until the success of *The Morals of Marcus* and *The Beloved Vagabond* had assured him some financial competency would he risk abandoning that safe salaried job.

Will's working hours gave him ample leisure to enjoy the days and the early evenings—mainly devoted to hospitality. He would appear at about eleven, always in spotless white flannels and the most expensive silk shirts. Midday would bring friends for a cocktail; and as many as a dozen would stay for lunch. Towards three Will would take his siesta. Other friends inevitably appeared between five and seven. Occasionally he dined at a restaurant, more often in company at home. Holidays, he spent either in London, or at some fashionable foreign watering place.

What this life cost W. J. Locke, Mary Chaldecott, who kept all his accounts and now has her own secretarial office in London, may know. Solly Joel and I once guessed it at a minimum of £15,000 a year.

The millionaire South African, I seem to remember, shook his head. But Will Locke paid his lavish way while the life was in him, and loved every minute of it. His chef, his butler, his chauffeur, his Aimée's jewels and his Sheila's clothes were all—as I see them—his forms of self-expression. He lived like a great gentleman of the old school because he was a great gentleman of the old school.

And how he laughed when I told him how I had led Solly away from that famous fight in which Carpentier floored Beckett with one knock-out blow while some of us were still looking at our programmes.

"I knew it", wailed poor Solly on that occasion. "I knew it. And I could have got four to one in hundreds. What a fool! What a fool!"

Yet at heart he, too, comes back to the recollection as a very simple man, one of whose hobbies was cooking, at which he excelled. Nor did he lack a sense of humour, as typified by this tale of him and Warwick Brookes, once M.P. for Tower Hamlets, but more famous as a financial filibuster.

The scene of that story was the cabin of Solly's yacht, then at anchor off Deauville. The bearded millionaire had just begun displaying a portion of his famous jewel collection to some half a dozen friends.

There was something of the poet in Brookes—he would often write verses on the back of the menu when we supped together.

"I say, you chaps", he cried suddenly. "There's *the* most marvellous sunset. You must just look at it. You, too, Solly."

"With you about?" snapped Solly. "And all these stones on the table! What do you take me for, Warwick? A complete mug?"

Whether I was a complete mug to establish myself in a remote corner of the Department of the Var at an eventual cost of some eleven thousand pounds sterling is left to the reader's judgment. The thought certainly crossed my own mind as I lay sleepless on that first night under my very own roof, listening to the drip-drip-drip from the cistern—one of the most irritating noises in the world.

§ 3

Castelvetri cured that noise next day, by the very simple expedient of attaching a piece of rag to the inlet pipe. This is a tip worth knowing.

Worth knowing, too, were our five painters, originally discovered by the dignified lady of the house doing a fine job of work on another new villa, just behind Sainte Maxime.

"I wonder who's going to live *there*", she kept asking. But Monsieur Buongiovanni, decorator from Monte Carlo, was a modest youth who kept his own counsel. Enlightenment as to the purpose of that new villa came from the Mayor.

"Our little corner so flowery and delicious", wrote the Mayor of Sainte Maxime to its more prominent residents, "may, one feels, be said to have launched itself. With the opening of the jolly little summer casino, we have lacked but a single amenity. Even this lack is now to be filled. Madame Rosa, of Paris, with several of her delightful lady colleagues, will be in residence at her Villa Cythère as from Thursday next. I have the pleasurable honour of inviting you to attend the formal opening of her establishment and to drink a cup of wine to the success of the enterprise."

Alas! Tickets for London were already taken; and I had to refuse.

CHAPTER FIFTY-FOUR

§ 1

WHEN Aimée and I arrived at the newly opened May Fair Hotel in Berkeley Street towards the end of 1927, I had not seen London—except for a brief ten days during the previous autumn—in eighteen long months. A few weeks, however, were to be the limit of the stay.

Memory recalls little of the time before Christmas, except various meetings with a very charming mother, son and daughter, Edith, Mark and Susan Harris, who had spent two summer holidays at the Golf Hotel; and interviews with Withers, rather worried at my decision to domicile myself abroad ("People will say you've only done it to avoid income tax", he protested, "and that may damage you as a political journalist"); with McWhirter, for whose *Sunday Pictorial* I was still writing regular articles; with Gundry; with Cork; and with the staff at Hutchinsons who were just about to publish the book which had worried Everett under the title, *So Much Good*.

That novel came out in January. Shortly afterwards Charlie Higham took my breath away with the most startling idea.

"Have you ever heard of William Harrison?" he asked; and when I admitted ignorance, he went on:

"Harrison started life as a solicitor. Now he's chairman of the Inveresk Paper Company and a lot more—Carrongrove among them. He's just acquired control of the Great Eight from Sir John Ellerman".

The Great Eight, I of course knew, included the *Tatler*, the *Bystander*, the *Sketch*, the *Illustrated London News*, and four similar weeklies, all sold at a shilling.

"Harrison has asked my advice about the *Graphic* and *Eve*", explained Charles, lighting yet another of the hundred fat Teofani King's Turkish he smoked every day of his life. "They're both losing money, and he wants to appoint new editors. I've suggested Ethel Mannin for *Eve* and you for the *Graphic*. With salary and expenses, it ought to be a ten-thousand-a-year job."

Not taking Charles very seriously, I suggested that a shilling weekly could never have a big circulation.

"Would he consider bringing it down to sixpence?" I asked.

"He might. Anyway, he wants to see you."

Two days later Charles brought Harrison up to my suite at the May Fair; and left us alone there for lunch.

§ 2

Riper experience has realised that any partnership—I use the word of set purpose—between myself and William Harrison must have been dangerous, if only because we possessed so many of the same characteristics.

We were equally ambitious, equally (and inordinately) imaginative, equally selfconfident, equally obstinate—and equally blind to the prime fact that we were both amateurs in the Street of Misadventure, where even professionals sometimes fail.

Accordingly we had taken to each other before we were through with our oysters; and began talking politics with our steaks.

We were both putting our best goods in the window by then. Fascism—I seem to remember—was merely hinted at, though the mutual Mussolini-complex would have been obvious to an outsider. About the need for protection of industry, neither of us—and how rightly!—cherished the slightest doubt.

Harrison's face is not easy to describe. It comes back clean-shaven, with a prominent nose, a wide thin-lipped mouth, and brown hair, kept a little too long for my military taste. The colour of the eyes has been curiously forgotten. Imagination paints them a lightish blue. His height must be a little less than my own five-foot nine. His speech betrayed the Yorkshireman. As such, he got down to brass tacks the moment the floor waiter had finished serving.

I did not realise that the *Graphic* was being edited by a man I knew and one with a fine war record in the Flying Corps—Alan Bott, now head of the Book Society and married to Josephine, daughter of the famous R. D. Blumenfeld. Even if I had known this, I doubt whether it would have made any difference.

William Harrison—though I took good care not to tell him so—seemed to be handing me all my dreams on a plate. He even agreed, before he scurried off to his next appointment, that the *Graphic* should be reduced to sixpence.

And, although memory suggests that he took just a little bringing up to the scratch, we were soon closeted with John Withers—slightly taken aback when W. H. broke the age-old ordinance of his sanctum by smoking cigarettes.

The secrecy of the subsequent proceedings, throughout which Harrison acted as his own lawyer, excited Withers' attention. But the contract appointing me editor of the *Graphic* for a term of years from May 1st, 1928, at the salary and expenses originally suggested by Charles, and guaranteeing my appointment as director to the two companies which controlled the Great Eight, came back duly sealed by the Inveresk Paper Company over its chairman's signature and that of his confidential secretary, also a director, by name Pyke.

During the continuance of this agreement Inveresk were to hold my life covered by insurance for £10,000. After a repetition of the old 1912 wrangle about a certain physical condition, I took out an endowment policy for this amount off my own bat. Inveresk, I imagined, would pay their share.

At long last, I could forget money, and concentrate on what seemed—even to Withers—"a lifetime job".

§ 3

It was already March 1928. A wiser man would have stayed on in England, the beat of whose pulses had changed considerably since the settlement of the General Strike. I returned, taking my wife and two friends with me, to Mas Natalie, imagining the quiet of my study the best place in which to work out my plans for remodelling the paper.

About this time Monsieur Autrechose sought satisfaction in the law courts at Draguignan, where I had seen some wonderful criminal trials. Civil actions in France are rarely attended by witnesses; and I did not go.

Autrechose's lawyer claimed at the action that I owed him some £500 in fees on the house he had not built, and that he was too good a citizen, having produced seven children for France, to be thus wronged by a foreigner.

My own Maître Mairin declared that the foreigner in question had been very welcome when he arrived in France with his fat cannons during the Great War and should be no less welcome now that he had re-arrived with his fat fortune.

Must the gallant captain of English artillery pay these demands merely because the celebrated architect had not practised birth control? Perish the unjust thought.

Mister the President, having heard out both advocates, remitted the case to an expert, who awarded Autrechose £100 for his unused plans. The costs of the entire action were less than £50. This was not the only case Mairin fought for me. In my experience French civil justice is every bit as fair as—and eighty per cent. cheaper than—our own.

Meanwhile my own plans for the *Graphic* had taken the shape of a dummy, and Harrison wired me to meet him at Marseilles, through which he would be passing to visit some esparto grass plantations in North Africa.

I buzzed over in the Yellow Peril, taking my dummy with me. Said Harrison, snatching a hasty déjeuner, "This looks all right. In fact, it looks so good that we won't worry about the *Graphic*. We'll start a brand new paper".

There was all the difference in the world between founding a new periodical and transforming one that had been established for more than fifty years. A wiser man than myself would have seen a red light then. I didn't. Neither did I take any notice of a confidence imparted by Mrs. Harrison just before they went on board.

"My husband", said that charming woman, "hasn't altered since he was a boy. He always liked playing with new toys."

Harrison and his wife—it seems to the mellowing mind—were always wonderful comrades, and cared little for the material trappings of success. But at the time mere happiness—in the accepted sense of that word—seemed to me the most contemptible of all objectives.

"You can say a cabbage is happy", I used to scoff. "Or a cow chewing the cud."

Chewing the cud of latter-day reflection, I am beginning to perceive that, up to this juncture—for it was the most definite juncture—in my life, every single one of my actions had been dictated by my emotions alone.

Whether these emotions were worthy or unworthy is of little account because—to myself—I nearly always managed to justify them. Eager for quick results, I never stopped to consider ultimate consequences.

In that mood I returned to Beauvallon after my fateful interview with Harrison at Marseilles.

§ 4

Three weeks of comparative leisure followed. The first of those thin blue Smythson diaries which I have used ever since shows regular tennis lessons from a professional at distant San Raphael.

Memory recalls pleasant meals with H. M. Harwood, the playwright, and his wife, Tennyson Jesse, who had brought a big house on the seashore; merry meetings with Sir Frederick Keeble and his lady, better known as Lillah McCarthy, the great tragic actress, also occasional Beauvallonites; chats with one Peiniger, secretary to the golf club; a trip to Monte Carlo; and more tennis with Frank Towle on the courts of the Metropole at Beaulieu.

But the diary entries are scant; and memory is no more to be trusted for the dates of such events than for the name of that second dog which accompanied me and Roy, most troublesome of bull terriers, and Aimée on our occasional walks.

While as for the names of those hundred odd (some of them very odd) merrymakers whose cars hurtled up the hill to Mas Natalie on the night of April 21st, 1928—I still meet ladies who say "But you must remember *me*! I came to the birthday party you gave at that gorgeous villa you had in the South of France".

Under that villa is safe cellarage for five thousand bottles of good wine. It was there, I seem to remember, that the last revellers forgathered to drink the last of those paltry hundred bottles or so we opened to celebrate my forty-fourth birthday.

Klepikoff, my Cossack butler, may have been abed by then; but a fire still glowed in the huge kitchen; nor did the dawn see us short of eggs and bacon to fortify late-goers on their homeward way.

§ 5

A grand party! Even the host did not seek his vast bedroom (complete, needless to say, with his own bathroom) entirely sober.

The mere body-satisfying exaltation of my own wine, however, was as nothing compared to the utterly soul-satisfying exhilaration of the thought: "My paper! My very own paper!"

"You'll never set the Thames on fire", Julia had been wont to chaff me.

Wouldn't I just? Wouldn't I set the whole Empire alight with the torch of my own patriotism.

A fool at the very height of his folly. Yet grant him this.

From Saint George's Day, the 23rd of April, 1928, onwards—when I came back to take up what then I imagined to be the rest of my life's work in London—right up to the very end of the misadventure, I never even stopped to consider my personal welfare.

Neither—I believe—did William Harrison, who was eventually to fare so much the worse of us two.

CHAPTER FIFTY-FIVE

§ 1

THE multitudinous ramifications of Harrison's papermaking concerns have little to do with this tale. His newspaper activities, when I joined him on the 1st of May, 1928, were still mainly confined to a financial interest in those shilling weeklies known as the Great Eight. It is important for you to realise that all his enterprises were controlled through the one company, Inveresk.

"We'll have to start another company for this new periodical", he told me at our first conference in his over-active legal office at 52 Bedford Square. "Think of a good name for it, and get Withers to draw up the articles of association. There are only two things you're not to interfere with. One's the supply of paper—I'm attending to that myself. And the other's the printing contract—I'm giving that to W. H. Smith."

Almost immediately Mr. A. J. Chalkley and "Billy" Welfare of W. H. Smith & Son called on me at the May Fair, and I told them my plans. High-speed printing on art paper was essential. I wanted to give up-to-the-minute news in magazine form.

"We'll need a special machine for this job", said Welfare. "I only know of one that's ever been made—and that's on its way to South Africa."

Memory suggests that the price of the machine was in the neighbourhood of £30,000. After a conference with Harrison which I did not attend, and the promise of the printing contract, Smiths ordered it from the makers. Faced with unparalleled difficulties, they were to do their damnedest throughout.

In the meantime I had thought of registering the new company as Imperial Newspapers Limited, an idea which appealed to Harrison; and Withers was busy on the articles, under which— this is even more important for you to realise—William Harrison and myself received appointments which amounted to joint governorships for our lifetimes with equal responsibilities for, and equal control of the new paper.

Snag number one was encountered when the competent authority refused registration of the word "Imperial". Confident in my acquaintance with the late Viscount Brentford, then Home Secretary as Sir William Joynson-Hicks—to whom I had once read a longish homily on the mistakes made by the government!— I wrote him a personal letter.

Sir William replied with his usual alacrity and courtesy, regretting that the coveted designation could only be sanctioned for large enterprises of proved imperial importance. We fell back on "British National Newspapers Limited"; and Harrison, for reasons still unclear to me, demanded that I should take the final draft of the articles personally to Berlin, where he happened to be conducting some negotiations.

There he gave me breakfast, his approval and an excellent luncheon. At his order, I returned to London by the night train.

§ 2

The extant diary does not give the date of my Berlin journey; but it does show that W. Crawfurd Price lunched with me on Friday the 4th of May, and William J. Studd on the following Tuesday.

The bald, clean-shaven, bespectacled Price was soon to write, "Men had looked upon me, I suppose, as one of those lucky dogs who could afford to shake the dust of Fleet Street from his heels, to sit back in lordly ease and pen pages about foreign politics at exorbitant rates when the spirit so moved him. Such was, in less fantastic measure, the truth".

Seeing before him, however (I quote from the same article), "not merely the old friend who had established a world-reputation as a brilliant novelist but a crusader fired with a definite mission", he decided to accept an editorial position only subordinate to my own at a salary which I do not feel to have been illiberal.

The handsome Studd, employed by an American advertising agency, decided after some deliberation to "cross the fence", as he called it, and become business manager. Both, with Harrison's sanction, were given longish agreements, and directorships of the new company.

Riper experience realises two risks. Price, older than myself, though an expert in foreign affairs, had never been more than a "foreign" editor. Studd, still in his thirties—though he has since justified my estimate of his abilities, being now in a good position with the Great Eight—had never been on a newspaper at all.

But greater risks had already been taken, when Harrison and I bought "Mussolini's Life Story" from Cork; and decided—largely on account of this scoop—that the new weekly should appear by the end of September.

Because in May the new weekly had no staff, no office, no business organisation—and no name.

Other risks, to put it kindly, were so many—and nearly all of my own taking—that the mellower mind refuses to catalogue them. If ever a man of forty-four played Johnny-Head-in-Air it was I through the succeeding months.

I did not even realise the inevitable hostility which Harrison had aroused in his own camp by the mere threat of publishing a sixpenny weekly to compete for advertising revenue with the shilling mediums of the Great Eight—soon to be housed in the hollow flatiron building of the *Morning Post* opposite the Gaiety Theatre, which his company had bought and was busy transforming. It is still called Inveresk House.

A top storey and a dome were being feverishly added.

"This ought to do you," said Harrison.

"The builders will have to hustle," said I, standing on bare concrete under those steel girders.

"They shall," he promised—and a few days later I called on him in Bedford Square.

§ 3

Memory suggests that the call may have had to do with the temporary offices we were taking—so far Studd, Price and I had done all our business from a couple of suites, one of them my own, in the May Fair Hotel. It may, on the other hand, have had to do with Gundry's appointment to audit the accounts of British National Newspapers—on which point I had been insistent from the first.

But Harrison, when I finally won my way to his sanctum, was in no mood to discuss trivialities.

"What do you think of these?" he asked—and pushed a pile of documents across his desk.

Then he demanded a Berlin call on the telephone; and even Johnny-Head-in-Air realised, while he scrutinised those documents, that they might mean this Napoleon's Waterloo. For they were the circulation figures of the liberal *Daily Chronicle*, and its stable companion, the *Sunday News*.

"Well?" he asked. "What about it?" And memory suggests he went on, laughing, "How would you like to edit a Sunday paper?"

"You mean, you're going to buy them?"

"If I can get 'em at the right price."

That price, I felt, could not be less than a million sterling. For all I knew, it might be double. And neither paper—to the best of my knowledge—had made a profit for years.

9*

A yes-man would have kept his own counsel. I spoke my mind at once.

"This paper I'm going to edit for you," I said, "is to go all out for protection of industry. The *Daily Chronicle's* pledged to free trade. You can't run both."

"Why can't I? I'm buying a paper, not a policy."

So far I had been on safeish ground. Now, deliberately, I stepped off it, begging him not to go on with the negotiations, not even waiting for him to ask my main reason.

"You're a clever man," I said. "But you're dealing with three of the shrewdest heads in England. If they saw any chance of running the show at a profit, they wouldn't think of selling it to you."

Actually, I said more. He said little or nothing. But it was patent even to my insensitivity that I had irritated him and that he thought me a fool.

§ 4

Once again the extant diary is not to be trusted for dates. I am tolerably confident, however, that Harrison's confidential disclosure—which I could not, of course, pass on to Studd or Price—took place before the night of July 20th, 1928.

On that night, at a banquet to our potential advertisers, we were to disclose the title I had chosen for the paper—so far a secret, even from Harrison himself.

I had two reasons for insisting on this secrecy. The first was a legal one, connected with the securing of copyright. The second was personal. Everybody in Fleet Street seemed to know my salary. It seemed highly inadvisable to risk a far more important leak.

Not accordingly until "devilled English mushrooms" and "fruits of the Empire" had followed the "cold red and white currant pie and Devonshire cream" of what I believe to have been the only all-British menu ever served at a public dinner, did Crawfurd Price announce:

"The band will now play you the name of the paper."

Simultaneously waiters carried round the first skeleton issue of *Britannia*—thus technically on sale.

§ 5

From Price's article in that first skeleton issue, I have already quoted. A paragraph from my own will serve best to show you the central idea of *Britannia*.

"We have no weekly paper", I wrote, "which can truly entitle itself either 'National' or 'Imperial'. We have Society weeklies. We have literary weeklies. We have political weeklies. But no comprehensive weekly; no paper which will keep the man or woman who is either too busy or too bored to read his daily in complete touch with all the worthwhile affairs of our British life."

The article concludes, "We have come through one Armageddon. We may—though pray God spare us from it—have to endure another. But whatever happens, *Britannia* will play its part in seeing that the older loyalties and the older decencies prevail."

My speech was to the same effect. Harrison followed me.

Despite the Pommery 1919, the Sandeman 1908, and the John Eckshaw brandy we served in balloon glasses, most of our potential advertisers were already deciding not to risk more than one insertion in the 100-page first number we were due to publish on September 28th.

CHAPTER FIFTY-SIX

§ 1

AIMEE, who had stayed on at Mas Natalie, returned to London just before that public dinner; and was soon on her way south again in a large new Siddeley with a Weymann saloon body built by Gurney Nutting, and driven by my English chauffeur, Knell. Charlie Higham and his third wife, a very lovely American woman named Eloise, were to join her for their summer holiday.

Knell, having turned the Siddeley over to my Beauvallon chauffeur, an ex-officer of Russian cavalry, came back by train; and was put on to driving the Hillman we had bought for *Britannia* from W. E. ("Billy") Rootes.

Billy and his brother Reggie, soon to rival Lord Nuffield as car manufacturers, were pals of mine. It was through them, I fancy, that I met Dehane Segrave, already planning that attack on the speed record at Daytona which was to win him his knighthood.

Twelve years my junior and a fellow Etonian, the tall sparse-haired blue-eyed Dehane fascinated me as much as any man I have ever met. We soon became friends. Memory recalls a night drive from the Café de Paris in Bray near Maidenhead—and a borrowed Stutz in which he brought me back to the May Fair at an *average* speed of a mile a minute. I never felt safer in my life.

On another occasion we spent a weekend at Bray; and I introduced him to my friends the Harrises, who had a house, Moana, near Boulter's Lock. They, too, were captivated by his charm.

Something of the Frenchman and something of the Irishman united in Dehane. All French was the cold objectivity with which he told me about the death of a young Guardsman to whom he sold that colossal Renault in which he would leave Biarritz after lunch to sup in Paris—no mean feat.

"I was afraid it would kill him", said Dehane. "I told him so. But he wouldn't believe me."

And his own end he prophesied to me that very summer, standing between his *Golden Arrow* and his speedboat, *Miss England*, in Rootes' Piccadilly showroom.

"I wouldn't drive that car for all the money in the world", said I.

"It's this boat that puts the breeze up me", said Dehane, patting the hull with one of his fine long hands. "Kill me before I'm through with her, I expect."

We were to meet for the last time some two years later. Strolling down Piccadilly, the badges on a Rolls-Royce attracted my attention; and I stopped to examine them.

"Hallo, Gilbert", called Dehane from the white wheel.

We chatted for a minute or so. He told me he was just off to Lake Windermere for another attempt on the water-speed record.

"How's the world otherwise?" I asked.

"Pretty bloody, old chap."

Less than a fortnight afterwards, Geoffrey Duveen—another pal I made while I was launching *Britannia*—switched on his radio; and it told us the worst.

§ 2

No pal of mine, that summer of 1928, proved Brigadier-General William Nevile Campbell, C.M.G., D.S.O., director and business manager of the two Harrison companies known as the Great Eight. Hardly had poor Studd begun his drive for advertisements, than Campbell disclaimed all connection with British National Newspapers in paid pronouncements to the trade press.

Promptly, the Street of Misadventure began to seethe.

Campbell's attitude, if not his action, was justifiable. The total sums available for advertising—especially for advertising in weeklies—are limited. The more *Britannia* managed to pinch, the less there might be for the *Tatler*, the *Bystander* and the rest.

Even at the time, I realised this. But what could I do about it? I couldn't even tell my old friend, Edward Huskinson, who is still editing the *Tatler*, that my agreement with Inveresk guaranteed my eventual appointment to the boards of both those companies which had just declared mutinous war on mine.

Harrison, I felt fairly positive, could not have disclosed that term in our contract to the directors of the Great Eight. So the mutiny was entirely his pigeon. I seem to remember telling him so, in forthrightish language; and doing my best to comfort the slightly shaken Studd.

My own sensitivities may have been a little worried about the new position. (Huskinson, you should remember, had done me a marvellous turn ten years previously.) But if the brigadier, whom I hardly knew, wanted a war, he must have it. Super-confident as always—we had £150,000 behind us, anyway, and my contract contained what I considered a definite obligation for Inveresk to provide more if necessary—not even the possibility of being defeated could cross my obsessed mind.

My job—as I saw it—was to make a success of *Britannia*, whatever the costs.

§ 3

Those costs, measured by the Great Eight standard, were already colossal when we moved, early in September, from temporary offices near the Embankment to the top floor of Inveresk House. That I instigated all of them, and that many of them were unjustifiable, I admit right away.

That great artist, C. R. W. Nevinson, for instance, might conceivably have taken less than I gave him for his design of the figure on our cover and the twin torches—our sign manual—which flared on her shield. My own room, in the dome, need not have been so expensively decorated and furnished. Many of the extensive editorial staff I engaged would have come to me for smaller salaries. Obviously, from the hardboiled business standpoint, I ought not have insisted that every scrap of furniture in that vast flatiron of an open office should be of British manufacture when it was cheaper to buy foreign.

Nor am I prepared to deny the good story of the young man who, approaching me in considerable trepidation, was promptly offered an agreement at double the money he had been nerving himself to ask.

I do not even propose to stress in this, my first written account of an adventure which caused a considerable hullabaloo a decade ago, that my own code prevents me from making satirical butts of those who have been too kind or too generous in their treatment of me—or my absurd horror of stepping into a dead friend's shoes.

The only thing I am still prepared to deny—and which I do wish to stress—is that either the salaries I sanctioned for my staff, most of whom were as loyally prepared to work their guts out as the man who had engaged them, or the amounts paid to such outside contributors as Lord Birkenhead, Edgar Wallace, Philip Snowden, Hilaire Belloc, and Arnold Bennett, to name only a few of many, had anything whatsoever to do with the eventual catastrophe.

Editorial expenses are the least costs of running any paper. One of the main reasons why the Street of Misadventure honoured its greatest name, Lord Northcliffe's, with a marble plaque outside Saint Dunstan's Church was because, realising this, he did more than any other, before or since, to raise the pay of the working journalist.

My reflective mind is not unproud of having earned a few score of brickbats in the same good cause.

Otherwise I have no pleas to offer. The good ship *Britannia* never made her landfall because—as I have already indicated—her captain, myself, was an untrained navigator.

Contributory causes were many; but the root cause lies there. I am not even prepared to admit that the owner of the ship, Harrison, should be blamed for engaging the captain.

Enthusiasm is contagious. I possessed enough for ten regiments; and my motives were as patriotic, as altruistic as his. But I needed balance, a greater faculty (and more time) for contemplative thought. I had no patience with, and no appreciation of, human frailties or sensibilities. Above all, I lacked technical knowledge.

It was sheer madness—and solely my own!—not to delay publication until Smiths had secured delivery of that machine. The whole scheme depended on our "Complete Imperial Weekly Newspaper" living up to its title.

From the first, we were a newspaper without news!

§ 4

In front of me, as I write this, lies "The First Copy of *Britannia*", signed by myself, Crawfurd Price, W. W. J. Studd, and Julia Cairns, now editress-in-chief of Weldon's Publications, whom I put in charge of our woman's section.

We had spent more than £10,000 to advertise that one number. Our title, our torches, and my own signature—this last, the Street of Misadventure found difficult to forgive—were flaring from the best site in Piccadilly Circus, now occupied by Guinness. Donald Riddell, our circulation manager—and nobody could have been assisted by a harder worker, a more loyal co-director or a better hand at his job—had secured orders for nearly 200,000 copies.

But already the ship was in jeopardy, if not doomed.

Experience, realising the root cause of eventual failure, can perceive several of the contributory causes by merely glancing at that first copy. The cartoon—entirely of my own instigation—was in itself enough to alienate every fanatical Baldwinite. And my own leader, passionately pleading for protection of industry, ends with a gibe at all parties. "How long", it asks, "can even the best balanced Empire sit on Three Rotten Stools?"

Even my inexperience, moreover, had realised—at least three weeks before that fatal 28th of September—one technical difficulty. Our raw material—the actual paper itself—hadn't been good enough then. It wasn't so very much better—though I had kicked and kicked about it—now.

Where the blame lay, I still don't know. What I most remember is the shock experienced when I handled that first copy; and head-shakings by my subordinates; and making light of the thing lest my own temporary feeling of despondency should infect them.

We had no stock of paper either; and within a week or so some accident at the mill—a fire, I think—nearly held us up altogether. The gap was filled just in time—though Billy Welfare had to blanket the old-fashioned machines they were still using, because the hastily made supplies were so "green" that they would hardly stand heat or take print.

§ 5

Yet nine little words of cold print in that first number may have done *Britannia* more harm than all our technical difficulties put together—and I do know exactly where the blame lay for that. In a smoking room, the double entendre might have been considered witty. In a sports page it was just smut, certain to offend the very people we should have been most chary of offending, the "family" public, and many of our advertisers. But I was never given the chance to put my editorial blue pencil through those nine words, written by a man who has since distinguished himself by signing at least one article in a prominent newspaper affirming his religious convictions.

Possibly he wrote what he did for a joke.

An unfortunate joke was perpetrated, more excusably, on poor Arnold Bennett, who had tried to help me with a really fine article, "Pernicious Politicians, Their Cause and Cure". The whole pith of Arnold's argument lay in his final paragraph. This was cut at the last moment.

Such cuts are not unusual. I have suffered from them personally. So I know how my distinguished contributor must have been feeling when he rattled off that letter giving me hell.

Real hell, however, had only just begun. The first number of *Britannia* carried fifty pages of advertisements. The second carried, including the back cover, less than eleven; the third —though I got Dehane himself to write up the Motor Show for us—a mere six.

And we had promised the public a hundred-page paper.

I did my best to live up to that promise—and all my others— for nine whole back-breaking weeks.

CHAPTER FIFTY-SEVEN

§ 1

J. L. GARVIN of the *Observer* is still with us, and still stands four-square for all worthwhile causes, including that of Anglo-American cooperation in world affairs. He is the kind of fighter I appreciate, and used to be myself.

In the first number of *Britannia*, I brandished a little hatchet at him—and he came back at me with a massed column of horse, foot and artillery. But that neither of us bear malice, time and extant letters—my own of apology and appreciation for a good review of one of my books answered by his, "That's the spirit, my boy"—have proved.

There is no need to dig up that rusted hatchet here. And that it was perfectly natural for Harrison to quiver, and Studd to blanch, at the thunder of the Garvinian barrage—he dragged up that old Philbert Swankau quip, and far be it from me to blame him—I see now.

What I still don't see is why Harrison insisted on my personally interviewing William Randolph Hearst. That interview appeared in our second number; and for sheer damned impertinence its opening beats the band.

"Mr. Hearst", I wrote, "you and I, as representative pressmen of two great and friendly nations, ought to be able to talk straightly. Not so very long ago you were definitely anti-British. Now, from what one reads, you are pro-British. Can I proclaim, through *Britannia*, that this is so? And will you tell me why?"

Deep speaking to great deep, you will observe. None of your damned truckling just because "the Farmer" happened to own a hundred odd American newspapers, a hundred odd million American dollars—and those American magazines which were paying novelists like my friend Locke fantastic prices for serial rights.

That I should soon be reduced to writing novels again had not occurred to me. I had even blasphemed my own craft publicly— proclaiming to some twenty colleagues when they called for a personal story that novel writing wasn't a "wholetime job for a man".

There was no need to say that.

Neither was there any need to tell Beverley Baxter, when he tried to explain that you can knock some of the people all the time and all the people some of the time, but that you can't knock all the people all the time, if you want to succeed as a newspaperman:

"Most of you chaps only run your bloody papers to sell patent-medicine advertising".

No wonder he and I were not exactly "en rapport" for the next twelve months!

Britannia carried no patent-medicine advertisements, in accordance with an arrangement I had made with the British Medical Association, who were conducting a page of hints on health and hygiene—the only such arrangement ever made.

This worried Studd. So did the non-letting of the back cover, always a sign of failure. Fortunately Bernard Baron of Carreras had commissioned me to write a booklet for him. I arranged with Eddie, the old man's nephew, to forgo most of my fee, on the condition that Carreras should spend a like amount in back-cover advertisements.

Charlie Higham and one or two others were still doing their best for us. George Royds, another big agent, actually brought one of his own experts along to help with our makeup.

But the rest of the crowd stood off. It began to look like a boycott—though our circulation was still way over a hundred thousand. Studd, naturally enough, began to get the jitters. So did Crawfurd Price.

My own reaction differed. The advertisers could go to hell—and stay there till they crawled back of their own accord. They'd do that all right, once they realised we could hold our circulation.

Inveresk hadn't put up half the agreed capital yet. They were pledged to more if necessary. Or so at least I read my contract with them. As long as I walked her bridge, therefore, *Britannia* wouldn't furl a topgallant sail. And who the blazes could kick me off?

"Harrison will", said my nervous coadjutors when, in his absence, I signed up the Earl of Birkenhead, at a thumping salary, to write for us exclusively every week.

But Harrison approved—and went even farther.

"Go and see Birkenhead", he told me, writing names and figures on a slip of paper. "Tell him I'd like him to join these companies as director at these fees."

The fees totalled five figures—somewhere between £10,000 and £15,000 a year. Within two days, I was driving myself down to Birkenhead's country house in Oxfordshire at a village called Chard.

§ 2

The Earl of Birkenhead originally excited my admiration, not long after the war, with a speech in which he condemned sloppy idealism and told a youthful audience that the world's prizes were still only to be won with sharp swords.

To me, he had seemed the greatest of all figures at the dinner, held some three years previously, to celebrate the signing of the Locarno treaties—attending which I had been overcome by a fit of cynicism, since justified, while I watched Austen Chamberlain place one arm round the French and the other round the German ambassador's neck after his speech.

British sentimentalism culled a basket of orchids from the slopes of Locarno, and flew them to that banquet as a gift for Lady Austen, who comes to the mind as a very lovely woman.

I may have thought of that dinner while I was driving to Chard. Mainly, however, I was thinking of a confidence once received from Tommy (still five years away from his own peerage) Horder.

"Birkenhead's pure eighteenth century", Horder told me. "He

belongs to the days of Fox and Pitt. Physically, he has all the strength of our best yeoman stock. Mentally, he's a colossus. But he'll tear himself to pieces by the time he's sixty."

When I braked the Hillman before that long low stone cottage, Galloper Smith—as the press of my youth was wont to call him—had just dismounted from a seventeen-hand horse.

"Have you brought your tennis clothes?" was the first question he asked me.

"I'm afraid I haven't, sir."

"Never mind. We'll lend you some. My boy's coming over and bringing one of the young Fords with him. I simply must have some exercise after lunch."

He went to change. His wife gave me a cocktail, and one or two confidences about him which there is no need to disclose. Memory suggests that both his daughters, Eleanor and Pamela, were at that luncheon table. Certain is the fact that I have never heard such rapid-fire talk or seen food disappear so quickly.

I eat too fast myself; but the Birkenhead family left me at the salt. Hurried into somebody's flannels, and shoes a size or so too large, I was soon rushed to the tennis court.

"We'll take on the youngsters", declared Birkenhead. "Though my old eyes aren't really up to it."

"Pi" Ford's son inherited the family genius for ball games. He and the present Lord Birkenhead knocked our heads off in straight sets. Afterwards I learned that he had only played lawn tennis four times in his life.

The governing director of *Britannia*, with many other things on his mind, did not exactly distinguish himself in that tourney.

"Aren't you supposed to play rather well?" said my host, not without a touch of bitterness. "We'd better talk business now. Come along to my study."

I put Harrison's offer to him in the fewest words possible. He heard me out in complete immobility and a judge's silence.

"Tell him I'll think it over and let him know", he said. And he too imparted one confidence, not about Harrison, which I shall not disclose.

I was kept for tea, and—very hospitably—for supper. My host's energy never flagged. I left him, a somehow-Neroesque figure in a soft evening shirt that gaped a little at the bosom, grasping a silver tankard in one huge hand as he disputed a Shakesperian quotation with his daughter Eleanor.

Even without that one confidence, every instinct in me knew that he had no intention of accepting the offer I had made.

"I think I'd better see him myself", said Harrison after we had waited a couple of days. "Do you think you could arrange it?"

A secretary who may have been Bechhofer Roberts, then helping Birkenhead with a book, telephoned, "You can bring Harrison down to lunch".

§ 3

Whatever his subsequent critics may have had to say about William Harrison, I am sure that he despised money for money's sake every bit as much as Lord Nuffield does. He neither fished, shot, hunted nor owned a yacht. The only outward sign of millionairedom he permitted himself was a blue Rolls. In this we were driven to Chard.

So far—though we had a bit of a dust-up about Garvin—we two life governors of *Britannia* were not actually at loggerheads. The *Daily Chronicle* deal, which I still disliked and distrusted, had been clinched—and financed. Harrison himself brought my city editor, a very sound man named A. G. Walsh, the first news of that fresh Inveresk issue, £1,500,000 worth of 6½% preference shares, all to be allotted for cash, half of them underwritten by the Cardinal Investment Trust.

Accordingly I read the financial barometer at "Set Fair".

Memory has not recorded our talk on the way down to Birkenhead's; but still holds a clearish picture of Harrison at the lunch table. I hope he will not think me unkind when I write that he seemed, to a novelist's imagination, a trifle out of his element and just a wee bit overawed. Birkenhead, in that mood, might have overawed J. D. Rockefeller.

He and Harrison had their business talk alone. Harrison and I left soon afterwards. All the way home—though we chatted amicably enough—I grew more and more conscious that the talk was utterly artificial.

That afternoon, insensitive as I still was in personal relationship, I could read Harrison's mind—you must remember in how many ways we resembled each other—like a book.

"Birkenhead? Frankau?" I could read. "Frankau? Birkenhead? I don't need both of them." And fifty-five realises, as forty-four couldn't, that he was absolutely and utterly right.

Nowadays, too, I can appreciate the full weight of the load he was already carrying on one solitary pair of shoulders, and that the chances—though we were improving with every issue—against *Britannia* beating that advertisers' boycott on the available capital were about fifty to one.

I can therefore write in all honesty, that, given Harrison's position, I should probably have decided to get rid of Frankau. Only, being and knowing Frankau, I should not have tried to use the big stick.

I, even at forty-four, should have tried to play on the sentiments of a loyal associate. If Harrison had only said, that afternoon, "I'm worried about *Britannia*, Gilbert. Come back and have a bite of dinner with me, and we'll talk the whole thing over"! But he didn't. He just dropped me—more on my guard than I've ever been in my whole life—at the May Fair.

An evening or so later he sent for me to the *Daily Chronicle* office, and showed me a letter from Birkenhead refusing the directorships. Whereafter certain words passed between us.

From that evening onward—call the date 7th November—it was war.

CHAPTER FIFTY-EIGHT

§ I

A FINANCIER living on the edge of his nerves, as William Harrison lived all the time we were co-directors, should be forgiven if he momentarily forgets his suavity under the stress of a sharp disappointment.

Birkenhead's refusal to come on the boards of Harrison's companies—especially after I had signed him up to write weekly articles for us—must have been a bitter blow. I realise this now. But at the time all I realised was that battle royal impended between us two.

The statement is intentionally dramatic; because, from that evening onward, I saw the whole thing as a drama and not from the business angle at all. Even from the personal angle, I could hardly see it. Reflection feels fairly positive that if anyone could have convinced me, "The paper, the creed you've been preaching and the people for whose livelihoods you conceive yourself responsible, will go on without you", I should have handed over my command.

But nothing could convince me of that once Harrison insisted that we curtail our press advertising of *Britannia*, a job which was being remarkably well done by Studd.

Rumours of dissension had been rife enough before. Now the whole Street of Misadventure became a street of tongues.

As first result of this, Geoffrey Duveen—with whom I was not as pally then as I am now—came marching into my private office under the dome. Great amusement, by the way, was occasioned for small minds by the red light which showed over the door of that office when I did not want to be disturbed—a trick borrowed from Withers, who had used it for years.

I clicked on the red light and offered Geoffrey a cigar. He asked me if there were any truth in the rumour that Harrison meant to stop the publication of *Britannia*. I told him something of the truth; and that Harrison, as yet, had not put up all the arranged capital.

"Will that be enough?"

"Not now we've begun to show the white feather."

Geoffrey ruminated.

"If I could find the money", he said, "do you think you could get Harrison to sell out?"

It seemed to me that Geoffrey's idea provided the one way out of an impossible situation. But before I could act on it, Harrison launched his attack.

§ 2

My whole battle with Harrison must have lasted the best part of three weeks. And no wonder, when you consider the obstinacy of our conflicting characters.

He, Yorkshire and hardboiled businessman to the backbone, simply had to get rid of me *and keep the paper* for his shareholders. I, largely the romanticist, didn't give a damn for shareholders, only for what I imagined to be my duty to my country, my employees, and my ship.

Poor Harrison. I must have made him sweat blood before we were through.

It is possible that he had already held private conversation with Crawfurd Price and Studd when we three were summoned to his house in Radnor Place, Bayswater, for the first phase of open warfare. If so, he was well within his rights, as we were both governing directors of the company.

But of this, I cannot be sure.

All I know is that—prior to our first conference that evening—I took Price and Studd into my confidence about my contract with Inveresk, and that I told them, in even more forthright language than my usual, "If Harrison thinks he can beat me, he's adjectivally well mistaken".

Reflection realises that this was hardly the way to make certain of a good time being enjoyed by all.

Memory of the ensuing interview between the four of us is not too trustworthy. My own part in the proceedings, I imagine, can be well summed up in the old phrase, "When gentlemen meet, compliments pass".

Only this year, asking Elsie Filby, my manicurist at the Savoy, whether she considered me bad tempered, I received the smiling answer, "Why, Mr. Frankau, you're the worst tempered client I've got".

And nowadays, except for occasional attacks of hasty impatience, I must be a perfect angel compared to the crazy fanatic of November 1928.

I was crazy. I was the fanatic. And I had worked myself up into a lasting condition of do-or-die obstinacy by the time I drove away from Harrison's modest little abode in Radnor Place that night. Aimée had rejoined me at the May Fair by then. We were just moving into Seymour (brother of Shaun) Leslie's house in Great Cumberland Place which I had taken furnished.

But it no longer mattered to me whether we moved into that house, Buck House, or two rooms in Wapping. The only thing that mattered to me was to whip Harrison.

You can imagine that this made me a little unsympathetic to the perfectly natural attitudes of Price and Studd, both completely human in their desires not to risk the substance of hard-boiled business for the shadow of an ex-poet's, a romantic novelist's, flag.

More abortive conferences followed. At a final and very private one with Harrison, I nailed my flag to the mast. If he would sell out, I would beg, borrow or steal the money to buy Inveresk's shares in British National Newspapers. If he wouldn't sell out, Inveresk must go on finding money as provided for in our contract until we had beaten the advertisers' boycott. Either way I'd see him boiled, sugared and served up with monkey nuts before I'd leave the bridge of *Britannia*.

His reply was to summon a formal meeting of the board of British National Newspapers which consisted of himself, myself, Price, Studd, Julia Cairns and Riddell. Frankau was then asked to resign his command.

The mellower mind fails to see what else Harrison could have done, and sympathises with any businessman who may have to deal with the kind of lunatic I was by then.

Lunacy, nevertheless, stopped short of handling a situation which now seemed desperate without legal advice.

I dashed to Withers.

"Whatever else you do", counselled that very wise man, "don't say anything which could possibly be construed as insubordination. Keep your mouth shut from now onwards."

For once, I did.

§ 3

The minutes of that board meeting should still show how often it was adjourned. My own impression is that it lasted, off and on, for the whole ten days between the 20th and the 30th of November, 1928. All that time I stuck to my guns, obeying Withers to the letter, refusing to quarrel but refusing to resign my life governorship. What I had to say about Harrison privately is nobody's business but my own.

Meanwhile the business of getting out two more numbers of the paper had to go on. And did.

By this time Harrison had managed to secure the services—primarily for his *Daily Chronicle* enterprise—of a man who really did know something about the newspaper game. His name is Jack Akerman—and we are still the best of friends.

Jack—whose philosophic attitude always strikes me as faintly Chinese—was still working for the *Times*. But he sat through that entire board meeting—mostly in the silence which befitted his slightly peculiar position. We had one private chat during the period. I manœuvred him into a position of extreme delicacy. He manœuvred himself out of it with consummate tact.

With my penultimate leader on sale—and even reflection, re-reading those two pages, feels them to be fairly adequate—I knew that the final showdown between myself and Harrison could not be delayed very much longer.

My original contract with Inveresk was ironclad. Harrison couldn't make me resign my joint life governorship of British National Newspapers. One move only remained for him. Would he risk that move? Or would he attempt a compromise?

He did attempt a compromise. If I would resign from *Britannia*, the Inveresk group would employ me as a writer for the whole period of the contract—and at the guaranteed income.

I refused this compromise—Withers agreeing—pointblank; and clicked on the red light while I wrote my last leader. How I know that those two pages were shown to Lord Birkenhead before they were printed—*and* before the showdown—is once again my own business.

Asked to give his opinion on one aspect of them, the finest legal authority we ever had in England failed to perceive how my opinions on "The Problem of Iron and Steel", and my plea for protective duties, could be construed into a breach of my agreement with Inveresk.

Almost immediately that prolonged board meeting of British National Newspapers held its final session. Present as directors: Harrison (in the chair), Frankau, Price, Studd, Miss Cairns, Riddell. In attendance: Gundry and Akerman.

Resolution, tabled by Harrison: "That Mr. Gilbert Frankau, having mismanaged the affairs of the company, is hereby removed from the board".

The actual words in the minute book, no doubt, read differently. I only give their effect. Memory suggests that I made the obvious answer. If—which I disputed—the affairs of the company had been mismanaged, I could not be held solely responsible. There were two life governing directors of the company, not one!

It is possible that I said just a little more. I seem to recollect reiterating my contention that *Britannia* was largely a patriotic enterprise. The resolution, however, was put; and eventually passed with one dissentient, the accused.

To a second possible dissentient, Donald Riddell, I whispered that it would be wiser to vote with the majority. We were the only two at that table who had seen active service; and I did not want him to lose his job.

He only agreed after a struggle. I have never seen a man look more unhappy in my life.

§ 4

The tenth number of the paper Harrison and I founded had gone to press while the board still sat. So whoever managed to cut my name off the front cover before it was actually printed must have been quite a live wire. To disconnect the wires which illuminated my name on the sign in Piccadilly Circus was, of course, merely an electrician's job.

I observed the second effort on my way home that very evening —and remember thinking it rather childish. The first I did not perceive until the morning of Friday, the 30th, when I received my own copy.

My last leader had been printed as written; but nowhere else did my name appear. That live wire had even removed the customary "Governing Director: Gilbert Frankau" from the contents page.

The "long and exclusive" contract into which I had entered with Birkenhead, however, was at last publicly announced. His lordship would contribute "a weekly feature".

"We feel sure", I can still read on page 822 of the big bound volume in my exiguous library, "that this announcement will meet with the general approval of our readers and still further enhance the prestige of *Britannia* both at home and overseas."

One reader, whose letters I had published in our "Open Forum", thought differently. Her name was Lucy Houston—and even Jack Akerman would have accepted her IOU for a quarter of a million sterling without batting a Chinese eyelash.

We were not to meet until six months later. But she took the trouble to find out where I was living and telephoned to me at Seymour Leslie's house that Saturday.

"I hear Harrison's chucking you? Is that right?"

"Yes, I'm afraid so, Lady Houston."

"Why on earth didn't you come to me? I'd have given you anything you wanted. Can't you get the paper back?"

Her subsequent conduct—she bought a weekly and ran it at colossal cost to the very day of her death—seems to prove that she meant business.

But by then it was too late for business. I could only sue Inveresk. This I did on Monday, asking for an injunction to prevent them from publishing *Britannia*.

CHAPTER FIFTY-NINE

§ I

GENERAL CAMPBELL of the Great Eight died some years ago. The mind resuscitates him as a thin gray badger of an Indian-army man smoking eternal cigarettes through a very thin holder. A day or so before the final breach, he and I declared a kind of armistice —as one result of which I obtained the valuable information that my promised appointment as co-director of his two companies had actually not been disclosed to their boards.

My life hadn't been insured by Inveresk either. A definite breach of contract.

By the time Withers took charge of the situation I was "neither to hod nor to bind".

In my black rage I could no more see Harrison's position than Studd's or Price's.

More than any financial compensation, I wanted the public, *and* the Street of Misadventure, to hear my version of the story of

Britannia. In imagination, I saw myself telling that tale to a sympathetic jury.

Shock number one, therefore, was the knowledge imparted by Withers that we must sue in the Chancery Court, which does not sit with juries. Shock number two was provided by my counsel, Alexander Grant, K.C.

Withers had warned me that Grant never minced words. Neither did I when he put it to me that we ought to accept the immediate money offer made, through Jack Akerman, by the other side.

"I want 'em in court", I said. "I don't want this thing hushed up."

Grant told me, in effect, that my proper abode was Hanwell asylum. He pointed out that the sum offered, properly invested, would bring me in a sufficient income to live on for the rest of my life.

When I pointed out that I needed more than double that income to pay my standing expenses of alimony and insurance, he called my attention to the fact that the emolument of a judge in Chancery was £5,000 a year less income tax.

"And you expect him to award you five times that, tax free!"

Years back, I had stood out against a distinguished barrister's opinion—winning a case he had told me was hopeless. But in that case—which established the precedent that Sunday is a dies non in the Mayor's Court—J. Frankau & Co. Ltd., the defendants, had been good for any possible damages that could be given against them.

Was Inveresk equally good? Today, yes. But tomorrow? The financing of the *Daily Chronicle*—it seemed to me—might eventually land them in queer street. And, if I refused their offer, the hearing of my own action for damages might be held up for a whole year.

The injunction for which we were asking was, of course, mere tactics. No judge would stop Harrison bringing out the next issue of *Britannia* merely because he and I had had a row.

I remember havering a little. I remember thinking, "In a year's time I may not be as keen on going into the box as I am now"; and of how much the Almack Case had cost to win. I remember how stoutly Grant persisted that we must accept Jack's offer. I fancy that it was at my instigation we insisted on £200 extra for costs.

The other side granted this demand; but insisted on secrecy. It must be an essential part of the settlement that I should never disclose the damages.

A few hours later, learned counsel threw a few public bouquets at each other. His lordship would not be troubled. An amicable arrangement had been come to, and would be endorsed on their briefs.

That morning my old friend, Eveleigh Nash, happened to be sitting in the office of another good friend, Sir George Sutton, managing director of Associated Newspapers, the company which controls the *Daily Mail*.

At the very moment I walked out of the Chancery Court—Eveleigh and I both happened to note the exact time—Sutton's telephone rang.

He listened for a few seconds. Then he turned to Eveleigh.

"You'll be glad to know", he said, "that your pal, Gilbert, is to be paid . . ."

The figure given by Sutton was exact to a pound. Some newspapers might have published it. The *Mail* didn't. Neither did any other paper. Neither shall I.

§ 2

The subsequent history of *Britannia* forms no part of my own tale. As a weekly, the ship soon foundered with all hands. Raised and refitted as a monthly, she was amalgamated with *Eve* (never edited by Ethel Mannin); and the joint venture is still prosperously asail under the captaincy of dark Jesse Heitner, who plays chess and drives speedcars in his spare time.

High among the many kindnesses I have encountered from colleagues, I rate Heitner's when he signalled his accession to the bridge of his new command by asking me for some articles. But no editor would have taken a paragraph from me in December 1928.

Charles Higham said then, "Here's a writer who's been front-page news for weeks and had his name flashing in Piccadilly Circus. Fleet Street's crazy. Some paper ought to sign him up right away". But poor Charles always understood mass psychology better than individual human reactions.

For all the foul temper I was in, I knew pretty well what I should be up against as a journalist when I walked out of the Chancery Court. You can't knock all the people all the time, and expect them to kiss you the moment afterwards.

Besides, I had different plans.

A general election pended. Just for once, I possessed enough money to do what I had always wanted. The very moment Inveresk's cheque was in the bank, I sought out a conservative member of the House of Commons whom I knew to be rather close to Mr. Baldwin.

"I want to stand for Parliament", I told him. "Give me any constituency you like—the tougher the better. I'll pay all my own election expenses."

My friend brooded for a moment. Then he looked me straight in the eye and said:

"I'd better be frank with you. As a divorced man, you could never be adopted by the conservative party. If you're so keen on a political career, I should try the labour people. They're not so particular".

Go labour? I—who'd spent ten solid years fighting socialism. "That's just about torn it", I thought—and it did, for keeps.

CHAPTER SIXTY

§ 1

WHAT with one thing and another—my domestic situation was again one of considerable delicacy—I must have been rather like a punch-drunk boxer by the time I left the office of the friend who had told me to go labour, and walked round to see a stockbroker.

"What are Inveresk Ordinary this morning?" I asked, puffing what must already have been my twentieth cigarette before lunch.

Call the price £3 10s. 0d. a share, and you won't be far wrong.

"How many do you want me to buy you?" asked my broker, when he had obtained the information.

"I don't want to buy. I want to sell."

"You mean—you've got some?"

"Not me. I wouldn't touch 'em with a pitchfork. I want you to sell 10,000 shares short."

"You're barmy."

"I'm not. You can have £1 a share cover if you're frightened."

"Sorry. But I don't think it's safe. And I won't do it."

Those shares never moved up again. Within the year they were to stand at a nominal shilling. In case you don't understand "bear" operations on the Stock Exchange, I explain that a bear sells stock he doesn't possess in the hope of buying it back at a profit. My profit on the suggested transaction would have been just under £35,000 if I had not taken my broker's advice.

And here let me confess that when Inveresk shares crashed, and Harrison lost every penny, I felt as glad about it as though I'd actually made that missed fortune.

The maturing mind realises that this was—to say the least of it—a most ungentlemanly emotion. But, then, I was still sore with him. Whereas nowadays, hearing he is on his feet again after what must have been a stupendous struggle, I wish him nothing but the best.

§ 2

I may have dwelt on the *Britannia* affair at more length than it deserves as a cause, because the mellowing mind understands just how profound was its effect. You must remember that my main aspirations from the day I felt myself capable of making my living by authorship had been political; and that hitherto my novels and my short stories had been mainly means to the desired end.

Still too angry to face up to the actualities, I could not even let myself contemplate, in those last weeks of the year which was to have seen me so triumphant as a political journalist, that my main aspirations must now go by the board.

I was still due to make various speeches—to an association of manufacturers in Leeds, to the Caledonian Society there, to some organisation or other in Liverpool. These appointments I kept in the January of 1929; and for the first weeks of that year I kept on the lady secretary who had followed me from *Britannia*.

Then I decided to do without a private secretary—and have never employed one since.

So far, I had not done one stroke of literary work. Now—seeking consolation, one imagines—I turned to the pen. Savage, I would write satire again—the story of a gigolo, told in the first person. I didn't know much about gigolos. But I could soon find out.

Hired for the evening session, a girl at the Palais de Danse, Hammersmith, gave me quite a few hints. "One of the boys from here did end up by marrying a countess", said that forthright young partner of mine. "But I believe she was a bit off."

Published, the new tale was to bring me my first rebuke from Kipling, "It's a regular beast of a book, and what's worse it reads like the truth. If you love me, don't do this sort of thing again".

I did love him—yet I doubt if even his personal influence, had he chosen to exercise it at this juncture, would have produced any mollifying effect. If I chose to "commit literary suicide" by foisting bitter satire on a public which demanded more romantic wares from me, who should say me nay?

That phrase "literary suicide" was subsequently coined in a review of the same tale by James Wedgwood Drawbell, who still edits the *Sunday Chronicle*. I am always grateful to Jim because his paper was the first to commission a few articles after my crash.

But devil another editor tinkled at my telephone through that bitter February.

"They will", said Millie Hulton, who had just married again after Edward's death. "Don't be so impatient."

As though patience had ever been my strong suit!

§ 3

All this time my domestic situation was growing more and more delicate—once again, maybe, through my own fault. Already, an observant spectator could have foreseen the end. But my own foresight must have been in complete abeyance. Bitter, obstinate, and still somewhat of a lunatic, I jumped to a new conclusion. Never again would I exile myself from my own country.

The leasing of a flat was suggested. Contemptuously, I began to look for a house—stumbling, by pure accident, on one within a stone's throw of Harrods Stores.

Negotiations ensued, and lasted the best part of a month. Meanwhile I committed myself to a last lunacy. I became vice-chairman of an advertising agency. The less said about this the better. "First National Advertising" lasted about a year, cost me a pretty penny, and my loyal partner a prettier—and never secured a profitable client. Eventually it was wound up.

Possessor, after considerable dickering, of my London freehold, I had another attack of "folie de pierre". The high, narrow, red brick house, built in 1897, must be gutted. It needed a new hall, a new staircase, three new bathrooms, lavatory basins and radiators throughout. On my American journey, I had discovered automatic heating by crude oil. The system was practically unknown for private houses in England—but no other would do.

Enter, therefore, an architect and a heating engineer, both relatives; the Marchese Malacrida, known to his intimates as Peter; and Rosita, more commonly Zita, Forbes.

Zita and Peter were associated in a building, decorating and furnishing business called Olivotti and Company. Peter has the best taste of any man in Europe. Zita's always seems to me just a little too exotic. But then so is her personality. Barring only Shelmerdine, she still exudes more glamour than any woman I know—and we had already known each other quite as long as either of us cared to remember in that March of 1929.

As in France, I stipulated for the best materials and no silly economies. Rebuilt, furnished and decorated from garret to basement, the new abode was to cost me . . . almost the figure given to George Sutton on the telephone.

It was to land me in a nice hole, too. The hole, however, was entirely of my own making, and I am still satisfied—with the four walls they made habitable still about me—that Zita, Peter, my architect and my heating engineer gave me a thoroughly good job.

§ 4

I have been a lucky man these last seven years in 17 Basil Street. Not quite so lucky proved that 1929 evening at 12 Upper Brook Street, where I had been invited to dine and play a little game of poker by Captain Cunningham-Reid.

He and I had played tennis together. I always found him charming—and always considered the lady then his wife a very attractive woman. She did needlework, I remember, while five or six of us sat down to the green baize.

The stakes were limited to five pound rises—not much of a gamble compared with that high game I had played twenty-one years previously in America. But the moment you limit the rise, not even the most careful, not even the most expert poker player can do much with bad cards.

From the moment I squeezed my first hand, I sensed the run of bad luck I might be in for. "This may cost me £300 before I'm through", I remember thinking—for, at a short session, sixty times the limit is the maximum one should lose.

Actually, playing my very tightest, I had kept my loss down to just a fraction over half that, when someone—my host himself, I fancy—dealt the last ace pot and it was opened.

My own hand contained two sevens. Thinking, "It happened once before. It might happen again. Anyway, I'll chance it", I came in; took three to the opener's two; and saw card history repeat itself, finding those same four sevens I had held nearly twenty-one years ago at the Holland House in New York.

The pot was worth about £130 before we'd finished betting. My fours took it. Walking back to Great Cumberland Place, I said to myself, "Don't be a b.f. However good you are, you can't afford to play those prices". And I have never played for anything except "chicken feed" since.

§ 5

Gambling at casinos, I had given up from the moment I made my domicile in France—to which country I returned with Aimée in March 1929.

The biggest gamble of my life was only just beginning. But of his, I had no idea. All my actions since I walked out of the Chancery Court must have been mere reflexes of a hurt romantic's pride.

CHAPTER SIXTY-ONE

§ 1

It was plain to me while I still meditated writing this story, that much would have to be omitted. The main omission begins here—and lasts until a day in October 1930. Gratitude to one who behaved kindly to me when I most needed kindness alone demands the reticence.

Nothing need be added except that any bitterness personally experienced has been turned to pity, if not to complete comprehension, by these mellowing years.

§ 2

The extant diary for 1929 seems to prove that I returned to London for a week in April; came back to Mas Natalie, and stayed there until the end of May. Memory seems to recall that my old crony, Henry Simpson—who has more friends the world over than any man I know—visited us, and sprained a tendon running races with Josephine Blumenfeld on the sandy shore. W. J. Locke, I think, spent his first, and only, night with us.

Certain is that I finished my satirical novel at Beauvallon, and returned to town again—alone—in the June. I was past forty-five then; but by no means past my financial follies. With one establishment built in France, another rebuilding in London, and the partial financing of an unsuccessful advertising agency on my hands, I still occupied a suite at the May Fair.

In that suite I made an expensive beau geste to Harpers—releasing them from the balance of the contract signed in 1926. From that suite, one June Friday, I set off to drive myself to Downside in a hired Buick. The moods of the day can never be forgotten—though their cause cannot be disclosed. Realise them from the fact that I came down the hill from Roehampton at nearly seventy; and overshot a policeman on point duty where the descent joins the main road by a brake-squealing hundred yards.

I was just beginning to learn that neither success nor money could ever make my particular life worth the living. But how to make it worth living, I could not see.

After a night with Millie and her husband at Downside, I drove on to visit the country house of a relative. There, playing "vicarage garden" tennis, I slipped a cartilage in my right knee. Presumably one of Godfrey Davis' men fetched the Buick from Goring. Because I certainly returned by train.

Weeks of lameness followed what I cannot believe to have been correct treatment. The diary shows me working at the advertising agency, supervising the work at Basil Street, correcting the proofs of my *Dance, Little Gentleman*, as I decided to call my satirical novel, and seeing *Journey's End* for the sixth time.

R. C. Sherriff, the author of that play, was also a Gallant— though we had not served in the battalion at the same time. Shortly after his first night he came—young, diffident and self-conscious—to one of our reunion dinners, started by two n.c.o.'s, F. J. Hardy and C. W. Harris, who still run them and whom I am very proud to call my friends.

It is curious that one temporary unit out of so many should have produced my own not-so-unsuccessful novel, *Peter Jackson*, and the most popular play on the 1914–1918 war. But Sherriff, unlike my overconfident self, could not bring himself to believe that *Journey's End* would ever be really popular.

He told me, as we sat together, that he had received a tentative offer for the picture rights.

"Do you think", he asked me, "that they're worth a thousand pounds?"

Write it down to the credit of an unsuccessful playwright that I answered, "Don't be a damn fool. You're on the biggest winner of the century. You'll get twenty thousand if you hang out long enough".

I have heard that my prophecy proved accurate; but would rather guarantee a favourite to win the Derby than the prices announced for films.

Guaranteed, however, is that Sherriff stood every one of his old comrades who cared to accept it a free stall at the Savoy Theatre —and the following story which he told, at another reunion, against himself.

"I'm afraid I wasn't much good as an officer", he began; and, turning to Lieutenant-Colonel C. A. Clark of the 9th East Surreys, who is known to all ranks as Nobby, he went on:

"I wonder if you remember, sir, what you said to me when I

reported to you that I had just been wounded, and that I was to be evacuated?"

"Afraid I don't", smiled Nobby.

"You said, 'Thank God' ", remarked Sherriff; and sat down to soldierly applause.

§ 3

My pencilled scribbles of appointments for the July of 1929 show at least three with General Campbell of the Great Eight. Memory searches vainly for the subject of our discussions; but is certain they were amicable. Clearer is the reason for many entries of the one word "Watt".

During my *Britannia* time Alexander Watt had been more assiduous and more helpful than all the other literary agents put together. My newspaper and magazine editors were still being rather sticky. Impulsively, and maybe not sufficiently considerate of Cork's feelings (nobody could have given more loyal service), I decided on a change.

There must have been quite a lot of legal business, too. As late as the 27th of the month I was seeing Withers. Meanwhile 17 Basil Street continued to take shape; and Aimée returned to begin buying furniture.

Still unable to play lawn tennis or take any other exercise, I conceived the plot of a new novel—the most sentimental I have ever written.

From the 1st of August until the 22nd of September the diary is blank. I must have been to and returned from Beauvallon about then, because the picture of a night on the Havre boat is so very clear.

The boat was packed out—not a decent cabin available. Emerging from my bunk when we arrived at Southampton, I ran into Claude Grahame-White, one of the very first ace airmen, and Ethel Levy, the revue star, to whom he was then married.

Almost equally tall, and equally dark, they were in the same furious temper. This being unusual, I asked the reason.

"Hatry!" answered both. "Haven't you read about it? He's just given himself up."

I had read of Clarence Hatry's arrest. But the news did not strike me as important. I hardly remembered it as I drove Aimée up to London. Neither did I foresee the impending slump.

Months back I had bought and paid for a few good British ordinary shares. Of American stocks, I held only one. Sold again, these could pay for the furnishing of Basil Street. Not that I imagined such a course would ever be necessary. I had always paid my way with my pen.

Still a victim of financial megalomania, I moved into my new house just as the American boom was collapsing, and gave the customary cocktail party—a form of entertainment I now eschew.

There must have been all of a hundred and fifty people at that party. I rather flatter myself I made a good host. My personal feelings were none of my guests' damned business anyway.

Those feelings, I am positive, were still unanalysed. Money and success, I must have fondly imagined, might still make my particular life worth the living. But, in one respect, I had already changed.

Acting on a sudden impulse as I unpacked three cases of books which had followed me from Beauvallon, I told the local dustman who happened to be at the back door, "Take these away and get rid of 'em. They'll only lumber up my study".

"These" being the books into which first I, and then my various secretaries, had been wont to paste my treasured press-cuttings ever since 1912.

Memory recalls both the event and the mood with precision. "Publicity!" I remember thinking. "You've been selling your soul for it. And it's only your work that really matters. Away with this rubbish."

I cannot recall how soon I remembered that every single one of my letters from Rudyard Kipling were among "this rubbish". But the sequel, already made public, seems worth repeating.

Nine years after the event, while I was at my evening spell on this very self-portrait, my telephone rang.

"My name's Doughty", said the voice at the other end of the wire. "Some time ago I bought a second-hand book. There's a letter from Rudyard Kipling to you in it."

Some of that letter, on which the column stripes of the first press-cutting book I ever used are still visible, has already been quoted here. Others, I feel confident, must be in existence.

But gentlemen as honourable as Mr. F. H. Doughty, schoolmaster of Streatham, are rare. I ask him to accept this further tribute of my gratitude for a truly altruistic deed.

§ 4

By a curious coincidence, I met Rudyard Kipling himself within a few hours of consigning his letters to the Chelsea dustcarts—to be precise, on Tuesday the 17th of December, 1929—

at the wedding of Charles Graves to the beautiful Peggy
Leigh.

Over-tall and slightly scornful of manner, the sleepy look in his
eyes entirely belying their powers of observation, Charles, who
now writes "I See Life" daily for the *Mail* (no mean feat in
journalism), must forgive me if I suggest that he spends a little too
much time endeavouring not to wear his heart on his Savile Row
sleeve.

His favourite pose is the hardboiled satirist's. Judge the
validity of the pose by the result of a personal encounter between
us while the Street of Misadventure still seethed with stories of
my escapades at Inveresk House.

"What are your plans?" demanded Charles for his gossip column.

"Why bother to ask? My name's mud. I'd have to commit a
murder to get a paragraph."

"Nonsense."

"It isn't. I made a speech at a restaurant last week, and a
waitress dropped dead in the middle of it. They wouldn't even
report that."

"Surely *you're* not developing an inferiority complex?" asked
Charles, who is fifteen years my junior.

I denied the cold truth with considerable heat, and gave him the
required information.

"But if you'll take my advice", I said when we parted, "you
won't try to make use of it."

He said, "You seem to imagine you're on a black list. I shan't
believe it till I've talked to the powers-that-be—and I propose
talking to them the moment I get back to the office."

He did so—and his three paragraphs were printed next day.
Latest information from the same stable is that my wedding
present—poems long since out of print—still holds "a place of
honour in his parlour".

Place of honour at Charles' wedding reception, a most social
affair, was Kipling's. I approached him diffidently. He greeted
me like an old friend; introduced me to his wife, and said, "I'm
very glad to hear you've gone to my man Watt".

Memory brings back the Rudyard Kipling of 1929 a little bent,
more than a little grizzled, half a lifetime older than the upright
figure in the wartime bar of the Grand Hotel, Rome. But the smile
had not altered; and he let me talk to him for some twenty minutes.

Over-emphatic, and completely forgetful that he and Mr.
Baldwin were first cousins, I begged him to lift up his voice again.

"You're the only man", I remember saying, "to whom the

whole Empire will listen. Won't *you* warn them that we shall soon be a second-class power if we go on disarming, free-trading, and scuttling away from all our responsibilities?''

He flattered me a little. Younger men like myself must carry the torch. Just before I tore myself away from him, he said the strangest, saddest thing.

"I don't understand England any more", he said. "Only India."

§ 5

What *I* didn't understand—as I drank the health of Charles and his young bride on that December afternoon—was that I should never talk with my master in craftsmanship, on this earth at any rate, again.

We cannot have met more than half a dozen times, or exchanged more than a dozen letters all told. Yet, when he was eventually taken, nothing would satisfy me but to give him my tiny tribute with my own hands.

He lay all alone, under the flag he served, in that exquisite little chapel of the Middlesex hospital. I put down my flowers, and meditated a little, and went out into the rain once more—"not unmindful of benefits", as he himself would so often write it, yet wholly conscious that so fine a spirit needed neither prayers nor praise from me.

CHAPTER SIXTY-TWO

§ 1

By New Year's day 1930 all the black birds of my financial megalomania were coming home to roost. For at least eight years, ever since I took that house in Lancaster Gate Terrace, I had never bothered to control my expenses. A balance sheet drawn at the period would have read something like this. *Assets:* Two houses complete with furniture, the London one already mortgaged to the limit, and a few shares already slumped to half the price at which the debtor bought them. *Known liabilities:* Several thousands more than the debtor can possibly find in cash.

The bulk of those known liabilities were to Zita and Peter, otherwise Olivotti. For the first and only time in my life, I gave bills—one due in April and the other in May. These I could only meet in one way—by finishing my novel. Curiously, I had planned that novel to end in a trial for fraud and the hero's imprisonment.

The Hatry case seemed made to my hand.

I had already attended the preliminary hearing of the Hatry case at the Guildhall. Now, by courtesy of a friend, I was given a seat at the Central Criminal Court. The newly knighted Attorney General, Sir William Jowitt, led for the prosecution, its principal witness Sir Gilbert Garnsey, the chartered accountant, since dead. Suave Norman Birkett led for Hatry; and three more K.C.'s, among them Roland Oliver, for the other defendants.

Until the last morning, no duller proceedings have ever been staged in any court. Even the speeches in mitigation of sentence —all four defendants having pleaded guilty—seemed useless displays of eloquence when one looked at Mr. Justice Avory, immobile and menacing in his robes.

"Can this", I remember asking myself, "be the same man who muttered that one word, 'Malicious?' when Carson led him and Rowlatt for my boyhood's self in the Almack Case nearly a quarter of a century ago?"

Speeches over, Sir Horace Avory adjourned the court for luncheon. Afterwards, I heard that he spent much of that scant hour on his knees. This I believe to be true. Indubitably, he must have been on the edge of his nerves when he encountered those of us who had sat out the whole proceedings crowding back to the seats which are in the gift of the City Lands Committee.

I cannot remember the exact words he rasped to an attendant when we seemed to be blocking his way to the bench. But they were spoken curtly, furiously, in a high rasping voice.

Not a paper rustled as he meted out sentence on Hatry.

I watched Hatry closely all the time—and the picture comes back clear-cut. A little bald man, dark-moustached, beady of large eye, his hands clasped behind his back.

Fourteen years imprisonment! He never flinched. He just turned away, the prison officer in blue at his elbow, down the staircase which leads from the glass-sided dock to the prison cells.

Then, awfully, Horace Avory called that one word, "Stay!"

Some further concurrent sentence had been forgotten. Hatry was turned about again. Still unflinching, he heard the final triviality, and disappeared.

The scene affected me even then. But a more affecting one was to follow.

Trials, I had seen before. And once I had visited a London prison—where a convict in broad arrows sat with one ankle chained, doing his "solitary". But the days of the broad arrows and the solitary confinement for the first months of certain sentences were long over. My novel must be factual and of today.

I put this to the friend, a man not without influence, who had secured me my seat for the trial.

"That ought to be easy enough", he said, and wrote to the Home Office.

"Not over the Home Secretary's dead body", wrote back, in effect, the competent authority. And to a personal letter in which I promised that I would not use anything I might be allowed to see for journalistic purposes, further pointing out the danger of letting any novelist portray the horror of prison purely from his own imagination, authority made the same reply.

As usual, the official attitude fretted me. Somehow or other, I would go all over . . . a certain gaol. And somehow or other—signing a false name in the visitors' register—I did.

Very fortunately, I knew none of the defendants in the Hatry case personally. One of them, he with the shortest sentence, I saw stitching mailbags. Hatry himself carried what memory brings back as a housemaid's tray and a brush, when we met face to face in one of those long corridors they call "landings". An officer walked by his side. Nearby was one of those ghastly lavatories with only the middle third of a door.

I have never experienced a sharper pang of pity. I remember thinking, "He may know who I am. I hope to goodness he doesn't. He may think I'm here just for curiosity".

A few months ago I received a letter from the schoolboy son whom I had seen talking to Clarence Hatry among those green leather chairs at the Guildhall. Would I sign a petition for his father's release?

"And did you, Frankau?" asked Sir William Jowitt, as we walked towards the Chamber from a cheery dinner party given at the House of Commons by my friend Lieutenant-Colonel H. J. Nathan, who represents—note the coincidence! Central Wandsworth.

"Rather."

"So did I", said the big man who had led for the prosecution. And Hatry is now free.

§ 3

It was rather a blow to learn from Russell Vick, not then a K.C., who afterwards did me the great favour of "vetting" my trial scene, and utterly refused to let me pay him a penny for it, that my comparatively innocent hero would have to serve his short sentence in a different prison.

But I managed to surmount the obstacles with first-hand information, to write my last two chapters—and to meet both my bills. Mas Natalie had been let for the summer season by then. This economy helped a little. Aimée, who had been sent out to prepare the house for our tenant, stayed on at the Golf Hotel.

Alone at Basil Street—the staff dismissed and only a daily woman to look after me—I passed the proofs of *Martin Make-Believe* for July publication; gave Olivotti another bill due in September; made out what I imagined to be a final list of my liabilities; fastened it to my desk with drawing pins, and sat down to write myself into solvency.

The task appeared within my powers. Magazine editors were commissioning short stories again. Fleet Street seemed to have forgiven me for *Britannia*. With any amount of commissions in hand, I adopted a new habit. Every week I noted how much I had earned in my little blue diary. Every time I received a cheque, I paid a bill, or part of a bill, and struck the figure off the liability list.

Debts shrank steadily; but so did the values of the securities I had pledged to the bank. My tether there, I knew, was pretty well exhausted. I had mortgaged everything I owned in the world, insurance policies and copyrights of my novels included, except Mas Natalie.

Hancock's charge on that property had been paid off long ago. But no French loan company would lend at reasonable rates, and no English one touch foreign bricks and mortar with a pitchfork. The villa which had cost me eighteen months' personal work and more than two years' income to build would have to be sold eventually. In the meantime, I could only hang on to my fountain pen like grim death.

At forty-six the fight merely stimulated me. My neglected knee was stronger again—thanks to Hugh Dempster, the osteopath. I could play tennis at Queen's Club any evening. Always a rabbit's, my game was now a standing joke for hardhitting young women like Susan Noel and Vera Finlayson. But I managed to have plenty of fun.

Plenty of country houses—Geoffrey Duveen's at Limpsfield, Rex Flatau's at Stoke Poges, Colin Cooper's in Northamptonshire, Edith Harris's at Cookham, Edgar Wallace's at Bourne End—welcomed me whenever I cared to show myself. The last two years had drawn me closer and closer to my two daughters, neither yet married. Stoke Country Club often saw us laughing together at the bar or dancing in the ballroom.

But underneath all my laughter must have lain the knowledge that my own youth was already spent. Spring had gone. Summer was passing. Presently I should be at my autumn, with only my two gods, money and success, left to worship.

Was success—even if achieved by the best work I had in me— such a satisfying deity? Could money ever bring me happiness?

For the first time in my life, I began to consider happiness as something quite apart from achievement.

Meanwhile, though, I had to go on achieving money, if only to pay off my creditors. And anyway, since I was now managing to keep my financial head above water, why shouldn't I treat myself to this bargain of bargains in used cars?

§ 4

Up to the day when A. H. Clarke drove that car to my door, I had barely heard of "the air-cooled Franklin"; neither had I even contemplated parting with my Siddeley limousine. But the red and black, thirty horse-power sports coupé was a revelation—and a temptation—from the moment I took her wheel.

Carried high in front of her thermostatically controlled, chromium-plated ventilating shutters, moreover, she showed a number plate with my own initials. That, even more than the persuasive brogue of a really honest salesman, clinched a deal never to be regretted—though "Frankie" spat at me like a wildcat the very first time I drove her down to Geoffrey's, and developed a shimmy in her full elliptic springing that made her solid steering column feel like indiarubber and nearly hurled me off the Colnbrook by-pass.

But that was before we learned to know and trust each other. Any car with Delco ignition will voice a protest if the distributor wires jump out of their sockets; and it seems unfair to blame Frankie for skittishness just because someone had not screwed home what the Americans call a "king pin". I made a goodish story out of that wheel wobble, too.

Comic memories! Yet it was to no scene of comedy that I hurled my thirty horses, on that sunny morning, the third in October, down the long gray roads of France.

I drove like a fool, the car open and my eyes ungoggled. I slept the night in Nevers. Mid-way between Avignon and Fréjus, where one swings right for Sainte Maxime and Beauvallon, the road switchbacks.

Down one of those switchbacks Frankie's slightly optimistic speedometer touched ninety miles an hour.

§ 5

I returned from Beauvallon more slowly—and not alone.

CHAPTER SIXTY-THREE

§ 1

WILLIAM CHRISTIE, who married Abe Bailey's eldest daughter, Cecil, and lived opposite to me in Lancaster Gate Terrace, had been my friend for many years but only doctoring me for one. I wondered why that kindly face should be looming above me and what those clean-shaven lips were trying to say as I came back to consciousness from under the anaesthetic.

Then I gathered that the hasty operation must have been successful, and drowsed off again. It seemed a longish while since I had pasted Frankie along the road to Calais, and re-shipped her across the Channel. I fancied myself still in Basil Street—and woke to realise myself in a bedroom at the May Fair.

The face of my surgeon, Alan Flynn's, now joined Willy's. I perceived the nurse's also. She gave me an injection of morphia —and I remember babbling to her. Then a night nurse came on duty—and my brain began to reconstruct the history of the last few days.

It appeared that I had spent just one night in Basil Street before coming to the hotel, and that a long-standing complaint had blown up too suddenly for Flynn to get me into a nursing home.

Shortly after my mind reached these conclusions, it became aware that my body was in pain.

§ 2

There is no measure of pain except the individual's capacity to bear it. Mark my own capacity zero; add a furious resentment against all concerned, including poor Willy, who refused the risk of turning me into a heroin addict when I cursed as "agony" what any normal person would have described as "discomfort"

—and you have a fairly accurate psychological graph of the patient's main reaction during the next ninety-six hours.

If I couldn't sleep, nobody should. Flynn's case book may show how often I telephoned Riverside 3099. Write it to his credit that I never called him up in vain.

A nursing home might have been excused for considering my demands troublesome. In a first-class hotel, with two of my own nurses in constant attendance, I could demand what I liked—including eggs and bacon at four o'clock in the morning. This peculiar procedure eventually restored the habit—lost since Whissendine days—of a "meat breakfast", which I still wolf.

During those first ninety-six hours in bed at the May Fair, my mind was far too concerned with bodily sensations to trouble about much else. Only intermittently did it even allow itself to consider either the past or the future. And, with discomforts waning, it concerned itself solely with the future.

To look back seemed utterly futile. (It still seems so.) Rightly or wrongly, but certainly without any legal cause whatsoever, I, and I alone, had taken the responsibility of breaking up my second marriage. On that decision, there could be no going back.

Jim Drawbell was on the phone while I still wrangled about heroin—the only drug that gave me any comfort—with Willy. I demanded a stenographer, dictated and sent him the commissioned article.

"Gone off your dot?" asked Jim, in effect, after he had read my effort. "You seem to think the *Sunday Chronicle*'s a fascist paper."

I told him to alter the offending paragraphs with his own fair hand; and he laughed back, "O.K., Gilbert. How soon do you think you'll be up?"

I was up in a week; and downstairs—slightly conspicuous with the air cushion suggested by Willy—inside a fortnight. To stay on at the May Fair while my overdraft dithered between £3,500 and £4,000 hardly seemed sound economics.

An advertisement of chambers to let in Clifford's Inn looked tempting; and I went to see them, past bare trees in a stone courtyard, past the only hall which the Great Fire left standing in the city, and along a roughly flagged path.

Two clipped yew trees guarded a tiny railed patch of turf and the entrance to that low brick house. On the ground floor I found three rooms—one panelled irregularly in figured oak.

I fell in love with the quaint abode at once, and was to make a good use of it as the home of my heroine, Felicity Darrington, in the book from which Hollywood adapted one of Katharine Hepburn's first successes on the screen.

Poor Colin Clive played opposite to her—in the name part, Christopher Strong.

§ 3

Clifford's Inn is now a vast block of modern flats. No. 17 in the old building—I soon discovered—belonged to Kyrle Bellew, the actress, then wife to John Beckett, a labour M.P., who had recently distinguished himself by attempting to do a Cromwell in the House of Commons. But he, instead of "taking away that bauble", merely laid hands on the mace.

The Bellew, a lovely large-eyed statuesque woman, who is more intelligent than most, let me have the chambers. I moved in at once with my few belongings—a trunkful of clothes, my pens and some foolscap paper. I moved Frankie from Lowndes Mews to Salmon's garage in St. Martin's Lane. She was now my only extravagance. Every other personal expense had been pared to the bone.

Adaptability has always been one of my strong suits; and I found my new existence more than tolerable. To walk straight out of my front door into the Street of Misadventure was a constant thrill. My daily woman cooked me my breakfast. The Cock Tavern, the Wellington Restaurant and the Savoy Grill became my haunts for lunch and dinner.

Meanwhile, on with the jobs.

By Christmas I was well away with the opening chapters of *Christopher Strong*. Remembering the good service of my old dictaphone at Gracechurch Street, I bought a new one on hire-purchase terms to deal with correspondence and journalism. My good friends, the Dixons, who own the English Dictaphone Company, used to send for and transcribe the cylinders at their office in Holborn. Even if I could have afforded my own secretary, I doubt if I should have engaged one. That phase was over, and my motto my father's, "Avoid artificial complications".

I had plenty of complications without a faithful amanuensis hanging—pencil at lip or notebook—on my lightest word.

Sooner or later my domestic situation would have to be clarified. But a friend's intervention had failed, and the easy proceedings of 1919 seemed out of the question. Writs for debts with which I could not cope—and for which Withers insisted I was not liable—pended.

Sound economics now demanded that Basil Street—where

Aimée was still living—must be let. By a stroke of good fortune, I let it at the drop of the hat to an American couple, Jack Harris, the orchestra impresario, and his pretty young wife, Charlotte, who were wonderful tenants and have been my friends ever since.

That George Gordon, of Gordon, Dadds & Company—who were acting in Aimée's interest—could ever metamophose himself into an even better friend appeared, at this juncture, slightly less possible than that I should ever learn to play master chess.

Twice before—at Hawtrey's and on active service—the one game in which luck plays no part had enfevered me. The present attack, originally caught at Queen's Club, proved so virulent that I could hardly keep my hands off the pieces before I sat down to my novel of a morning. And when Alekhin, then champion, came over to play in a tournament organised by the *Sunday Referee*, I made him autograph his book for me. Thus some English schoolboy with Jack Hobbs, or his American counterpart with Babe Ruth.

Fellow addicts were Mark Harris, and two well-known tennis players—that grand veteran, Greville, of whom and Miss Ingram, his wife these forty years, I still possessed a photograph taken with my Bullet Kodak at Eastbourne in 1897—and O. V. Forbes.

Forbes knew the classic openings and defences by heart. He taught me how to study the master games. Only with difficulty could I hold him for more than thirty moves; but we had some grand evening tussles in that oak-panelled room of mine, nearly jumping out of our skins if the telphone rang.

Chess demands as much concentration as novel writing; and the effects of an interruption—in my own case—are similar. Fortunately there were two telephones in my Clifford's Inn chambers; and my daily woman could deal with any morning calls.

§ 4

The first quarter of 1931 saw little or no change in my domestic situation. Withers, busy in Parliament, already meditating retirement from the law—and not too happy at the thought of my name reappearing as a respondent's in the divorce list—had entrusted my affairs to his partner, Francis Covell, now also retired from the firm through ill health.

Covell and I had known each other since the Almack Case. Little, gray and bald, he always wore a cross in his watch-chain. Alike in our devotion to our jobs, how much we differed in another respect can best be gathered from the following scrap of dialogue at one of our many conferences.

Myself: "It'll have to come to it sooner or later. I expect I could manage to provide the usual evidence. Why don't you let me take the bull by the horns?"

Covell: "Don't you mind going through the divorce court again?"

Myself: "I'd rather go through the divorce court ten times than go through the bankruptcy court once. Wouldn't you?"

Covell: "If I had to make my choice, I'd far rather go bankrupt."

I could respect the conviction. But the viewpoint struck me as strange. Granted one proviso, that the evidence should be the customary fiction, I could see nothing wrong in allowing myself to be divorced. I was willing to do—was already doing—my utmost financially for my "deserted" wife.

But Gordon, Dadds & Co., unlike Barkiss, didn't seem to be willing. So there was nothing to do except get on with my work, and let the domestic situation ride.

The hero of my novel being a multiple shopkeeper and his lady-love a speed queen on land, sea and air, I needed a lot of expert assistance. S. C. H. (Sammy) Davis, who writes under the pseudonym of Casque in the *Autocar*, promptly behaved like the sportsman he is.

"These motor racing scenes are all right now", he said, after providing me with all the information I required and correcting my subsequent effort. "But you'd better know what it feels like to go flat out. Get yourself some goggles first though."

I bought a pair of racing goggles, complete with an insurance policy for my eyes, from Meyrowitz in Bond Street. I drove Frankie down to Brooklands. It was a gray afternoon, with the Mountain Course due to be closed for practice within half an hour.

"What the hades has happened to the Invicta?" asked Sammy. But a mechanic drove her over the bridge and into the paddock while he was still apostrophising.

They ran her on to the concrete, and I climbed in beside S. C. H. Davis. He is pretty well my own age. He had never had an accident in his life. But I'd never worn goggles before, my feet couldn't reach the floorboards, we jumped away to a real racing start—and the low door by my side wasn't latched.

Sammy does not suffer—as motor racing slang has it—from floating foot. My breath left me as we shot up the Mountain. That blasted door swung open—and I couldn't close the thing. Sammy reached over and did it for me with his tyres squealing on the black danger line at the top of the grade. Then we were round the corner, and diving—flat out—for the Fork.

Memory suggests we did five circuits at an average that approached record.

"It's always worse for the passenger", grinned Sammy, who had been coolly reading the instruments on our headlong dashboard while I was gritting a set of my friend John Gow's very best uppers and lowers in frantic fear lest I should disgrace myself by howling, "For the lord's sake, stop. This b. car isn't safe".

I held my tongue and did not disgrace myself unduly.

But that the fears of a tyro had not been entirely unjustified were proved within the next twenty-four hours. That Saturday, I watched Sammy hurl the very same car he had tried out with me once up the Mountain. But it never reached the Fork.

§ 5

When I subsequently visited Sammy Davis in Woking Cottage Hospital, one of his legs was suspended in a cradle.

"Looks like being a six months' job", he said. "Funny, isn't it? The same thing happened to me in the war."

Surgery substituted a steel joint for the bone one. Some years later, a correspondent suggested in the *Autocar* that Casque, competing in the "Old Crocks" race to Brighton, might have been overdoing valour when he pushed his mount the last ten miles to the Ship Hotel by hand!

CHAPTER SIXTY-FOUR

§ 1

ON Sunday April 19th, 1931, Frank Towle and my cheery pal, Clifford Whitley, husband of Elsa Macfarlane, once of the Follies, invited me—and some few hundred others—to a publicity party at the Dorchester Hotel, due for public opening next day.

Chef de restaurant of the new enterprise, built on the site of the old Dorchester House, was the celebrated Charles, of whom it is related that he once bent proud to whisper in Solly Joel's ear, "We have five queens dining with us tonight".

"Have you, though," said Solly, who did not number snobbery among his failings. "That's why this b. soup's cold, I suppose."

Charles, whose hobby used to be riding, greeted me with his usual courtesy that April evening. So did others. Just as I was leaving, however, I fell in with a many-pearled lady who behaved rather like Frankie with a loose Delco wire. I told her, as charmingly as circumstances permitted, to mind her own business and leave me to mind mine. Courtesy withholds the name—remarking only that people who inhabit conservatories should not heave rocks.

§ 2

Similar attitudes of hostility were encountered—naturally enough—throughout this period. Friends and acquaintances of couples in matrimonial difficulty rarely refrain from taking sides.

Meanwhile my living still had to be earned, and I earned it; speeches were still due to be made, and I made them—at the Poets' Club, at a luncheon of the newly formed Kipling Society (from which Kipling's modesty shrank in affright), and at a legal function where I evoked a certain amount of laughter by maintaining that, as a constant client, I could never pass the door of any courtroom in the Probate, Divorce and Admiralty Division without the usher touching his hat.

By no means as insensitive to the tragedy of the situation as I pretended to be—and considerably more exercised about its outcome than I ever admitted—insouciance seemed the only possible public attitude.

My insouciance, however, was rudely shattered when Covell received a certain document from the solicitors for the other side.

"Do you mean to say", I stormed, "that they can make me produce my bank books?" And he assured me that they could.

This infuriated me. I dashed off to E. W. Gundry, and told him to get out a complete statement of my earnings for the last three years and my financial position.

"Don't forget the overdraft", I said. "Or the mortgage. Or the debts I still owe."

"Keep your wool on, Gilbert", advised Gundry.

A few days afterwards he and some half a dozen of us sat at a long table in a private room at the Law Courts. I was livid and shaking with temper—some of which had found expression—by the time I emerged into the sunlit air.

Covell and my counsel drifted away. Gundry, who had not seemed his usual self, stayed with me. A young man, partner in Gordon, Dadds & Co., approached us smiling. His name is John Jassman Dykes.

Minded to give Dykes the rough edge of my tongue, I lit a cigarette instead. He and Gundry began to talk.

"You don't understand Gilbert", I heard Gundry say. "I've

known him for twenty-six years. But I've never known him try to escape a financial liability."

It was almost the last service poor Gundry was to do for me. Presently he went back to his office in Great Winchester Street. Presently Dykes and I were dodging traffic on our way across the road to tea.

It struck me, as we sat down to a marble-topped table, that he was quite a decent chap, that he had only been doing his duty, and that the figures extracted from me hadn't got him very much forrader.

He admitted this, adding, "There's one thing I can't see anyone in your position doing. And that's getting married again".

The president of the Law Society himself, had he been present, could not have found a word spoken by either of us during our subsequent talk worthy of his censure—unless it be collusion for a husband to say to his wife's legal representative, "Would it make matters any simpler if you had evidence of infidelity?"

But all I could get out of Dykes was, "You can't expect me to answer that".

§ 3

Up to this point—maturity realises—I had been acting in my old slap-dash, haphazard, semi-inspirational, semi-idiotic way. Not once had I sat down to consider the exact consequences of my action in leaving Basil Street. Now, cold anger must have succeeded hot. Dykes might be the best of good fellows—but costs were piling on costs, I could neither sell nor mortgage my French villa, and these constant worries, even if they did not succeed in getting my tail down, were bound, in the long run, to have the worst possible effect on my work.

Say that I was still incapable of seeing anybody's point of view except my own—and the more balanced judgment of these mellowing years will not disagree with you. Neither will they argue with you if you happen to be one of those many people who disapprove, on religious grounds, of divorce.

One country, at least—Eire—does not permit divorce. Nowadays I can sympathise with that; just as I can sympathise with those of my own countrymen who say, "Marriage is the basis of the family, and the family is the basis of the nation. You cannot, therefore, make divorce as easy as marriage without jeopardising the whole social fabric".

What strikes my maturity as so utterly futile is that—in a country like our own which does allow the dissolution of the marriage contract—any mutual agreement between the contracting parties should be legally barred.

I had known that for years. I knew—as I sat alone in Clifford's Inn after my talk in the teashop—how utterly futile it would be to say to Covell, "Go and see Dykes or Gordon. Tell them I want to be divorced. Tell them I'm quite ready to pay for the privilege. Tell them just how much I'm prepared to do".

Rightly or wrongly, there was only one thing I could do, take the law into my own hands—and cheat it to the top of my bent. The gamble was a twofold one. Given the only evidence I intended to provide, neither Gordon, Dadds & Co. nor a judge might care to act on it. But if the double gamble came off, I should be out of my troubles. I refused to let myself look farther than that.

The thing had been done before. It has been done ever since. Recent reforms may have made it a trifle less necessary. But until the law says, in effect, "Marriage is a civil contract, dissolvable like any other by mutual consent", men will continue to stage farces for its benefit.

The best of all such farces was put on by a member of the House of Commons, who subsequently admitted to that august assembly how he obtained his freedom by spending a night in a hotel bedroom with his own sister.

But I could hardly ask my sister to do that.

CHAPTER SIXTY-FIVE

§ I

THE problem of finding a correspondent was complicated by the fact that judges were growing a great deal too curious about names.

Cautious inquiries, however, seemed to prove that this risk might be run. And good staff work eventually discovered a coadjutrix of unimpeachable virtue, also two witnesses of unimpeachable integrity. The farce of breaking the necessary commandment was then staged.

Witness number one had not been warned. Slightly surprised at the sudden alteration in my ascetic habits, he unlocked the main gate of the Inn towards two o'clock of a summer's morning—and let the "guilty pair" through.

Witness number two had been advised that I should not be alone for breakfast. My coadjutrix said just before we retired to our separate rooms, "As you don't seem to possess an alarm clock, you'd better bolt your front door".

Fortunately, I took her advice. We were both fast asleep when my daily woman rattled at the knocker. The blameless lady woke first—and scuttled from the sofa on which she had spent the intervening hours. She woke the blameless gentleman. The blameless gentleman opened his eyes; said "Hop in"; hopped out; drew the bolt of the front door, and hopped back to bed again.

My daily woman, bringing tea for two, found the little scene conjugal enough.

Miss X dressed in the bedroom; I in the bathroom. We breakfasted together, and I embraced her—gratitude and necessity alike demanding—before her suitcase was carried to the summoned taxi.

We have never met since.

§ 2

That pseudo-adulterous morning, I did my usual quota of pen work. Nothing more happened—except one event laid down in the preliminary staff work—for the best part of a fortnight.

Then, just as offices were due for weekend closing, and I for a motor ride into country air, my telephone rang.

"In view of certain evidence which has come into my hands", said George Gordon, "there's no reason why I shouldn't talk to you."

We then talked.

Having assured me of his good will, Gordon further assured me that he was only anxious for his client's welfare. I said that I shared his anxieties on her behalf. It transpired that we were also anxious to make each other's acquaintance; and we arranged to meet in company with Covell.

Covell, seen on the Monday, expressed himself at some length about clients who took the law into their own hands. I remember thinking, "If either you or Gordon knew that the whole evidence I sent him was faked, you'd both chuck up your cases".

Poor Covell went on to say that my attendance at the suggested meeting, though within the law, would be highly irregular. I may have remarked that I was an irregular person. Anyway, we kept an appointment at Gordon's office—of which I was subsequently to make good use as a setting in a novel.

Dickering might or might not have been within the law, on

which I do not pretend to be an expert. But I had no intention of dickering.

"Those are the terms I think fair", I said. "And they're the maximum I can afford. You must take them or leave them."

George Gordon could only promise to take his client's instructions.

If this part of my story shocks your sensibilities, blame neither the truthful self-portraitist nor those many who have laboured to reform our divorce laws. The blame lies deeper—in the roots of our national character.

Compromise between opinion and opinion is the very heart of England. But as long as our legislators continue seeking for a compromise between the principles of the churches and the behaviour of the free-thinking laity—so long will our divorce laws remain a muddle.

Marriage is either a holy sacrament or a legal contract. Unless and until Parliament decides this main issue, the individual must continue to act according to the demands of expediency and the dictates of his or her conscience.

That I acted expediently is indubitable. That my own conscience has not yet begun to reproach me is presumably intrinsic to my own character.

Anyway, Aimée's petition was soon on the file.

§ 3

My aunt, Eliza Aria, came to dine with me at the Savoy Grill shortly after I had been served with my divorce papers. Nearing seventy, she looked a mere fifty—and was still the best company a lonely man could desire.

I told her the main item of news while she glanced at the menu.

"Are you shocked?" I inquired.

"I am rather. One divorce ought to be enough for anybody."

"You introduced me to both my wives", I reminded her.

"Is that meant to be a reproach?"

We bantered on. Suddenly she grew serious.

"Your father", she said, "would have hated it."

"I know."

We dropped the topic. She asked me about my work. I told her that I had finished my novel.

"And started another, I suppose?"

"Not yet. But Watt has sold the serial rights."

Eliza smiled.

"If only your morals were on a par with your industry!" she continued. "What's happening to the house at Beauvallon?"

"It's let for the summer, thank goodness. I'm going out there to see if I can possibly sell it."

"Alone?"

I told her that Edith Harris had taken rooms for herself, Mark and Susan at the Grand Hotel, Cap Ferrat; and that I was motoring Mark out there. Just for a second, her light eyebrows lifted.

"Let me see", she said, with another smile. "Did I introduce you to Susan?"

The implication was obvious. I told her not to be silly.

"Susan", I protested, "is hardly older than Ursula. And I shan't be free for at least a twelvemonth. And even if I did want to get married again then, I couldn't."

"Why couldn't you?"

"Because I'm broke to the wide."

Eliza ruminated.

"You've always put too high a value on money", she said at last. "Look what a happy life I've had. And I never even know where the last quarter's gas bill is coming from."

She went home early, having made me promise that I would bring Mark to her birthday party on the 11th of August. He and I were to sleep in Dover that night.

We arrived at Buckingham Gate about teatime. Eliza had been holding similar "salons" for more than thirty years. Both rooms were crowded—with her family, with friends of her Victorian days, of her Edwardian days, and the youngest theatrical set in London.

She greeted Mark—this being one secret of her charm—as though he was the one person she most wanted to meet. She introduced him to Margaretta Scott and Diana Wynward. When the time came for us to leave, I could hardly drag him away.

"I think she's the most wonderful person I've ever met", he told me as he climbed into the Franklin. "She said I was to come to see her as soon as ever we got back. Do you think she really meant it?"

"Yes. I'm sure she did."

Mark, who is dead, lost a leg while he was still a child—and with it many enthusiasms. But he talked about Eliza all the way down to Dover. I had never known him take such a fancy to anybody.

"I believe you're in love with her", I chaffed him.

Most people were. Let that be her epitaph. She was to die in the place she most loved—a theatre—before we returned.

CHAPTER SIXTY-SIX

§ I

My daughter Pamela, no mean novelist herself, has told the full story of Eliza's passing in the self-portrait of her own youth, *I Find Four People*. I never leave an address when I take a holiday, so she could not telegraph to me. A wire from my Aunt Esther at Monte Carlo eventually reached me at the Majestic in Cannes, whither I had moved from Cap Ferrat.

By catching the first possible train, I might just have reached London in time for the funeral. The idea seemed extravagant—I should have to come back for the car. It seemed sentimental—my presence couldn't do poor Eliza any good. And I discarded it right away.

Within a few hours of my decision, the Banque King telephoned from Sainte Maxime. There were two people after my house!

The news was thrilling. I drove over at once, taking Edith, Mark and Susan with me. A Monsieur Jeantet—who had rented Mas Natalie for the second summer running—had just moved out, leaving an offer behind him. He wanted the place lock, stock and barrel, down to the kitchen cloths, for considerably less than half its cost. A Monsieur Roux, also of Paris, wanted to rent the place for the winter, with an option of purchase—at a better price—by the spring.

Monsieur Roux was in Cannes. I looted the last two bottles of my 1812 Sazerac de Forge brandy from my own cellar; picked up my passengers at the Golf Hotel, and dashed back across the Esterels.

Roux, interviewed at his hotel, materialised as the best type of Frenchman—charming, educated, honest and acute.

"Your house is a jewel", he began. "Unless you are really in need of the money, you should not think of selling at the price I am willing to offer for it and the furniture. And please remember that I am only taking an option. I am not promising to buy."

Then we got down to figures.

"You will be losing the best part of £4,000, I'm afraid", he said shrewdly. "That's to say if I exercise my option. But I can't give you a franc more."

I accepted, and we exchanged letters—neither of us caring

overmuch for feeing lawyers—which took rather a long time to write. The letters stipulated for advance payment of the rent.

"You'll send me a cheque?" I suggested.

"But no, my friend", laughed Roux, as we shook hands; "I shall send your Barclays a good bill on the Bank of France."

Leaving him, I dropped in at the local branch of Barclays Bank (France) to tell them my news, and deposit the letters.

"You'd better send these on to Albert Chunn in Monte", I said to the Cannes manager. "He'll be glad to know I look like getting rid of the house, though it will have cost me rather a packet."

The manager stared at me, and asked:

"Haven't you heard?"

"Heard what?"

"That Britain's just gone off the gold standard."

It took me a minute or so to grasp his meaning. I had to ask the nominal rate of exchange before I realised that the deal I'd just done in francs would mean—if Roux exercised his option—that I should make a profit and not a loss, reckoned in pounds, on the sale of Mas Natalie.

And if only I made that profit, if only the judge accepted my little farce at its face value . . . Eliza's implication might yet come true!

§ 2

I am always sorry when I think of the way I drove Mark back to England. It is conceivable that the possibility—it was still only a mere possibility—of being able to ask Susan to marry me, made me too anxious to see her again.

Anyway I did most of that trip at seventy-five—and took the wrong road from Dover harbour, landing up in the narrower cul-de-sac of the Castle there, and the ugliest temper because I could not perceive any place in which to turn Frankie. Blame the last of the 1812 brandy, which I had drunk on the *Townsend.* Praise some gallant lads in khaki who lifted Frankie round for us; and cheered the remounted driver and his lame passenger as we hurtled down the hill.

September was almost over by the time I returned to Cliffords' Inn. Another winter on the ground floor of that unheated seventeenth-century house hardly seemed advisable. An acquaintance of my cigar days—Robert Middlemas, the racehorse owner—wished to sublet a portion of his flat in Lincoln's Inn.

I took those two rooms, complete with a bath and a kitchenette, forthwith. The financial position was not yet rosy enough to allow the buying of a wardrobe and a work table for cash. But £3 down and a hire-purchase agreement with Woodhouse's saw my few suits hung up, and the tools of my trade in their places.

Almost immediately I struck a baddish snag.

A certain friend had given me a great deal of help in the business technicalities of *Christopher Strong*. Innocently—with Hutchinsons' presses waiting to run off the first twenty thousand copies—I sent him a set of page proofs.

"You'd better just look through these", I wrote, "in case I've got some detail wrong."

Frantic telephoning ensued. Summoned to my friend's offices, I found his entire board in session and the company's solicitor in attendance.

Our proceedings were private; and resulted in an agreement which I must still respect. As a result, I reconceived and rewrote —admittedly not without compensation—the whole business plot of that novel in less than seventeen stretches of fourteen hours apiece. Unless you are a professional storyteller who plods away, like I do, at an average of twelve hundred words daily, you will not realise the strain this implied.

And the strain of preparing my defence to a test action brought by a dressmaker which might bankrupt me if I lost it, the fairly persistent thought, "Supposing my staff work wasn't quite good enough when I staged my little farce for the divorce court", and a bank whose patience seemed to have grown more than a little restive—and, even if you are not a professional storyteller, you may realise some of my difficulties in getting down to the first chapters of my next long story.

By Christmas 1931, however, Mr. Justice McCardie had decided the test action in my favour. And a while later the Court over which my one-time crossexaminer, Lord Merrivale, presided was satisfied that I and my blameless coadjutrix had made a sufficient breach in the necessary commandment. Within six months, I should be a free man. Happiness beckoned. How great a happiness I did not even then foresee.

§ 3

Happiness was marred, at the end of January, by the shock of Gundry's death. You should know, by now, why almost the last coherent word he said was, "Gilbert". Two of us loved him better than most men—myself and Charles Higham, who is also gone.

Obstinate men both, Gundry's advice was always law to us.

I wondered what that advice would have been as I sat staring—a few days later—at a letter from Roux.

"This tears it", I remember thinking. For Roux had decided against exercising his option. And how could I contemplate a third marriage with bankruptcy staring me in the face?

I did my usual morning's work; and spent most of the afternoon drawing up a kind of balance sheet. Figure as I might, the result was the same—a net debit of £5,000. To pay this off out of income would never be possible. Reckoning three hundred days' work in the year, my earnings were already pledged—as they still are while I write this—to the tune of £10 a day.

My estimate of £5,000 did not include the mortgage repayments on Basil Street or the increasing French taxes on Mas Natalie. Basil Street was still occupied by Jack Harris, and therefore unsaleable. If Jeantet wouldn't renew his offer for Mas Natalie, it looked as though I were sunk.

I wrote to the Banque King that night, telling them of Roux's decision and to approach Jeantet. Two days later, a last complication occurred. The Society of Authors, Playwrights and Composers, having promised to fight an action against a cinema company for me, decided to throw up the case long after they had actually issued the writ.

"We're advised that the Sale of Goods Act will be against us", they told me.

That Act, originally passed to prevent the monks being swindled out of their lands when Henry VIII disestablished the monasteries, had already cost me several packets. A barrister, met by chance, consented to examine the letters exchanged between Watt and the British cinema company. In his opinion, they constituted an actionable contract.

An older friend, George Cran the solicitor, agreed with this opinion. Watt seemed rather dubious. But the Society had entered the action in my name—and I decided to continue it at my own expense.

By the time we redrafted the pleadings, another good man had passed on.

§ 4

That good man, whose name was Edgar Wallace, would have cleaned up my little financial tangle with a fortnight's intensive work. He had told me, the previous summer, how much he was paying off for arrears of income tax alone. Memory brings back the figure as £1,000 a month.

Recently Margaret Lane, then his daughter-in-law, wrote Edgar's biography. She must excuse me for doubting if she put his best goods in her shopwindow. To me—whatever his literary merits—he will always remain a Herculean figure, and far more kindly than her book suggests. I happen to know of one particular kindness which I cannot bring to light, and of another which I can.

It was Edgar Wallace who first encouraged the author of *I, James Whittaker* to write. Only after Edgar's death did I carry on with the good work. Jimmy Whittaker—whom Susan and I are proud to call our friend—no longer labours in a cotton mill. His book, with the preface I wrote for it, is still obtainable. Read it for yourself.

My acquaintance with Edgar—it was never much more—began just after his first success as a playwright with *The Ringer*. Lunching next to me at Ciro's, he introduced himself with a typical, "You're Frankau, aren't you? I'm Edgar Wallace". That must have been in 1926.

In 1928 he contributed to *Britannia*. Nineteen thirty-one had seen us drawing closer. We meditated forming a Storytellers' Club, I recollect. He made the suggestion at Chalklands, his house near Bourne End, after I told him, "If your play *On the Spot* had been written by Eugene O'Neill the highbrows would be as crazy about it as the lowbrows". To this judgment, I still adhere.

His *Sanders of the River* tales, too, take a lot of beating. But Walter Scott himself could not have carried the burdens Edgar's temperament laid on him—and no man, least of all an author, can jump out of his own skin. Secretly, I had sometimes felt—when he would prowl in on us, his hat, which he never seemed to abandon while at Chalklands, rammed well down on his head as though he were one of his own gangsters—that his end would be untimely.

Yet the news of his death that February in Hollywood might have been almost as great a shock to me as Gundry's if I had been less absorbed. And even in my self-absorption—this is still altogether clear—I could not help thinking, when rumour began to whisper that he had died in financial difficulties, "There, but for the grace of God——"

Even Susan and her mother—though I had taken to telling them most things—didn't know how worried I was, or how determined to postpone marriage until I could see my financial way clearly.

Since I couldn't afford to pay for my elder daughter's wedding, how the blazes could I afford another of my own!

§ 5

My daughter Ursula, who has since made me a grandfather, married Harry d'Arch Smith of the Hampshire Regiment, still years too young to draw "married" pay, at a London registrar's on Passion Sunday, March 1932.

Pamela provided the reception—and I remember thinking, as I drove to the Stafford Hotel, "What a mean devil they must be thinking me. This ought to be my show".

And as I drove back alone to Edith's house at Cookham I thought, "You can't expect the bank to carry you much longer. What'll happen to those two if the bank stops paying Ursula her allowance?"

Then—abruptly and amazingly—the whole financial picture was altered. Jeantet wanted to buy my French house.

CHAPTER SIXTY-SEVEN

§ 1

THE more I consider that kaleidoscopic change of fortune which occurred just before my forty-eighth birthday the more I feel justified in subtitling this self-portrait, *The Novel of His Own Life*. For no old-time novelist could have timed the sale of Mas Natalie more opportunely for his denouement. And that Susan and I have "lived happily ever afterwards" is still true in this summer of 1939.

Yet the fact that Jeantet bought a house he had been coveting for two years—for slightly fewer francs than he offered previously —is not particularly strange.

Far more strange is my present conviction—only reached after much thought—that the biggest gamble of my life, though its many hazards worried me from time to time, never really panicked me. Subconsciously, I must always have known that it would come off.

§ 2

With Jeantet on the hook, but not yet landed, I knew some nasty moments, through most of which I was seen by my legal friend, René Monsarrat, who practises half the week in London and the other half in Paris.

But with the deal clinched and the money paid over, a real spot of humour was provided by Lloyds Bank. Acknowledging the

cheque which eliminated an overdraft of fourteen years' standing,
another friend—A. R. Woollacott, since retired from the manager's
room of R Department at the Cox's and King's branch—asked in
some surprise why I had not advised him of my "future requirements".

Almost at once Beverley Baxter telephoned from his managerial
sanctum in Shoe Lane, "We hear you're engaged to be married,
Gilbert. Would you like to give me an advance story?"

This may or may not have been a leg-pull. I may or may not
have suggested that if the *Express* were to publish the name of a
bride-to-be before the wife of her husband-to-be had applied to
have her decree made absolute the resultant damages might pay
for a long honeymoon.

Anyway, Bax held his hand.

§ 3

Susan and I announced our engagement in earliest June and
fixed our wedding day for the 14th of July. I had finished one of
the novels of which I am not too proud by then. My luck, once
turned, seemed unending. Journalistic commissions poured down
my telephone. Jack and Charlotte Harris—dear people!—surrendered their agreement for Basil Street, not only refusing to take a
penny compensation but spending lavishly to put the place in
apple-pie order for us. (They are no relations, though their
surname did happen to be the same as Susan's.)

While to cap all—as it seemed—Jeffery Bernerd used his good
offices to settle my feud with Herbert Wilcox, who came up to me
in the Grill a few days after we had agreed on the compensation
his company was to pay, said he was jolly glad about the whole
business, and congratulated me on my engagement. A sporting
act which he may have forgotten, but I never shall, even if I live
for "Sixty Glorious Years".

So what more luck could one expect—with every bill receipted,
including those four-figure law costs, and enough ready in the
bank to pay for a six-weeks' tour of the continent, with a few
pennies over to start housekeeping on when we came home, and
little more than a fortnight to the happy day?

"I don't see why I shouldn't chuck work for the last few days",
I told Susan over the telephone one evening. But as I hung up it
rang again.

"Warden of the *Mail* speaking", I heard. "When are you off?"

"On the fourteenth."

"Good. Then you'll just have time to report the Barney case for us. The trial's set down for Monday."

And he named a fat fee.

§ 4

At ten o'clock on Monday the 4th of July, 1932, I squeezed myself into a seat at the Central Criminal Court.

"Standing room only"—and precious little of that except behind the glass-sided dock down whose steps I had seen Hatry disappear—was the order of the following three days.

Elvira Barney is dead now; and the very name of that boy who predeceased her, with a revolver bullet through his heart, forgotten by most of us. Patrick Hastings led Walter Frampton for her successful defence. To see Hastings demonstrate how easily the fatal revolver—never examined by the jury and of the only make which has a safety spring let into the back of the handle—could go off by accident, was a revelation in histrionics.

Telling, too, was that last speech in which he slashed at "famous novelists sent to gloat over the sufferings of an innocent woman".

James Douglas, who had given me my first review for *One of Us* twenty years before, my mother's old friend, Seymour Hicks, and I lunched together before the verdict.

"She never did it", said soft-hearted Jimmy.

Seymour said, "Did you notice the way Pat's wig kept slipping? It made him look exactly like the Widow Twankey".

The jury returned a verdict of "Not Guilty"—with which tens of thousands disagreed. Hundreds blocked my way as I went for a taxi.

"Carmelite House", I said. "And as fast as you can."

A. L. Cranfield, afterwards to sit in W. L. Warden's chair, and now of the *Evening Standard*, had first charge over my intrepid pen. The final word lay with Kenneth Henderson of the legal department.

You should have seen their faces when they read, "Sir Patrick Hastings, with his wig awry, looks a little like the Widow Twankey".

§ 5

Cranfield's pencil hacked out that borrowed phrase and every hint of my real opinion.

But what did I care—I who still cannot see what I have ever done to deserve that sweetest, loveliest, most sensible of companions whom I married within the week?

EPILOGUE

SUSAN and I spent the seventh anniversary of our wedding day at one of the grandest spots on earth, the Broadmoor Hotel, Colorado Springs, Colorado.

Twice, that day, we swam in the warm lake, six thousand five hundred feet above sea level. And after our second bathe, she left me alone.

The sun was just setting beyond the old road to Cripple Creek. From the memorial tower to Will Rogers sounded the bells.

"Seven years of complete happiness", I thought. "Can any man ask for more?"

Then, for a while, my mind repictured those years—flattering itself, maybe, that their accomplishment in mere words, two million of them at the least, might not be so altogether unworthy. Till laughter took me at the thought of an American lady who had said, only the night before, at the end of a longish conversation about modern literature during which many names of British authors were mentioned:

"You're not a writer by any chance, are you, Captain Frankau?" Which laughter, it seemed to me, was very good for the soul.

And after that my mind, turning away from mere accomplishment, pictured the many other journeys Susan and I had taken during those few weeks of leisure my many burdens allow me each year.

Once more, in my imagination, we tooled that good motorcar we christened Frankie up the Furka, still snow-piled for our honeymoon; and bathed at Rimini from sand so hot that it burned our naked feet. Once more—in 1933 that was—we drove the Stelvio, with its eighty-seven hairpin turns, and the Katchberg (still Austrian) whose last miles are as steep as the Brooklands test hill.

Once more we toiled those four thousand miles through Spain —still outwardly at peace, though subconscious foresight already warned me of the doom to be.

And after that, still living in my imagination, I saw flashes of many another European journey, and the whole film of our American one—now nearing its end.

"Less than a month", I thought, "and we shall be back in our own little house, in our own London."

Nor was the thought—despite all the kindnesses we had received, and all the good friends we had made—unsweet.

The sun was almost set by then, and the beacon of the memorial tower alight. I went in to the hotel. The elevator boy smiled at me. We talked for a moment as he took me up.

"Is there going to be a war, Captain?"

I gave my stock answer. If there were no war by the fifteenth of September there would be peace for a generation. Personally—I told him—I felt very confident. But, later the same night, talking with Susan, that subconscious foresight of which another generation may find some traces should any of the work accomplished in these last seven years survive ephemeral popularity, fell on me again.

Susan, too, was feeling a little homesick. She wanted—even more than I, though Edie is almost as dear to me as Julia once was—to see her mother again; and "Granny" who, at ninety, can still recall how she heard the servants in "Uncle Bessemer's" (Sir Henry Bessemer's) kitchen talking of the Indian Mutiny; and all that large family, so reminiscent of the Forsytes in Galsworthy's *Saga*, who displayed such fortitude when "Edie's girl" promised to become the third wife of that twice divorced novelist, myself.

"I'm so glad", said my Susan, "that we didn't have to stay in Hollywood. It was a lot of money; but I don't feel we should have been happy there. Even if there is going to be a war, I'd rather be in England."

Whereupon I said, "If it breaks out before the twenty-ninth of this month, the *Mauretania* may not sail. And even if she does, we shall have to stay in America. I can't disobey orders".

"No", agreed my Susan. "You can't. And that means we may have to spend the whole war in Washington."

"Safely!"

My Susan meditated for a moment.

"You wouldn't like being out of England any more than I should", she said at last.

"No. But I should hate to feel that you were in any danger."

That is still my predominant feeling as I write these final words of a tale that may be altogether out of date, just the dry bones of one insignificant individual's totally unimportant struggles for solvency and happiness, by the time you read it.

For these final lines are being penned in Basil Street, London, on Thursday, the twenty-fourth of August, nineteen hundred and thirty-nine; and tomorrow I must offer myself, once again, for service.

This time, if this thing must be, let all who survive see to it that no puling politician betray our victorious dead.